J. G. Ballard

Modern Masters of Science Fiction

Edited by Gary K. Wolfe

Science fiction often anticipates the consequences of scientific discoveries. The immense strides made by science since World War II have been matched step by step by writers who gave equal attention to scientific principles, human imagination, and the craft of fiction. The respect for science fiction won by Jules Verne and H. G. Wells was further increased by Isaac Asimov, Arthur C. Clarke, Robert Heinlein, Ursula K. Le Guin, Joanna Russ, and Ray Bradbury. Modern Masters of Science Fiction is devoted to books that survey the work of individual authors who continue to inspire and advance science fiction.

A list of books in the series appears at the end of this book.

J. G. Ballard

D. Harlan Wilson

UNIVERSITY OF ILLINOIS PRESS
Urbana, Chicago, and Springfield

1 2 3 4 5 C P 5 4 3 2 1
∞ This book is printed on acid-free paper.

Library of Congress Cataloging-in-Publication Data
Names: Wilson, D. Harlan, author.
Title: J. G. Ballard / D. Harlan Wilson.
Description: Urbana : University of Illinois Press, 2017. | Series: Modern masters of science fiction | Includes bibliographical references and index. |
Identifiers: LCCN 2017017824 (print) | LCCN 2017033297 (ebook) | ISBN 9780252050039 (ebook) | ISBN 9780252041433 (hardback) | ISBN 9780252082955 (paperback)
Subjects: LCSH: Ballard, J. G., 1930–2009—Criticism and interpretation. | Science fiction, English—History and criticism. | BISAC: LITERARY CRITICISM / Science Fiction & Fantasy. | BIOGRAPHY & AUTOBIOGRAPHY / Literary.
Classification: LCC PR6052.A46 (ebook) | LCC PR6052.A46 Z94 2017 (print) | DDC 823/.914—dc23
LC record available at https://lccn.loc.gov/2017017824

Contents

ACKNOWLEDGMENTS

This book would not have been possible without the many scholars and friends who provided me with guidance and support. I am particularly grateful to Rick McGrath, David Pringle, and Simon Sellars, maestros of the Ballardian; they responded to my many queries almost before I conceived of them, and their feedback was essential to the accuracy of my information and the development of my ideas, not to mention Simon's Ballardian.com and Rick's JGBallard.ca, the two most comprehensive and edifying Web sites on Ballard. Talented critic and novelist James Reich was nice enough to read through an early draft of my manuscript and point me toward clearer skies. Dominika Oramus gave me valuable advice, and Jeannette Baxter, Beatrice Ballard, Mike Bonsall, Dan O'Hara, James Goddard, Mike Holliday, Umberto Rossi, Pippa Tandy, and David Paddy all corresponded with me in some capacity; I am grateful for their attention as well as the work they have published on Ballard. While I never communicated with them personally, I am indebted to Peter Brigg, Andrzej Gasiorek, Samuel Francis, and Roger Luckhurst, all of whom have written superb books on Ballard that I looked to for inspiration and direction. Additionally, I should mention the Facebook pages devoted to Ballard, where I often encountered some of the aforesaid intelligentsia alongside other enthusiasts, aficionados, and detractors; I learned more here than I ever thought possible.

I performed much of my reading and research during a sabbatical granted to me by Wright State University–Lake Campus in 2014. Special thanks to the emeritus dean of the campus, Bonnie Mathies, who took a genuine interest in my writing projects and entertained me with stories about deranged librarians.

I must acknowledge the assistance I received from all the University of Illinois Press editors and external readers—namely Willis Regier, who worked with me on my proposal, and Marika Cristofides, who advocated for my manuscript and helped me refine and polish it in the latter stages of the writing process. Julie Gay skillfully honed and sharpened my prose at the end of the line. Commentary from one reader in particular, Gary Westfahl, gave me the insight, acumen, and confidence to map out my critical agenda. I'm so appreciative of everybody's time and input.

I can't forget my mentor and friend, Bob Crossley, who introduced me to the study of science fiction when I was working on my M.A. in English at UMass-Boston in the 1990s and set me on the course I have taken in my professional life. These pages would not exist without him.

Finally, I'm thankful for my daughters Maddie and Renee. Life took several dark turns for me during the composition of this book, and they invariably brought me hope, joy, and strength. No matter what I do, they are always my foremost inspiration.

J. G. Ballard

INTRODUCTION

In 1975, J. G. Ballard revealed the working thesis of his stories and novels to date: "My fiction is all about one person, all about one man coming to terms with various forms of isolation" ("Interview," Goddard and Pringle 89). His interest in this theme didn't end in the mid-1970s. It spanned the length of his career, culminating in his autobiography, *Miracles of Life*. Published the year before his death from cancer in 2009, the autobiography closes the door on a body of work that includes hundreds of stories and essays and nearly twenty novels, not to mention the accumulation of Ballardian scholarship that continues to gain a fierce momentum. The terminal subjects that populate his fictions were often extrapolations of his life as an outsider in prewar and wartime China and later in postwar England. As an author, Ballard was an outsider, too, writing against the codes and norms of the science fiction genre. Beyond the genre, the pathology of American media waged a special influence on his *sole*-seeking protagonists, who capitulate to "the apotheosis of all the fantasies of late twentieth-century man—the transformation of reality into a TV studio" (Ballard, "The Future" 225).

Ballard's career spanned six decades. A child of war, his interest in science fiction can be traced back to the destructive technologies of World War II, during which he was interned in a Japanese prison camp. Later he entered the military himself, and his imagination started to churn. In the 1950s he published his first stories in science fiction magazines, quickly distinguishing himself as a unique voice and destabilizing the traditions established by editors like Hugo Gernsback and John W. Campbell and authors like A. E. van Vogt and Isaac Asimov. Instead of hard, heroic space operas, Ballard wrote soft, antiheroic psychodramas.

His early disaster novels reimagined the postapocalyptic subgenre of science fiction. He went on to compose provocative, often inflammatory narratives that experimented with form and reveled in "dangerous visions" of sexuality, morality, and ontology; works like *The Atrocity Exhibition*, *Crash*, and *High Rise* continue to rouse the rabble even today. He became a figurehead for the New Wave, an avant-garde movement in the genre spun from the wheel of literary modernism and catalyzed by the UK magazine *New Worlds*. Other authors associated with the New Wave (contemporaneously or retroactively) include Michael Moorcock, M. John Harrison, Brian Aldiss, and John Brunner in the UK, and Harlan Ellison, Philip K. Dick, Ursula K. LeGuin, and Joanna Russ in the US; together they didn't change the face of science fiction, but they did give it a facelift, marshaling it in new directions. In his later, postmillennial career, Ballard fixated on consumer-capitalism and the culture machine, spending the final decade of his life writing almost exclusively about the pathology of rich, technologically overloaded suburbanites in novels like *Super-Cannes*, *Millennium People*, and *Kingdom Come*. Time after time, his characters must come to grips with an implosion of real and cinematic landscapes, whether they are scurrying through the deepest jungles or sunbathing atop the tallest tower blocks. A diegetic uncertainty stigmatizes them, and they experience pain and suffering in concert with liberation, agency, and power. Revered by critics and fans for his prescience, Ballard's oeuvre maps the unfolding of the mediapocalypse from the dawn of the Space Age into the twenty-first century.

A bird's-eye view of his progression as a writer shows him emerging within the science fiction genre, growing disconcerted with the confines of the genre, slowly turning away from it, and abandoning science fiction in the end. A recurrent portrayal casts Ballard as a one-of-a-kind genius who never fit into any genre, a shrewd enfant terrible unlike any other writer, a virtuoso driven to abandon science fiction so that he could fully explore the incomparable labyrinth of his own imagination. Fantasy author China Miéville strikes this pose in an introduction to the American edition of *Miracles of Life*, reveling in Ballard's "irreducibility" to one category and *mode d'écriture*. Ballard's fiction is distinctive, almost matchless. The editors of *Collins English Dictionary* validated it when they installed the term "Ballardian," which denotes anything "resembling or suggestive of the conditions described in Ballard's novels and stories, especially dystopian modernity, bleak man-made landscapes, and the psychological effects of technological, social or environmental developments." But his relationship with science fiction has not been as tenuous, strained, or knotted as some critics would have us believe. There is little doubt that he was "ex-centric."[1] As I argue in this book, however, Ballard began as, and always remained, a science fiction writer.

Ballard's writing diverges from science fiction of the Golden Age, a period that began in the late 1930s when Campbell took over the editorship of the American pulp magazine *Astounding Stories*, founded in 1926 by Gernsback. Campbell changed the title to *Astounding Science-Fiction* in 1938 and cultivated authors like Asimov and van Vogt as well as Robert Heinlein, Theodore Sturgeon, Clifford D. Simak, L. Ron Hubbard, Jack Williamson, C. L. Moore, and Lester del Ray, among others. In *The Encyclopedia of Science Fiction* the Golden Age is described as "the period in which genre sf belonged primarily to magazines rather than books" and stories "were by and large written by men for young male readers" with "soaring ideas . . . too often clad in an impoverished pulp vocabulary aimed at the lowest common denominator of the mass market" (Ashley and Nicholls). Combining technological realism and the masculine, adventure-story ethos of the preceding pulp era, Golden Age science fiction began to splinter after World War II as authors deviated from the customary storylines, tropes, and characters. Ballard was an exceptionally sharp splinter whose highly literary writing made the Golden Age look like the child's play it often was, if only by juxtaposition and association/dissociation. Likewise with other authors in the fold of the New Wave, which turned the Golden Age on end, favoring "achronology, stream of consciousness, and metaphor, and its visions of the future are usually dark: the belief that progress and technology are inevitably positive is gone" (Gordon 109).

When Ballard sold his first stories in the 1950s, American magazines dominated science fiction. Relegated to the UK for his innovations, Ballard spent years breaking into the US market. Ironically, American science fiction editors perceived it as *the* genre of innovation. They still do, especially in the US. Major publishers like Tor and Ace continue to insist that authors stick to narrative formulas and avoid unsettling readers' comfort zones. Except for *The Atrocity Exhibition* and several other experimental short fictions, Ballard was a storyteller first, but much of his work clearly delights in unsettling (and in some cases trashing) comfort zones. The purpose for this deviation is not mere shock value. It is a Poundian endeavor to "Make It New." Fellow British science fiction author Brian Aldiss had this to say about his authorship in 1965: "Ballard's attitude is such that we are often reminded of SF by the very things he is ostentatiously not doing. Ballard likes to regard himself as something of an outcast among the SF fraternity. He avoids most other authors, he believes . . . that 'H. G. Wells has had a disastrous influence on the subsequent course of science fiction,' he seems to regard William Burroughs as the greatest of SF writers, and of course he is the apostle of Inner Space" (41).

Aldiss's depiction of Ballard is somewhat overblown but fair. There's no doubt about his being "the apostle of Inner Space." Uninterested in the worn-out Golden Age themes of space exploration and alien invasion, he wanted to marshal the genre in a new direction; instead of pointing it at the stars, he would point it at the human psyche and our intricate, uncanny technologies of desire. Ballard's rampantly cited maxim, "The only truly alien planet is Earth," typifies this sentiment, which he explicates in "Which Way to Inner Space?" Originally published in 1962—the same year he published his first inner-spatial novel, *The Drowned World*—the essay is a short manifesto about the condition of science fiction and how he wants to refine it. Ballard writes:

> First, I think science fiction should turn its back on space, on interstellar travel, extraterrestrial life forms, galactic wars and the overlap of these ideas that spreads across the margins of nine-tenths of magazine s-f. Great writer though he was, H. G. Wells has had a disastrous influence on the subsequent course of science fiction. . . . [S]cience fiction must jettison its present narrative forms and plots. . . . The biggest developments of the immediate future will take place, not on the Moon or Mars, but on Earth, and it is *inner* space, not outer, that needs to be explored. The only truly alien planet is Earth. In the past the scientific bias of s-f has been towards the physical sciences—rocketry, electronics, cybernetics—and the emphasis should switch to the biological sciences. (197)

Over the years, Ballard has said different things about science fiction and its practitioners, sometimes contradicting himself or putting forth alternate views. His conception of inner space remained relatively constant. In a 2005 interview, over forty years after the publication of "Which Way to Inner Space?," he retrospectively explains: "Inner space—I meant the invented space that you see in dreams and surrealist paintings in particular, but also in highly dislocated realities such as war zones, sites of plane crashes, earthquake aftermaths, derelict buildings, where the observer imposes his own fears, dreams, phobias" ("J. G. Ballard," Francis 179).

Ballard's conception of inner space may have been the single-most important apparatus in New Wave science fiction, a narrative speakeasy that flouted pulp prohibitions and celebrated modernist subversion. Initially Ballard aligned himself with the New Wave, but by the mid-1970s, mainstream science fiction had commercialized and assimilated it. "The New Wave, along with almost all the more intelligent magazines and anthologies," reflected Ballard in 1981, "has long since been inundated by a tsunami of planet fiction, sword-and-sorcery sensationalism, and *Star Wars* rip-offs, propelled by a reactionary s-f writers' guild closely interlocked with the New York publishers" ("New Means Worse" 190). Literary movements are the construction of fans and critics who publicize iconoclastic stables of authors involved in a similar enterprise. Sometimes the authors labor to construct themselves as figureheads of movements, such as Ezra Pound (Imagism), André Breton (Surrealism), Jack Kerouac (Beat), and, more recently, Carlton Mellick III (Bizarro). Ballard had no interest in this—he wrote what he wanted to write with little concern for group aesthetics or objectives, be it the New Wave or science fiction at large. Nonetheless his fiction will forever be associated with it, particularly that which appeared in the 1960s in *New Worlds*, the "ideological center of the . . . movement to rejuvenate conjectural literature" (Levin 254).

Surrealism played a central role in Ballard's line of flight. The canvases of Max Ernst, Marcel Duchamp, Giorgio de Chirico, Paul Delvaux, and Salvador Dali provided him with an imaginative toolkit for storytelling and stylization. He was more inspired by visual artists than authors, unmoved by most fiction writers (dead or alive) with the enthusiastic allowance of William S. Burroughs and a few others,[2] and he sometimes referred to himself as a "frustrated painter" who became a writer because he wasn't good enough with a brush.[3]

Like the Surrealists, Ballard had a keen interest in depth psychology. Many of his stories and novels demonstrate an active engagement with Freudian dream analysis and theories of the unconscious. As Jeanette Baxter notes, "The thrust of Surrealism's transformative thesis lay in the breaking down of repressive boundaries between the unconscious and the conscious, self and object, the irrational and the rational, reason and the imagination" (*Surrealist* 3). Ballard consistently implodes the same dualities while spurning the ogre of cultural repression. In the process, he foregrounds media pathology and the ways in which we are (re)produced as desiring-machines by consumer-capitalist technologies and architectures. Ballardian inner space hinges on these factors.

Ballard is usually reputed to have coined the term "inner space," but English novelist J. B. Priestley first introduced it in 1953. In "They Come from Inner Space," Priestley critiques science fiction for similar reasons and advises "moving inward, exploring ourselves, the hidden life of the psyche" rather than "travelling to the other side of the sun" (25). He says that UFOs are symptoms of cultural anxiety and manifestations of the collective unconscious, predating Jung's 1958 study *Flying Saucers: A Modern Myth*. His champion of inner space is Ray Bradbury, whom Ballard refers to as a "poet" in "Which Way to Inner Space?" and regarded as a nearly peerless science fiction writer (195).[4] James Pardey contends that "Which Way to Inner Space?" advances "They Come from Inner Space," even if Ballard doesn't acknowledge Priestley's essay:

> Ballard did more than merely echo Priestley. He also argued that for sf to avoid falling by the wayside it must discover new routes to inner space that draw on more abstract, speculative and experimental techniques like those used in other media such as modern art. As such, he was not just offering a commentary on the state of sf, he was issuing a manifesto that would need to be adopted if the genre was to secure its place as "the literature of tomorrow."

What emerged from Ballard's singular desire for the future of science fiction was a literature of affirmative pathology and alarming foresight that polarized readers, producing devoted fanatics and raw antagonists. This came to a crux with the postmodern turn[5] he took in *The Atrocity Exhibition* (1970) and the techno-erotic, paraphilic aesthetics of *Crash*, both of which incited heated controversies. Explorations of inner space became more common among New Wave science fiction writers, but it by no means took over the genre, and nobody could do it like Ballard. Even in his earliest short fiction, he shows that he was not just a gifted storyteller and wellspring of ideas. He was also a superior narrative stylist, a technician of prose with a powerful command of rhythm and sound (despite Michael Moorcock's insistence that his prose was not poetic[6]). He streamlined a vocabulary of math and science with an intense permutation of imagery, fabricating a language that is esoteric and artful yet highly readable. A reviewer of *Cocaine Nights* christened him "a man who [could] turn a sentence like a Nijinsky pirouette" (Dowell 1).

Ballard cultivated a sense of inner space until the end—even in the fictional autobiographies and so-called "crime novels" that comprise the bulk of his output in the second half of his career. He admitted that he had stopped writing science fiction, and he once said that, after *The Atrocity Exhibition*, he "abandoned the genre for good" ("I Really"). This wasn't because he disliked science fiction. In his eyes, science fiction had expired; the futures it once envisioned had been ingested by the present. "I think science fiction has come to an end," he remarked in 2007. "It's simply because the world that science fiction envisaged is already here in many respects" ("Historian" 471).

A similar experience befell William Gibson, who rose to fame as a cyberpunk author in the 1980s and 1990s, then began writing what qualified as mainstream novels in the twenty-first century. His reason had to do with the state of the present. "I found the material of the actual twenty-first century richer, stranger, more multiplex, than any imaginary twenty-first century could ever have been" ("Talk" 46). As with many science fiction authors, Gibson venerated Ballard, whose voice echoes throughout cyberpunk literature.[7] Ballard had signaled the assimilation of the future by the present long before Gibson published his first science fiction story, however, let alone before the turn of the twentieth century. And, curiously, Gibson has recently returned to the carcass of science fiction with *The Peripheral* (2014), a novel set in the far future.

Whether or not science fiction "has come to an end" depends upon how we view, define, and assess it. I tend to think the genre is very much alive—with the same limitations, regulations, redundancies, and imaginative deficiencies that irked Ballard. Something can be said for the snowballing science fictionalization of reality, an undeniable phenomenon that Ballard capitalizes on, but his "non," "anti," or "post" science fiction still functions as science fiction.

In *The Metamorphosis of Science Fiction*, Darko Suvin established a classic (and still viable) definition of science fiction, which is distinguished by a *novum*, a "totalizing phenomenon or relationship deviating from the author's and addressee's norm of reality" that is situated in a futuristic, alternate, or unusual context (64). In effect, readers experience "cognitive estrangement," recognizing the social conditions of their own present and existence while processing the new textual landscape. Ballard employs rational *novums* that defamiliarize and alienate readers in the context of conceivable, technologically advanced dystopias. He may have stopped writing science fiction according to a certain rubric and modality, but he never stopped reaching for the genuinely New, even as he recycled and retooled old storylines and leitmotifs, and even as he autobiographed himself. From start to finish, his body of work is coded by the cognitive estrangements, affective technologies, and latent desires of science fiction.

There are many fine book-length studies on J. G. Ballard, including over twenty monographs and critical anthologies, plus John Baxter's biography, *The Inner Man* (2011), and numerous peripheral studies, such as Colin Greenland's seminal analysis of the New Wave, *The Entropy Exhibition* (1983), and Iain Sinclair's 2008 pocketbook study of David Cronenberg's film adaptation of *Crash*. Among the strongest recent studies are Jeannette Baxter's *J. G. Ballard's The Surrealist Imagination: Spectacular Authorship* (2009), Samuel Francis's *The Psychological Fiction of J. G. Ballard* (2011), and David Paddy's *The Empires of J. G. Ballard: An Imagined Geography* (2015). Important precursors are David Pringle's *J. G. Ballard: The First Twenty Years* (1976) and V. Vale's periodicals for RE/Search Publications that, between 1984 and 2005, devoted four volumes to Ballard. Without the contributions of Pringle and Vale, Ballard scholarship may have taken a different course. Peter Brigg's *J. G. Ballard* (1985) deserves a strong nod, too; the chapters in which he thematizes the full breadth of short fiction (up to 1982) is an impressive feat, and his views of Ballard predate the more progressive scholarship of the twenty-first century, but this primer ends just over halfway through Ballard's career with the book that made him famous, *Empire of the Sun*, an autobiographical novel about his childhood in wartime China.

The present book focuses on the science fiction apparatus and how Ballard makes concerted attempts to defuse it—even when he claimed not to be writing it. After all, as he chirps in a 1970 interview by James Goddard: "Everything is science fiction!" Ballard isn't talking about garden-variety science fiction, of course, but rather the type defined by the realm of electronic media and capitalist technologies, which increasingly affect and pathologize subjectivity. It is the science fiction of reality studios, commodity fetishism, social entropy, and implosion. His assertion that science fiction is "everything" corresponds with the pop media philosophy of Canadian professor, cultural theorist, and public intellectual Marshall McLuhan, whom Ballard admired and whose work can operate as a theoretical equivalent to Ballard's fiction.

Coming into prominence in the 1950s and 1960s, McLuhan hypothesized that electronic technologies are a projection of the human sensorium, rendering the sphere of culture a sort of exfoliated inner space where the spacetime continuum has fallen by the wayside. He makes this proclamation in *Understanding Media: The Extensions of Man*, which broke new ground in the field of media studies:

> After three thousand years of explosion, by means of fragmentary and mechanical technologies, the Western world is imploding. During the mechanical ages we had extended our bodies into space. Today, after more than a century of electric technology, we have extended our central nervous system itself in a global embrace, abolishing both space and time as far as our planet is concerned. Rapidly, we approach the final phase of the extensions of man—the technological simulation of consciousness, when the creative process of knowing will be collectively and corporately extended to the whole of human society, much as we have already extended our senses and our nerves by the various media. (149)

In many of Ballard's diegeses, the external reality of consumer society is an illusion perpetrated by the central nervous system to the degree that we become fixtures (sometimes fluid, sometimes static) in the virtual space of billboards and signage, movies and TV shows, transportation and communication networks. Cyberpunks pushed this state of being further, extrapolating it into dystopian, hypercapitalist, technophilic futures where the body and mind have been invaded by machines. Ballard was concerned with the present—not the New in the Next, but the New in the Now. And the Now (socially, culturally, psychologically, ontologically) had become a geometry of electronic media. Representation was as good a tool as extrapolation for his efforts to "reach the imaginative truth" ("Visitor" 266). Even when he sets narratives in tropical places, such as the Pacific island of *Rushing to Paradise* or the African jungle of *The Day of Creation*, the "extensions of man" materialize in the form of pathological documentarians, camera towers, satellite dishes, television screens, and the niggling sense that the landscape, no matter where it is, may be a stage-set.

Throughout this book, I have tried to minimize specialized terminology and literary theorization in the interests of clarity and all-purpose accessibility. Ballard's fiction often invites (if not demands) theoretical consideration and rhetoric, however, and I think a scholarly examination of his entire canon will benefit from some application. Periodically I refer to four main figures. McLuhan is one of them. The others are Sigmund Freud, a major influence whom Ballard extolled as "one of the great surrealists" (270), and Gilles Deleuze and Félix Guatarri, the French philosopher and psychiatrist whose writings on capitalism and schizophrenia, respectively, help to map the contours of Ballard's narrative topography and the postmodern landforms that occupy it. As Paul March-Russell states, "Ballard's stories arguably represent the apotheosis of Deleuze and Guattari's writing machine, a principle of repetition, assemblage and modality that echoes the classical avant-garde as well as the proficiency of Edwardian short fiction" ("Writing Machine" 125).

Overall I am less concerned with Ballard's ideas about his fiction (what he thinks it "means," what his authorial intent is, and so on) than how that fiction operates within the sphere of culture and the science fiction megatext. I will provide background information on Ballard's life as well as the conception, production, and reception of his work with regard to his alleged flight from the field of science fiction. Unlike, say, Kurt Vonnegut, who began writing conventional science fiction but did in fact get sick of the genre and left it, cutting all ties to the community and devoting the rest of his career to literature that was not clearly science fiction, Ballard *always* wrote in the tradition of the genre, even when the genre failed to recognize it, and even when Ballard himself discounted it. How he defined himself in 1968 stands true until the end of his career: "I don't consider myself a science fiction writer in the same sense that Isaac Asimov or Arthur C. Clarke are science fiction writers. Strictly speaking I regard myself as an SF writer in the way that surrealism is also a scientific art" ("Interview," Storm 17).

This book is the first full-length monograph on J. G. Ballard since his death in 2009 that accounts for his career from beginning to end. For readers and critics new to Ballard, it will function as a primer; for veterans, there are fresh readings informed by some of the most recent Ballardian scholarship. I take a somewhat revisionist look at the author, resituating him in the science fictional milieu from which some scholarship has attempted to remove him. It is true that Ballard shook up a number of readers with the publication of *The Atrocity Exhibition* and *Crash*—they are unapologetically graphic, ultraviolent, and bizarre, and they deviate like hellions from the structure and content of the fictions that preceded them. Thereafter many readers were perfectly content to buy his novels and read his stories in magazines like *Ambit* and *Interzone*, often praising them. In 1980 he won the prestigious British Science Fiction Association Award for *The Unlimited Dream Company* for best novel of 1979, and subsequently he received five other awards and over thirty nominations for the Nebula, John W. Campbell, and Locus Awards, among others. This is hardly the record of an author who has been shunned by the field or turned his back on it. Furthermore, there are hundreds of scholarly articles about his writing, his novels were regularly reviewed in science fiction publications to the last, and reviewers typically regarded him with great respect, not with suspicion, as if he were a turncoat or deserter. Ballard didn't like conventions and he wasn't gregarious, but he remained devoted to the science fiction community and the project of science fiction as a source of innovation and original energy.

Ballard's writing evokes powerful emotions and visceral reactions; readers tend to feel strongly about it. People still spit venom and sing hallelujahs when they review *Crash* on Goodreads and Amazon, for instance, and they frequently project the techno-erotics of the novel onto the rest of Ballard's canon, having read little else by him and ignorant of the fact that sex doesn't figure that prominently in most of his fiction. Readers are also put off (or enlivened by) the moral and narrative ambiguities that lace through his fiction, because they like (or don't like) either the prospect of a creative pathology or the gray area into which Ballard collapses good and evil. Even Jeannette Baxter agonizes over the ambiguous framework of *Crash*, which, she says, "remains maddeningly, fascinatingly open to various and paradoxical readings" (*Surrealist* 5). But ambiguity is precisely the point—Ballard erupts from the vanguard of implosion, from the convergence of televisionary and psychic landscapes, from a matrix that problematizes and plays with the vicissitudes of the real, the good, and the true. Any definitive assertion of clarity or fixedness would belie the very nature of the petri dish in which he encases his characters.

Ballard said that he stopped writing science fiction in the late 1960s more than once. Of the longer works, he really only categorized the first four disaster novels as such. When he made these claims, he was talking about his work within the borderzones of genre science fiction and the rules of its editorial sentinels. His career maps a long and "lonely struggle trying to get a broader . . . and more elastic . . . definition of science fiction" ("Conversation," Verniere 234). He saw the great potential of the genre and wanted to innovate its better, braver expressions, embracing it as "a fiction of paradox" that straddles the divide between amusement and intellect, adventure and philosophy:

> It's thought of as escapist entertainment, but in fact in its naive way it's concerned in all its different varieties with a metaphysical understanding of the nature of human existence, especially at a time of change. Science fiction is the literature that responds to change. It's a dynamic form of fiction, whereas most mainstream fiction (which is very retrospective) is rather static. . . . Science fiction assumes a sort of dynamic flux. Nothing is certain, nothing is sure, everything is relative. (235)

These are the terms of J. G. Ballard's science fiction. In the chapters ahead, I will examine the dynamic flux that defines it.

CHAPTER 1

J. G. BALLARD, A.K.A. SHANGHAI JIM

DISCLAIMER

In a review of John Baxter's problematic biography, Roz Kaveney writes:

> J. G. Ballard would not have liked the idea that he could be summed up in a standard "life and works." He was far too savagely pessimistic a Futurist to welcome the inevitable explanation of his work and life in mutually reductive terms of each other. . . . On the other hand, much as Ballard disliked the process of having his portrait painted, he liked the sense of having been captured. Although he played off potential biographers—including John Baxter—against each other, and never committed himself to any, it is possible he would have welcomed a biography in the same spirit as a portrait—part of the due paid by the world to a writer who had forced it to see things through his eyes, at least some of the time.

Likewise does Simon Sellars express misgivings about a biographical effort in his introduction to *Extreme Metaphors*, the most comprehensive collection of Ballard's interviews to date. In the first few pages, Sellars collates a series of chronological "facts" that form a "potted history" in order to show how Ballard's "career is almost impossible to summarise" given the variable nature of his writing (xiii).

> In reality, if your first introduction to Ballard is by way of, say, his short story "The Drowned Giant," then you might think you have stumbled on to a master magical realist in the Swiftian tradition. If *Crash* is the initiation, then you might think twice before proceeding further, unless your palate is already sufficiently developed with a taste for the blackest intellectual meat. And what if your introduction is via one of the many interviews he gave across the arc of his career? (xiii)

Kaveney and Sellars aren't alone. While certain themes, motifs, images, and characterizations run the gamut of his library, Ballard does seem to spread himself all over the map, exploring a wide diversity of subject matter and evolving across different physical, social, and psychological landscapes. In a sense, this chapter is doomed to failure. As fun as it would be, I will not attempt to biograph Ballard in the vein of, say, a surrealist montage. Nor will I make any unfounded claims or speculations about his personality, desires, emotional condition, and so on, as Baxter does in his biography.[1]

Ballard's fictional autobiographies, *Empire of the Sun* and *The Kindness of Women*, have been mined as codings for his science fiction as well as documents of his real life. They both take significant liberties. Andrzej Gasiorek calls them "teasing explorations of narrative form as much as they are accounts of the writer's life" (19). Ballard himself has said that the books are largely inventions.[2] Even his "real" autobiography, *Miracles of Life*, wears the grin of the sphinx. That said, Ballard didn't live in Pynchonesque obscurity. He was a private man, even a reclusive man, like many professional authors with robust work ethics who do their writing from home. He wasn't inaccessible, however, and he didn't experience the deep sense of isolation that affected many of his protagonists, whose actions and desires, he once said, have "nothing to do with any quirks of my own" ("Interview," Goddard and Pringle 25).

I have appropriated the alias in the title of this biographical chapter, *Shanghai Jim*, from the 1991 BBC biopic that casts Ballard's work against the background of his origins in China and expatriate residency in England. The film documents his first and only return to Shanghai, and he figures prominently in it. Combining names that belong to two distant and very different cultures (in other words, the names of a decidedly non-Western city and a definitively Western male), the title substantiates Ballard's self-confessed feelings of alienation and unbelonging that punctuated his life and fiction. He never felt at home in England and had a strong distaste for British culture.[3] And, as he concluded in the biopic, he thought of Lunghua Camp, where he was interned during the war, as his real home, the place "to which I've always referred in my imagination."

BIRTH AND PARENTS

James Graham Ballard was born on November 15, 1930, in Shanghai, China. His father, also named James, and mother, Edna, were English natives, but work brought James Sr. to China shortly before the birth of their son and, in 1937, the birth of their daughter, Margaret, James Jr.'s only sibling.

Ballard profiles his parents in *Miracles*. They met on holiday in the 1920s in northwest England's Lake District, the picturesque stomping ground of the Romantic poets. His father held a degree in chemistry and worked for the Calico Printers Association, a British textile company based in Manchester that specialized in cotton production and goods. The year after their marriage in 1929, he transferred to Shanghai to run the CPA's overseas operation, the China Printing and Finishing Company. It paid well. At the time of the registration of James Jr.'s birth, the Ballards lived in a modest apartment inside the expatriate International Settlement, but they soon moved into a large, three-story house at 31A Amherst Avenue outside the settlement. They enjoyed many bourgeois amenities, including ten Chinese servants, a cook, a chauffeur, and a country club. This was in dire contrast to the native Chinese living in greater Shanghai, thousands of whom were impoverished and homeless. There were some wealthy Chinese, Japanese, and multinational gangsters, but the poor far outnumbered them, incessantly replenished by the influx of refugees from greater China. Ballard calls Shanghai "a media city before its time" (*Miracles* 5). Among his most vivid memories is the great divide he witnessed between rich and poor, excess and dearth, glitz and misery, even though as "a small boy aged 5 or 6," he wrote, "I must have accepted all this without a thought" (14).

In *The Inner Man*, Baxter says that Ballard had a bad relationship with his parents, who were indifferent to him. "With infant mortality high, it didn't pay to become too attached. Also, James and Edna were still young and enjoying their privileged life. They took little notice of Jim, meeting his numerous irritating questions with a blank stare and silence. His status, he wrote bitterly, was somewhere between a servant and the family Labrador, and even the servants never looked him in the eye" (11). As with much in Baxter's would-be torrid biography, his claims—sometimes wild and unfounded, casting his subject as a pathological maniac—should be taken with a grain of salt. True, Ballard often found himself left to the company of his imagination, but the fact is his early boyhood was reasonably happy and duly pampered. Not until the breakout of war and the internment of the International Settlement residents by the Japanese did he feel a disaffection toward his parents.[4] It would last their entire lives. There never seemed to be a major falling out, but Ballard remained ambivalent about them. Shortly before the end of his life, he divulged: "I think I have to face the fact that I didn't really like them very much. I tried in my earlier fiction—and in my earlier life . . . to maintain a kind of neutral stance, particularly towards my mother. I mean it is perfectly possible she wasn't a very nice human being; I don't think she was. I don't think either of them had that big an influence on me. One habit I'd learned from the war was that I'd have to look after myself" ("Marinated").

Ballard mentions James Sr.'s interest in science and science fiction in *Miracles*, underscoring his esteem for H. G. Wells and his belief in "modern science as mankind's saviour" and "the power of science to create a better world" (8, 43). It's tempting to read his fiction as a reaction to or revolt against the proverbial Law of the Father. After all, the fiction, while far more positive and hopeful than it has been given credit for, customarily extrapolates "science" into various internal and external architectures of dystopia. Ballard was adamant about the ways in which science had become a fictional enterprise. In 1968 he suggested that the social and psychological sciences are "the major producers of fiction. It's not the writers anymore" ("Interview," Storm 17). His father came from a generation whose ideology of optimism deliquesced in the wake of two world wars. James Sr.'s belief in the primacy of science belonged to the nineteenth century and the Victorians, who had yet to experience the technological horrors initiated by the Great War. In contrast, his son's beliefs reached for the future and the consumer-capitalist media technologies that would unhinge the studios of reality and desire.

PREWAR SHANGHAI

Ballard accentuates the capitalist dog-eat-dog way of life that dominated the "bright but bloody kaleidoscope that was Shanghai" (*Miracles* 6). As a boy, with one eye he witnessed great wealth and comfort, with the other the deepest and darkest blight. It wasn't uncommon for him to see corpses littering the pavement. "Chinese roamed the streets of Shanghai, ready to do anything to find work. Every morning when I was driven to school I would notice fresh coffins left by the roadside, sometimes miniature coffins decked with paper flowers containing children of my own age. Bodies lay in the streets of downtown Shanghai, wept over by Chinese peasant women, ignored in the rush of passers-by" (14). Civil war, floods, and famine had driven millions of peasants from their villages to Shanghai. "Unlimited venture capitalism rode in gaudy style down streets lined with beggars showing off their sores and wounds" (5).

Shanghai struck him as an oneiric and mystical society, much as England did later, but for different reasons. He always asserted that his fiction was, first and foremost, an invention, yet he wasn't reluctant to discuss the real-world experiences and phenomena that informed it. Reality itself proved to be an evolving fiction, and in a way, his novels and stories merely channel their own essence. All told, Shanghai was "a self-generating fantasy that left my own little mind far behind. . . . I think a large part of my fiction has been an attempt to evoke it by means other than memory" (6).

Ballard attended a prestigious boys' school affiliated with the Holy Trinity Cathedral, an English-speaking Anglican church. The Japanese invaded in 1937 and established a stranglehold on Shanghai, inaugurating the Second Sino-Japanese War. They left non-Chinese residents alone, and life in the International Settlement continued as usual adjacent brutal fighting in the countryside just a mile from the Ballards' home (24). They fled and rented a house in the French Concession, which was not part of the International Settlement and better insulated from warfare. The sneak attack on Pearl Harbor in December 1941 ushered Japan into the World War with Europe and America. That same month, the Japanese occupied the International Settlement, and by 1943 they had detained British expatriates and other civilian Allies in internment camps. The Ballards entered one such camp, Lunghua Civil Assembly Centre.

LUNGHUA

On the grid of Ballard's personal and narrative life, Lunghua is a seminal co-ordinate. It is the primary setting for *Empire of the Sun*, his most widely read and bestselling novel, and it is the traumatic kernel for the alienation, violence, dehumanization, and psychological terror that flares up again and again in his fiction. I'm disinclined to make any allegations about the state of Ballard's actual psyche. I will submit to Umberto Rossi's argument that "the suggestion remains that J. G. Ballard's mind—and the minds of his fictional alter egos—is a battlefield, a complex psychological landscape of violent images, memories and histories, some of which are real and some of which are fictional" ("Mind" 68).[5] If this is the case, surely the greater part of that landscape owes a debt to Lunghua and what the young Ballard experienced during his internment.

Located several miles from the city, Lunghua was a middle school and former university campus that had been damaged earlier in the war. It encamped nearly two thousand people, mostly European and American civilians. There wasn't much to the complex. As Baxter explains in his biography, it consisted

> of seven three-storey concrete buildings, with three large wooden barracks, standing on an area of open ground. . . . The surrounding land, so flat you could see the distant towers of Shanghai, was paddy fields, infested with mosquitoes. The most visible landmark, a Buddhist pagoda, with a giant and threatening statue inside, bristled with anti-aircraft guns to protect the nearby airfield. In addition to installing a barbed-wire fence around the camp, the Japanese refurbished fifty-nine dormitories to house about a dozen individuals each, and 127 family rooms. (21)

This is similar to the way Ballard describes the layout of Lunghua in a 1975 interview[6] and *Miracles* (58) as well as *Empire of the Sun*.[7] Each description evokes a sense of desolation, wilderness, and looming violence. In Ballard's memory, though, Lunghua was a playground and, ironically, a site of literal and imaginative freedom. He loved it. For two and a half years, he lived in relative happiness.

> I thoroughly enjoyed my nearly three years in Lunghua camp. It was a huge slum, and the people who really relish life in a slum are of course the teenage boys. They run wild. I ran wild. I was totally out of the control of my parents. And that's why I left them out of *Empire of the Sun* when I came to write the book, because it wasn't psychologically true to have had my parents in the novel. To all

intents and purposes in Lunghua camp between the ages of twelve and fifteen, I was a hooligan. ("Memento" 276)

Ballard didn't skulk through the camp in a gang like the teenage droogs of Anthony Burgess's *A Clockwork Orange* (1962). His "hooliganism" consisted mainly of innocuous horseplay with other boys, playing chess with bored internees, bartering for copies of popular magazines from American sailors, snatching the odd sweet potato, and so forth. He attended school regularly, and there were rules and discipline for children in the camp, but not like there had been in the International Settlement. Ballard gained a sense of independence and autonomy that few children his age ever experience. Coupled with the atrocities he was exposed to, it changed him dramatically, forcing him into an early adulthood.

Unlike his elders, he didn't mind the ramshackle state of the camp, which worsened over time. Food and water, on the other hand, concerned everybody. He didn't starve to the extent of his protagonist in *Empire of the Sun*. The denouement of his actual internment wasn't as apocalyptic as the novel's either. But he was often hungry, and rations steadily depleted as the Japanese lost footing in the war. Near the end, there was almost no food left. Melancholy and despair accompanied a fear that the Japanese would close the camp and execute everybody in it. Then, one day in August 1945, the internees awoke to find that the Japanese militia had fled during the night. By September the Ballards had returned to 31A Amherst Avenue. Shanghai was an eerily different place. No longer a multicultural, futique, mediatized city of excess, it became an insignia of "the strange surrealist spectacles that war produced" and a reminder that "the unrestricted imagination [is] the best guide to reality" (Ballard, "Nothing" 384).

"RETURN" TO ENGLAND

In November 1945, Ballard, his sister, and his mother traveled by ship to England. His father stayed in Shanghai and resumed his job with the CPA for several years before joining them. Ballard expected to return to and live in Shanghai when it was rebuilt, but it wouldn't be until 1991, in his sixties, that "Shanghai Jim" would see his birthplace again.

Contrary to the self-history Ballard spun (or allowed to be spun), his "return" to England, according to shipping records, was not the first time he had been there. The Ballard family visited England for an extended stay in 1934 (when he was three years old) and again in 1939 (when he was eight and attended school for a term in Sussex). He never lied about these visits, but he never mentioned them. By omission, he facilitated the growth of the legend of the fifteen-year-old boy raised entirely in China with no real knowledge of his parents' homeland beyond popular magazines and books.

He didn't like England. It was hardly the place he had read about in China. Rather than a country of promise and futurity, socially and topographically it was a bombed-out wasteland with buildings in rubble and a population in dire moral and emotional straits. Ballard recollects being taken aback by how "the English talked as if they had won the war, but acted as if they had lost it. They were clearly exhausted by the war, and expected little of the future. . . . [H]ope itself was rationed, and people's spirits were bent low" (*Miracles* 111). More troubling was the system of stratification in which the shell-shocked middle class treated the working class "as almost another species, and fenced themselves off behind a complex system of social codes" (113). He despised these divisions, and whereas his fiction often favors the dynamics of American culture, *High-Rise* and his final four novels directly engage and critique this fundament of English society.

Life in England paled in comparison to life in Shanghai. A Freudian might say that Ballard's writing symptomatizes the proverbial return of the repressed, an unconscious delirium fired through the shotgun of his imagination, or perhaps one form of a desire to "return to the womb" and reclaim the rapturous feelings produced by near-death episodes. Ballard has implied that his writing is an effort to repossess or tap back into his boyhood self, projecting the imaginative glories and actual horrors of his own past onto narratives of the present and the not-too-distant future. Whatever the case, even by normal standards, he led a peaceful, uneventful adult life, riding the wheel of monotony in his day-to-day affairs. And he liked it that way.

SCHOOLING

From 1946 to 1949 Ballard attended The Leys, an English boarding school in Cambridge. In *Miracles*, he explains that, unlike many institutions of its type, The Leys "was liberal and progressive" and "well-equipped, with superb physics, chemistry and biology labs, so much so," he said, "that I rather looked down on the tired and broken equipment I later found in the University science laboratories" (115). It was here that he acquired a basic understanding of science, literature, and art. Living in Cambridge also provided ample outlets for going to theaters that played American film noir and B-movies, which fascinated him.

Ballard said he wrote his first book (about how to play contact bridge) when he was around twelve years old ("J. G. Ballard," Linnett 48). He composed his first stories at The Leys, writing "in idle moments during evening prep," and once he started, he didn't stop: "I persisted with my short sketches, gnawing away at the inner bone" of the past (*Miracles* 117). "[At sixteen,] I discovered Freud and the surrealists, a stick of bombs that fell in front of me and destroyed all the bridges that I was hesitating to cross" (120). This was a vital discovery that paved the road to science fiction he wanted to take. "Surrealism and psychoanalysis offered an escape route, a secret corridor into a more real and more meaningful world, where shifting psychological roles are more important than the 'character' so admired by English schoolmasters and literary critics, and where the deep revolutions of the psyche matter more than the social dramas of everyday life, as trivial as a tempest in a tea cosy" (121).

In 1949 he went to King's College to study medicine. He wanted to study psychology, but it was still a minor discipline and he would have had to major in philosophy. Moreover, to pursue any kind of career in psychology, he had to acquire a medical degree. He liked the idea of becoming a doctor and decided to give it a shot. It didn't last. After two years, he realized that medicine wasn't for him and left the program. King's College is significant for being the place where he published his first story, "The Violent Noon," in a student newspaper. It also grounded him in the principles of anatomy and technological discourse that distinguish his prose and galvanize his marque of cognitive estrangement. More generally, his medical studies showed him the power of the imagination: "My years in the dissection room were important because they taught me that though death was the end, the human imagination and the human spirit could triumph over our own dissolution" (*Miracles* 131).

After the publication of "The Violent Noon" Ballard knew he wanted to become a writer. His father was skeptical. In terms of income and prestige as much as practicality, making up stories for a living was a far cry from practicing medicine, and he didn't know how his son might bring it to bear.

He encouraged him to pursue a degree in English literature at University of London's Queen Mary College. In spite of himself, Ballard began in 1951. This, too, he regretted and in fact utterly disparaged, calling it "the worst possible preparation for a writer's career" (136). He left after his first year. He was done with academia, and he no longer wanted to be economically dependent on his parents, who had subsidized his studies.

ODD JOBS AND THE ROYAL AIR FORCE

For the next two years, Ballard worked odd jobs, among them a stint as a copywriter for an advertising agency, as a porter for a street market in the chrysanthemum department, and as a door-to-door encyclopedia salesman. The latter job seems exceedingly odd, but he claimed to be "surprisingly successful, partly because the *Waverly Encyclopedia*," he said," was the one I had read as a child in Shanghai—I knew it backwards and genuinely believed in it" (144). By no means was it a career he wanted to pursue, though, even to support his writing habit.

Ballard's lifelong obsession with flying and aviation recurs in his fiction. In 1954 he joined the Royal Air Force. He was twenty-three years old and his writing career showed little promise of taking off; he thought the experience would be good imaginative fodder for the development of his craft. Basic training for the RAF began in Lindsey, Lincolnshire. He was posted to a Canadian base in Moose Jaw, Saskatchewan, where he remained for less than six months before transferring back to England in 1955, at which point he resigned from the RAF. In *Miracles*, he says that he worked diligently on his writing and composed his first science fiction stories in the service. There is no evidence of any literary output; he probably spent most of his time reading science fiction magazines. Nevertheless, when he returned to England again, he was confident in his abilities as a writer and keen on starting a career.

Ballard came late to science fiction. He had not been a big fan or reader in his early teens beyond the few items he could get his hands on in Shanghai, such as *Flash Gordon* and *Buck Rogers* comic books. Science fiction's popularity surged after World War II, and magazines were plentiful and close at hand in Canada. He read them voraciously, turned off by the boyish genre conventions of most pulps but inspired by "magazines like *Galaxy* and *Fantasy & Science Fiction*, where the short stories were set in the present or very near future, extrapolating social and political trends already evident in years after the war" (150). Science fiction also "looked searchingly at the abuses of psychiatry and at politics conducted as a branch of advertising" (150), features that became crucial motifs in his work. The seed of inner space had been planted. He saw the great untapped potential in the genre and vowed to "interiorise" it, "looking for the pathology that underlay the consumer society, the TV landscape and the nuclear arms race, a vast untouched continent of fictional possibility" (152).

Awaiting discharge from the service in May 1955, Ballard wrote his first bona fide science fiction story, "Passport to Eternity," at RAF Booker near High Wycombe in England. It didn't come out in print until 1962. His stories began to appear with regularity in 1956, not long after he had left the RAF and married Helen Mary Matthews ("Mary"), whom he met in 1954 before being stationed overseas.

SHEPPERTON

At the time of their marriage in September 1955, Mary was pregnant with their first child, Christopher James ("James"), born in 1956. They had two more children, Caroline Fay ("Fay"), born in 1957, and Beatrice ("Bea"), born in 1959. During these years, Ballard wrote and submitted many stories to UK and some US science fiction magazines. American publications paid more, but they rejected the stories he sent out, and he sold his earliest pieces to English magazines. The income he received wasn't enough to live on. He continued to work other jobs and became the deputy editor for *Chemistry and Industry*, a trade journal aimed at working chemists and industrialists.

In 1960 Ballard and his family moved south of London to Shepperton into a two-story, semi-detached house at 36 Old Charlton Road. Asked in 1984 if he enjoyed living there, he replied:

> I don't really *live* here—in a way it's just a sort of *grid reference* on the map. I came here 20 years ago with my wife simply because we didn't have any money. We'd had three children by then, so we moved . . . down the sort of price scale which coincided, by and large, with the distance from London, and found a small house here. Suburbs are nice places to bring up kids in England. I stayed on here out of inertia once the kids went to schools and all the rest of it. ("Interview," Juno and Vale 14)

In spite of the arbitrariness of Shepperton—Ballard could have moved to any number of suburbs outside of London—it became a central inspiration for his fiction, and he set multiple narratives there, most notably *The Unlimited Dream Company*. He champions Shepperton for being child friendly and "a great place to work" because "it's isolated" (ibid.). The physical and psychological landscape became a fertile source of extrapolation for him. With Heathrow Airport seven miles to the north and Shepperton Studios several blocks away, he cultivated two of his most iconic themes: flying (as agency) and the mediatization of reality (via film and television). The growing sprawl of expressways and malls in the area factored significantly into his vision. Shepperton fostered Ballard's exploration of the effects of capitalist media and technology on subjectivity. He viewed this liminal place (and suburbs in general) as "the real psychic battleground—it's on the wavefront of the future, rather than a city area. I keep an eye on all the social trends that develop," he said. "I would almost call it an *airport culture* that's springing up around in suburbs like this—a very transient kind of world" (ibid.). It is no surprise that the characters he invented in that modest home on Old Charlton Road, where he lived until he died, were almost always transients, physically and figuratively, wandering through labyrinths of the earth and the mind.

For all Shepperton's modernization, it reminded Ballard of Shanghai, as he notes in the biopic: "The river, which winds through Shepperton like a sort of great snake, all the gravel lakes here and the great reservoirs of the Metropolitan Water Board—you realise when you fly from Heathrow and look down on the place, this is a marine world. I think it was the right choice at the time, because Shepperton has insinuated itself into my fiction over the years." The topographic (and by extension psychic) ghost of Shanghai haunted the London suburb, but it wouldn't be until the early 1980s, over twenty years after he published his first science fiction stories, that he actually wrote about Shanghai in *Empire of the Sun* (and the novel's seed-story "The Dead Time)," an experience that reminded him just how much his writing had been shaped by the circumstances of his Chinese boyhood.

In 1986 Ballard said: "Obviously this house and this quiet suburb where I work doesn't have a real grip on my imagination. Its great appeal for me is that it is nowhere, that it represents the minimal context in which I can credibly feel part of a landscape, but it's not one from which I draw anything, imaginatively speaking" ("Future" 230). At face value, the sentiment seems like a wild inaccuracy, if only considering that the engine of Ballard's imagination revved for the better part of his life in that quiet suburb. *The Unlimited Dream Company* alone undermines his conviction that the suburb "doesn't have a real grip on my imagination" in that it can be read as *a fable about the grip of the imagination*. In so many ways, Shepperton was instrumental to his fiction. Here Ballard is probably talking about the dull grind of daily life in Shepperton, which didn't possess the sensory stimuli of, say, Camden or Westminster in Inner London. As a symbol for his own past along with the external and internal causeways of the future, Shepperton, on the contrary, *fueled* his imagination.

WRITING CAREER AND FAMILY LIFE

In "The Pleasures of Reading," Ballard says that he was twenty-six years old when he published his first story and thirty-two when he composed his first novel, *The Drowned World* (181). In fact, he published "The Violent Noon" when he was twenty and wrote his actual first novel, *The Wind from Nowhere*, when he was thirty, but later he disavowed both works as juvenilia and always foregrounded *The Drowned World*. It came out in 1962 after he had settled into family life and sold nearly twenty stories exclusively to the British science fiction magazines *Science Fantasy* and *New Worlds*.

Reviews of *The Drowned World* were overwhelmingly positive, and it was translated into multiple languages. *The Wind from Nowhere* came out the same year. He didn't make a lot of money on either novel, but he made enough. He took a gamble and quit his job at *Chemistry and Industry* to focus full time on writing. That same year, he wrote a guest editorial for *New Worlds*, and in the late 1960s he began editing *Ambit*. For decades, he composed scores of nonfiction essays and reviews for magazines and dabbled in other "extracurricular activities," some of which included "full page, sexually charged ads in magazines; acting in a surreal short film with Gabrielle Drake, based on *Atrocity* fragments; attempting a multimedia play based around the car crash; and staging his notorious exhibition of crashed cars, which managed to enrage its audience of drunken guests" ("Sci-fi," Barber 22). After *The Wind from Nowhere*, however, his primary income came from writing fiction. The gamble worked.

Not only did *The Drowned World* lay the foundation for his career and establish Ballard as a major talent, grabbing the attention of the broader literary establishment, it brought greater interest to the science fiction genre, especially among publishers in the UK. It was a strong, auspicious beginning for the budding novelist, whose career was as healthy and promising as his young family.

Tragedy struck in 1964 when Mary died unexpectedly from pneumonia during a vacation in Spain. Ballard was devastated yet determined to be strong for his children. He did his best "to be both mother and father to them, though it was extremely rare in the 1960s to find single fathers caring for their children" (*Miracles* 182). In his biography, Baxter plays up the compensatory drinking and womanizing that allegedly took place after Mary's death, and he contends that Ballard's fiction became the product of his crazed bereavement. Surely he was grief-stricken, and losing Mary influenced his narrative choices, but Baxter's book often reads more like a chintzy celebrity gossip column than a legitimate, properly documented life history intent on exposing Ballard as a reckless boozehound and sex maniac. Ballard was no angel, but he was a good father, at least according to his children. As Fay once said, "Daddy sacrificed everything to bring us up. We had a lady who came in to change and wash the sheets every Friday, but apart from that he did everything, and he did it brilliantly. Our home was a nest, a lovely, warm family nest" (Pringle, "Obituary").

A proud single parent, Ballard raised his children at 36 Old Charlton Road and continued to produce novels and stories at a steady pace with some extended gaps between them (for example, a four-year hiatus between the publication of *High-Rise* in 1975 and *The Unlimited Dream Company* in 1979). By the time *Empire of the Sun* was published in 1984, after the children had left home and began their lives apart from him, Ballard had over ten books and almost one hundred stories to his name.

LATER LIFE AND DEATH

With each new novel, Ballard became more financially stable while leading a sparing life. Steven Spielberg's adaptation of *Empire of the Sun* in 1987 elevated Ballard to new heights of fame and fortune, yet he continued to live frugally for the rest of his days. When he died in 2009, he possessed a net worth of £4,019,809—over $6 million, most of which was left to the children.

At the end of *Shanghai Jim*, Ballard reflects on his past from a room in a building erected on the site of Lunghua Camp. Sitting next to a set of old wooden bunks in a white linen suit and fedora, he says:

> In many ways, [Lunghua] is the most important place in my life. . . . I came to puberty here . . . and I came to something close to an adult mind in this camp. . . . There is no doubt that [coming here] is a kind of settling of accounts for me. It is a coming to terms with the past and with the sort of dreams that to some extent have sustained me during the last 45 years in England where I was never really all that at home. . . . This camp has been my real home to which I've always referred in my imagination.

The final shot of Ballard in the biopic shows him leaning over the handrail of a boat in the Bund, a waterfront area in central Shanghai that was once part of the International Settlement. He would never return to China. Here, in 1991, his life had come full circle. But his life (and career) were far from over.

Between 1991 and 2009, he wrote only a few essays and stories, but he published six more novels and his autobiography, averaging about one book every three years. As I will discuss in chapter 6, many of these novels center on the theme of crime, violence, and pathology as a means of agency from the ennui that afflicts the elitist residents of assorted postcapitalist European communities. They are at once weird and provocative contributions to Ballard's canon, demonstrating clear thematic obsessions and narrative recyclings to the degree that his final four novels can be read as revisions or remakes of one another, although each new installment builds and riffs on its predecessor, and they remain under the spell of Ballard's trademark estrangement.

In his personal life, he spent time with longstanding partner Claire Walsh, whom he met at a party hosted by Michael Moorcock several years after Mary died. Ballard speaks highly of Claire in *Miracles*, emphasizing their deep intellectual and emotional connection, their extensive travels together, and the importance of Claire's knowledge of the publishing industry. (When they met, she was a publicity manager for an art books publisher, and later she worked for different publishers, namely Gollancz, before moving on to other pursuits.)

Claire died of cancer in 2014, five years after Ballard himself succumbed to the disease, mistaking back pain for arthritis over the course of a year. By the time he consulted a specialist, it was too late: the cancer, originating in the prostate, had spread to his spine and ribs. He and Claire never married or lived together, and he moved into her flat in 2008 so that she could assist in his treatment. He continued to deteriorate until passing away on April 19, 2009, at age 78.

In "Remembering J. G. Ballard's Science Fiction Legacy," Alasdair Wilkins writes: "Ballard's iconic voice . . . infused his ideas with a literary style few of his science fiction contemporaries could truly match. . . . [He] was the very best a certain strand of science fiction—equal parts literary, dystopian, edgy, and endlessly experimental—could ever hope to be." Wilkins does well to put him on a science fictional pedestal. Like many readers and critics, however, he wrongly brands Ballard "endlessly experimental," hinging too much of his prose on *The Atrocity Exhibition* and perhaps some of the more playful stories in *War Fever*. Ballard hardly ever experimented with style. For the most part, he was a storyteller and wrote straight narratives for serious readers. At the same time, he broke the rules, chased the wiles and whimsies of his mind's eye, and repeatedly extrapolated his personal history. The result is a body of work that, above all, explores the fears and compulsions of a bruised, technologized psyche.

CHAPTER 2

THIS WAY TO INNER SPACE
Short Fiction and Nonfiction

OVERVIEW

According to John Clute and David Pringle, "Ballard is regarded by some as a better short story writer than novelist" ("Ballard, J. G."). I think he had a talent for both forms in their own rights. If nothing else, his short fiction shaped the contours of his authorial identity, ingenuity, and style. This is especially true of the stories published in the 1960s, which "drew an enthusiastic audience" and were "masterpieces of melancholy and desolation" (ibid.).

Most of this book focuses on the novels. They contain the real meat of Ballard's legacy. The stories, though, are crucial building blocks, test sites for his craft and the emergent flows of inner space as well as seedlings for book-length works.[1] Peter Brigg writes:

> Ballard's early intentions and methods made the short story an ideal realm for his development as a writer. His highly pictorial imagination made it easy for

> him to develop arresting scenes. Short stories require compact presentation of image with necessary information carefully arranged like the objects in a small painting. His relative dissatisfaction with the methods of the telling in the pulp era of science fiction frequently fitted well to the short story writer's opportunity to begin with a clean "canvas." . . . Ballard's stories soon developed into compacted, dense, atmospheric, psychologically intense tales that benefit from the brevity of the short story as their moods would be difficult to sustain over hundreds of pages. (19)

He published upwards of one hundred short stories over the span of five decades. Not including best-of anthologies, they were collected in eighteen volumes, beginning with *The Voices of Time and Other Stories* (1962) and ending with *War Fever* (1990). The stories treat many of the same themes as the novels. Most of them appeared in the science fiction magazines *New Worlds, Science Fantasy, Fantastic Stories of Imagination, The Magazine of Fantasy of Science Fiction, Interzone,* and *Ambit.* He sold his last story, "The Dying Fall," to *Interzone* in 1996. Until his death in 2009, he focused on novels and, last, his autobiography. He stopped writing short stories because of market changes.[2] In the 1950s and 1960s one could scrape together a living selling stories, but in the 1990s and beyond, it was no longer possible—although Ballard once confessed, "in some ways [these final novels] are extended short stories. But please don't tell anyone" ("I Really").

Ballard composed and sold his first stories in the 1950s. They were published in *Science Fantasy* and *New Worlds,* UK magazines both under the editorship of E. J. Carnell. He wasn't the advocate for experimentation and innovation that Michael Moorcock would be when he took over *New Worlds* in 1964. Then again, Carnell didn't fully subscribe to the Campbellian brand of Golden Age ethics seen in most American science fiction magazines, which favored linear narratives, hard science, space opera, and alpha male heroics.

In 1951, while studying medicine at King's College, Ballard published his first story, "The Violent Noon," in *Varsity,* Cambridge University's student newspaper. He was twenty. The story won first prize in a writing competition; he'd written it as a "Hemingwayesque pastiche" to appease the judges (Sellars, "Collecting"). Years later, he disavowed "The Violent Noon" as his inaugural story, just as he disavowed his first published novel, *The Wind from*

Nowhere, calling it a "piece of hack work" ("Interview," Goddard and Pringle 23). Portraying a covert terrorist attack, the story nonetheless reveals "a basic Ballardian theme: the surprising characteristics that emerge when people are immersed in unexpected, brutal situations" (McGrath, "In the Beginning").

Years later, after quitting medical school and the RAF, he sold his first stories as a professional writer. In December 1956, "Prima Belladonna" appeared in *Science Fantasy*, "Escapement" in *New Worlds*. Technically "Prima Belladonna" is the maiden story, since the December issue of *Science Fantasy* was released two weeks before *New Worlds*. These publications came after much rejection, predominantly in American magazines whose editors "bought almost entirely from people they knew. Since many doubled as agents, the writers were also their clients, while the book publishers to whom they sold were also old pals" (Baxter, *The Inner Man* 78). Persistence paid off, however, and Ballard started to make steady sales in the UK.

There are some gaps in the history of his short story production. In the late 1950s, for example, a two-year hiatus resulted from attending his first and only science fiction convention and getting a taste of fandom, which turned him off to the genre.[3] But a look at Ballard's primary bibliography reveals a consistent and adamant output, typically with multiple stories published almost every year between 1957 and 1992.

Ballard's early stories were instrumental to the New Wave, a movement actuated by the short fiction published in *New Worlds* under the editorship of Carnell and then Moorcock. Carnell's publication of "The Terminal Beach" in 1963 was a momentous trigger-pull for the New Wave, although what Ballard and like-minded authors were doing wasn't new to literature. In essence, they applied modernist techniques to science fiction. Ballard led the pack with stories that aroused hostility in both UK and US fans who preferred old-guard science fiction and thought literary experimentation didn't belong in the genre. In 1968 Ballard jokingly said: "I *am* the New Wave!" ("Interview," Storm 17). He didn't really care about the label, or rather, he cared insofar as it encouraged more newness and originality.

> People like Tom Disch, John Sladek, Michael Butterworth, Pam Zoline, the young American painter over here. They're starting to write a different kind of science fiction, but whether they will stay within science fiction long enough to consoli-

> date the so-called New Wave or whether—as I think will happen—they'll just move out of science fiction altogether and begin writing a speculative fiction that doesn't owe anything to science fiction, I don't know. (Ibid.)

Ballard understood that the New Wave was more a symptom of the shortcomings of science fiction than a new, vibrant subgenre. He also understood that it couldn't possibly last. There are many novels associated with the New Wave, but it was engendered and propagated by the short form, and "the great dying-off of the magazines" that began in the 1970s ensured the slow dissolution of the movement that, not coincidentally, accompanied the slow dissolution of Ballard's short story production ("Interview," Fuchs and Körber 138).

In the Starmont Readers Guide, Brigg provides a careful and concise overview of Ballard's stories through 1982, organizing them by subject matter and themes that include the arts, dream states, time, urbanity, outer space, psychology, sex, and the mythic. He expresses trepidation about having limited room to survey the material, but his discussion is perfectly sound as a primer. Rather than cherry-pick representative stories for deliberation or mimic Brigg's approach, I concentrate on what I believe to be Ballard's most important fiction collections, writing detailed abstracts for each of them in hopes that less familiar readers and scholars can get a sense of the context out of which they arose, what they contain, and the themes they exhibit. No critic has ever looked at the collections collectively, so to speak, and I think this approach will offer insight into their confluence as I appraise the major short works. Together these collections feature the better part of Ballard's sizable output of short fiction. Among my selections is *War Fever* (1990); all of the stories in it were published after Brigg's book came out in 1985. Titles I don't mention tend to recycle stories originally published in other collections. I end this chapter with a précis on the nonfiction Ballard published between 1962 and 1995, most of which appear in *A User's Guide to the Millennium*.

Many of Ballard's fiction collections are iconic as individual volumes and revered as such by Ballardians for the interrelations of the stories therein. Before researching and writing this book, I had read the better part of Ballard's short and long fiction, but I didn't have a strong grounding in secondary criticism, nor did I realize how fanatical his fans truly are. Far from the costumed role-players who roam the hotel hallways, dealer rooms, and street blocks of Comic-Con, Dragon Con, and other conventions, many of them are university professors, literary critics, artists, and authors who operate as executors of Ballard's literary "estate," preserving it with tenacity while promoting new modes of commentary, interpretation, and creativity. These are the true Ballardians, and much of this book takes a cue from this small but emphatic subculture of critical obsession.

Due to market forces, editorial demands, and magazine readerships, Ballard's stories approximate genre science fiction far more than his novels do. The evolution of the novels demonstrates a progressive rejection of convention and a freedom of narrative and thematic choice, but the stories are central to an understanding of the author's development. "The Terminal Beach" is the jewel in the crown. Ballard said,

> It is certainly one of my most important stories. Even though it was published in *New Worlds*, it wasn't a science fiction story at all, but rather conveyed merely a certain science fiction atmosphere. It described a landscape that was the expression of a particular psychological state—our fear of nuclear war. . . . I think "The Terminal Beach" is the first real "inner space" story and it leads directly to *The Atrocity Exhibition*, but also to novels like *Crash*, *High-Rise* and *Concrete Island*." ("I Really")

There are some standalone gems, but short stories served Ballard best as the imaginative sparks for longer works.

THE VOICES OF TIME (1962)

The Voices of Time • The Sound Sweep • The Overloaded Man • Zone of Terror • Manhole 69 • The Waiting Grounds • Deep End

In Ballard's first collection, we see the advent of his distinctive style and tone. The titular story deals with psychic, actual, and narrative time, a theme that ripened in his early novels. John Baxter claims that "The Voices of Time"

> transgressed every rule of science fiction by behaving as if there were none. Fiction traditionally aims to lure readers into a consensual fantasy; to involve them in a story and have them identify with a protagonist. Jim broke with this method. He distances us from identification by fragmenting the narrative into numbered chapters, printing some passages in italics, and interrupting the text with tables

> of digits and the single out-of-scale word "YOU"—techniques learned from *Limbo 90* and *The Stars My Destination*, and anticipating *Naked Lunch*. (107)

Baxter's argument is hyperbolic. The story isn't terrifically experimental or transgressive. It doesn't come close to the word-image experiments with synesthesia that Bester practiced in *Stars* (published four years earlier than "Voices" in 1956) or the scatological, surreal, sex-charged bravura that Burroughs unleashed in *Naked Lunch* (published one year before "Voices" in 1959 and thus not anticipatory). But it does break fresh ground and employ minor experimental techniques. A product of the Atomic Era, "Voices" might be Ballard's most important rookie story, depicting a surrealist future endangered by an entropic force, describing one man's descent into a symbolic underworld, and standing tall as an example of inner space.

Other stories or "voices" in this collection science fictionalize the time motif. Set in a mediatized near-future, "The Overloaded Man" concerns an axiomatic Ballardian alien (in other words, a male subject alienated by and within a hostile socioeconomic matrix) who believes he "may actually be stepping out of time" and possesses the psychic ability to escape life in the hypermodern consumerist village he lives in and despises (247). He wants to achieve "pure ideation, the undisturbed sensation of a psychic being untransmuted by any physical medium" (253). In the process, he absentmindedly murders his Stepford-like wife, an insignia of the culture that has interpellated him.

The stories in *The Voices of Time* take place in well-defined future and/or alternate worlds. They represent the impermanence of time and raise issues that would become Ballardian staples. "Deep End," where we see the first meaningful occurrence of Ballard's iconic empty swimming pool, touches on the Adam complex he foregrounds in the natural disaster novels and embeds in almost every subsequent novel. On a moribund Earth, most of whose occupants have migrated to Mars, the main character determines to "stay behind and keep alive a sense of what life here has meant" (238), pathologically clinging to a world polluted beyond repair with designs of remaking it into a kind of "New Eden" (242). "The Sound-Sweep" introduces themes of celebrity and music that would be cultivated in *The Atrocity Exhibition* and *Vermilion Sands*, whereas the highly Freudian "Zone of Terror" thematizes psychosis, "Manhole 69" sleep and the unconscious, and "The Waiting Grounds" alien races and relics.

Ultimately, it is not time but *pathology* and *affect* that governs *The Voices of Time*. The stories noticeably belong to early Ballard. Their treatment of subjectivity threads through his entire canon, however, and in and of themselves, they have not really aged. Unlike much science fiction, which extrapolates the present into an alternate or future world that bears the skid marks of the uterine present, it is difficult to tell that these stories were written in the 1950s and 1960s; stylistically and narratively, they could have just as easily been written in the twenty-first century. Here, then, is a retro-speculative play on the title: the stories in *The Voices of Time* are *timeless*.

THE TERMINAL BEACH (1964)

US EDITION (as *Terminal Beach*)

End-Game • The Subliminal Man • The Last Word of Mr. Goddard • The Time-Tombs • Now Wakes the Sea • The Venus Hunters • Minus One • The Sudden Afternoon • The Terminal Beach

UK EDITION (as *The Terminal Beach*)

The Terminal Beach • A Question of Re-Entry • The Drowned Giant • End-Game • The Illuminated Man • The Reptile Enclosure • The Delta at Sunset • Deep End • The Volcano Dances • Billennium • The Gioconda of the Twilight Noon • The Lost Leonardo

Published the same year, the US and UK editions of *The Terminal Beach* share only two stories, "The Terminal Beach" and "End-Game." Otherwise, they contain different content with mutual themes of consumerism, perceptual implosion, and the Atomic and Space Ages. Four stories had never appeared in magazines before and saw their first publication in the UK edition: "The Delta at Sunset," "The Drowned Giant," "The Volcano Dances," and "The Gioconda of the Twilight Noon" (Holliday, "Short"). Clute and Pringle think the US edition is "perhaps Ballard's single strongest collection of stories" ("Ballard, J. G.").

As in *The Voices of Time*, the titular story carries the most weight and is a vital organ in Ballard's body of work that depicts a concerted journey into inner space. Allegorizing Cold War pathology and signaling his brief turn to more fragmented and experimental fiction, Ballard considered it a watershed piece of fiction (Brigg 15) in terms of the "very abstract, almost cubist way" he stylizes it, a procedure that foreshadows the "condensed novels" of *The Atrocity Exhibition* ("Interview," Storm 19). Set on a Pacific atoll, Eniwetok, where nuclear tests were conducted between 1948 and 1958, "The Terminal Beach" diagrams one man's psychological compulsion for discovery/recovery. Traven, a former H-bomber pilot harrowed by the untimely death of his wife and son, absconds to Eniwetok in an effort to find himself, but he ends up losing himself as the ruined, labyrinthine landscapes of the island and his mind implode. The story is a pastiche composed of short, subtitled segments ("The Blocks," "The Corpses," "The Lakes and the Specters," "Traven: In Parentheses," "The Catechism of Goodbye," and others) that move back and forth in time. Nebulous and arcane, they map Traven's "terminal" decline as he wanders across the ramparts of the island through a maze of concrete bunkers and blockhouses, negotiating visions of his wife and son and "the river of his memory" (594). In a broader sense, the story accomplishes something similar to "The Voices of Time" by underscoring the motif of "historical amnesia" and addressing "complex questions of nuclear decimation and the ethics of science in the long shadows cast by Auschwitz and Hiroshima" (Baxter, *Surrealist* 21). Such concerns pervaded Ballard's short fiction of the 1960s, but no story so effectively embodies the disorienting, alienating effects of the H-bomb.

The Space and Atomic Ages are overlapping and intimately linked (but not synonymous) historical periods that both involve the scientific development and use of high technologies in the name of empire and global dominance. They provided impetus for a wealth of science fiction, the result of which was an increasing mythologization of both ages that persists to this day. In addition to "The Terminal Beach," "Deep End" (the one reprint from *The Voices of Time*) and "A Question of Re-Entry" express Ballard's view that the Space Age had lapsed in the public imagination.[4] "A Question of Re-Entry" is a good example of how he uses the short form to gestate and nurture ideas for longer works. A NASA official travels upriver through the Amazon jungle in search of a crashed space capsule and encounters a Kurtzian potentate who lords over a tribe of natives. He partakes in a terrestrial, psychological, and symbolic journey analogous to Marlow's in Joseph Conrad's *Heart of Darkness* (1899), a paradigmatic text for Ballard that he channeled in the natural disaster novels (especially *The Drowned World*) and later in *The Day of Creation*.

The dominant theme in both the UK and US editions of *The Terminal Beach* is perceptual implosion—the blurring of reality and fantasy, of subjective and objective worlds, almost exclusively through the perspective of one man, which we see in "The Terminal Beach" (Traven) as well as "The Last Word of Mr. Goddard" (Mr. Goddard), "Now Wakes the Sea" (Richard Mason), "The Sudden Afternoon" (Elliot), "The Gioconda of the Twilight Noon" (Richard Maitland[5]), "Minus One" (Dr. Mellinger), and "The Delta at Sunset" (Charles Gifford). The latter story, an account of a misanthropic archeologist's "dig" into the loam of the unconscious, includes a sentence that could be a mantra for Ballard's concept of inner space, which is contingent on implosion: "The only real landscapes are the internal ones, or the external projections of them" (631).

Elsewhere Ballard reifies the formative power of the media spectacle, a singularity in his oeuvre that would become essential to almost all his novels after *The Crystal World*. Located in an "over-capitalist" (422) autogeddon where "the roadways and car parks covered more than a third of the country's entire area" (414), "The Subliminal Man" extends Vance Packard's *The Hidden Persuasion*, a sociological study of media control. Ballard presages the explosion of advertising technologies that have become commonplace in the twenty-first century (such as massive electronic billboards on the highways and multiple TVs in every home). A panorama of signage dominates Dr. Franklin's waking life; he finds himself psychologically obligated to spend money and consume products for the sake of it, underlining the illusion of choice that typifies consumer-capitalist subjectivity. It isn't a complicated story, but it is among the most prescient in the collection.

"The Drowned Giant" takes on a similar concern. Irreal, absurdist, and told in a matter-of-fact tone by an emotionally distant first-person narrator, it is a "kind of fairy tale in reverse" (Burke) in which a dead, colossal humanoid washes onto a beach and becomes a media sensation whose popularity surges, drawing enthralled crowds, then dwindles to nil, as meaningless as the passing of a celebrity spat on TMZ. In the end, the giant is altogether forgotten, and its body is dismantled and taken away, leaving only "the clutter of bleached ribs like the timbers of a derelict ship" (648). While it hasn't generated the attention of other stories in these collections, "The Drowned Giant" is quintessentially Ballardian, featuring "many of Ballard's perennial themes—physical grotesqueries and society's fascination with them, alienation, the juxtaposition of life and death, and a sense of bleakness that pervades the human condition" (Burke).

The Kafkaesque tenor of "The Drowned Giant" reminisces "The Metamorphosis" in the unaffected voice of the narrator and the way the grotesquerie around which the narrative turns is initially alarming and then accepted as a matter of course. "End-Game" sees Ballard syphoning inspiration from Kafka's *The Trial* (1925), namely the central chapter/parable in the novel, "Before the Law." Like the rhetorical struggle between Josef K. and the mysterious gatekeeper who bars his way to the ever-elusive "Law," "End-Game" portrays a tête-à-tête between Constantin, a man on death row, and his executioner, Malek. During a series of chess matches, Constantin tries to talk Malek out of killing him, just as K. tried to finagle his way past the gatekeeper and thus "save" himself. Constantin dies only after confirming his innocence, and K. dies only after he realizes he could always pass through the door, which existed for him alone.

Ballard didn't admire that many authors, but he really liked Kafka. In many respects, the Ballardian reveals itself to be the Kafkaesque in modernized form, situating the Czech-German irrealist in front of a TV set. Paul March-Russell explains that both authors accord with Deleuze and Guattari's concept of the writing machine, an assemblage of parts, "a mimicry that is designed not simply to replicate but to magnify the workings of desire and expand upon its operation to a point of collapse" ("Writing" 140). Ballard's chronic use of the term "mimetize" in *The Atrocity Exhibition* is the signature of this theoretical dialectic. Theory aside, both authors institute a chronic emotional detachment in their characters, thrive on moral ambiguity, problematize meaning-making, and punctuate the absurdity of existence. In short, Ballard, like Kafka, teases out the Abyss.

VERMILION SANDS (1971)

The Cloud Sculptors of Coral D • Prima Belladonna • The Screen Game • The Singing Statues • Cry Hope, Cry Fury! • Venus Smiles • Say Goodbye to the Wind • Studio 5, The Stars • The Thousand Dreams of Stellavista

Ballard wrote *Vermilion Sands* over a period of fourteen years between 1956 and 1970 when he was in his twenties and thirties. It is his most surreal collection. The stories all transpire in the place-name of the title, an oneiric, ultramodern holiday resort populated by bizarre artists and disillusioned yuppies who fall prey to various social and psychological afflictions. The dominant affliction is "beach fatigue," "that chronic malaise which exiles the victim to a limbo of endless sunbathing, dark glasses and afternoon terraces" ("Studio 5" 209). First mentioned in the 1959 "Project for a New Novel," an experimental compilation of magazine spreads that evolved into *The Atrocity Exhibition*, beach fatigue runs rampant in *Vermilion Sands* and serves a dual purpose, numbing "the senses insidiously, blunting despair and hope alike" (228). Still, Ballard's protagonists are never without desire and the animus of obsession.

In "Portrait of the Artist as a Jung Man," William Schuyler enumerates the production and arrangement of the stories in *Vermilion Sands*, saying that they

> must be taken as a group. They were written over a period of fourteen years, and they came in clusters, which suggests otherwise. On the other hand, Ballard rewrote an early story ("Mobile," 1957, which became "Venus Smiles") to put it in the sequence, and he arranged them in an order which is not the order in which they were written and which is not in chronological order for Vermilion Sands either. The sequence has a larger plan than those of the individual stories. It may have been imposed by Ballard after some of the stories had already been written. . . . When we read through the stories in the order in which they are placed in the collection, what appears is a meta-narrative in symbolic form constructed by the juxtaposition of disjoint parts. (18–19)

Brigg calls the stories "finger-exercises on the theme of a future, bored, narcissistic society where people do strange things for pleasure and act out even stranger plots and revenges to satisfy the needs of their psyches" (22), and Ballard makes light of the science fictional aspects of the collection in a short preface:

> Vermilion Sands is my guess at what the future will actually be like. It is a curious paradox that almost all science fiction, however far removed in time and space, is really about the present day. Very few attempts have been made to visualize a unique and self-contained future that offers no warnings to us. Perhaps because of this cautionary tone, so many of science fiction's notional futures are zones of unrelieved grimness. Even its heavens are like other people's hells.

> By contrast, Vermilion Sands is a place where I would be happy to live. I once described this overlit desert resort as an exotic suburb of my mind, and something about the word "suburb"—which I then used pejoratively—now convinces me that I was on the right track in my pursuit of the day after tomorrow. (7)

Apart from "The Screen Game," every story contains at least one soft science fictional novum, usually in the form of esoteric and baroque low tech. "Sonic sculptures," which "externalize the internal emotional responses of the characters" (Schuyler 16), pervade the book and serve as centerpieces in "Venus Smiles" and "The Singing Statues." Mutant, melodic flowers and plants take the lead in "Prima Belladonna" and have a small role in "The Singing Statues." In "Studio 5, the Stars," automated poems antagonize the main character, who displays symptoms of anomie and creative deficiency—a common thread. "The Cloud Sculptors of Coral D" features "painted gliders" that make art out of clouds, carving "seahorses and unicorns, the portraits of presidents and film stars, lizards and exotic birds" (744). Finally, "Cry Hope, Cry Fury," "Say Goodbye to the Wind," and "The Thousand Dreams of Stellavista" incorporate these sentient or otherwise hypersensitive objects: paint, clothing, and architecture.

By way of these estrangements, of these surreal bio-media that arbitrate human relations, Ballard dives headlong into inner space, mixing internal and external elements like a chemist. These stories beg for psychoanalytic inquiry, as if tailor-made for it. Moreover, they showcase the rhetorical and narrative replications that are, as Roger Luckhurst observes, "a mark of the oeuvre as a whole: the nine stories virtually repeat the same plot, a plot that is itself about repetition compulsion. . . . *Vermilion Sands* has perhaps the most extreme concentration of Ballard's idiomatic tic: his use and abuse of the simile" (169). Once again, Ballard manifests the deleuzoguattarian writing machine.

Schuyler argues that *Vermilion Sands* "in ordinary terms make[s] little or no sense" (19). On the contrary, Ballard relates a clear sensibility and rationale in every story, each of which extrapolates known phenomena. His extrapolations simply deviate from the science fictional norm. They still make sense "in ordinary terms" under the aegis of cognitive estrangement. And while Schuyler admits that, in spite of the stories' alleged futility, "the reader gets the distinct impression that there are good and sufficient reasons why all these weird things are happening" (19), he feels compelled to defend his assessment. Schuyler doesn't dislike the book, but he seems to want to apologize for the disorienting narrativization. It is one of many emissions / admissions of critical anxiety and agitation instigated by Ballard's fiction.

Reflecting on the collection in 1992, Ballard said: "Where is Vermilion Sands? Somewhere between Palm Springs and Ipanema Beach" ("Second"). In the 1950s when he wrote the first stories, a leisure-based society was a fantasy, but after spending time in North America and witnessing US progress and prosperity firsthand, he imagined that "work . . . would one day become the ultimate play, and play the ultimate work. . . . I will wake up and realise that the world I longed for all those decades ago had taken concrete shape around me" (ibid.). Not only did that world take shape in reality, it consumed his later fiction with viral intensity. Four years after these comments, Ballard published *Cocaine Nights*, the first of his last four novels, all of which converge on leisure and the ethical conundrums it raises. The stories in *Vermilion Sands*, then, symptomize a dragon that Ballard chased with terminal devotion for the last fifteen or so years of his life.

MYTHS OF THE NEAR FUTURE (1982)

Myths of the Near Future (1982) • *Having a Wonderful Time* (1978) • *A Host of Furious Fancies* (1980) • *Zodiac 2000* (1978) • *News from the Sun* (1981) • *Theatre of War* (1977) • *The Dead Time* (1977) • *The Smile* (1976) • *Motel Architecture* (1978) • *The Intensive Care Unit* (1977)

These stories came out in magazines between 1976 and 1982. Only the title piece had never been published elsewhere. Several debuted in the literary magazine *Bananas*, for which Ballard served as associate editor under novelist and editor-in-chief Emma Tennent. During this period, he published *The Unlimited Dream Company* and *Hello America*, solidifying for some critics that he had given up on science fiction, a terrific irony in that *Hello America* takes place in the twenty-second century and returns to the spirit of his natural-disaster novels. Ballard did confess to pursuing new subject matter and called *Myths of the Near Future* "pure imagination, so [the stories] range about in the zone of free, fantastic literature," he said, "like both of my last novels" ("Interview," Fuchs and Körber 144).[6]

Facetious and near-futuristic, "Zodiac 2000" is a McLuhanesque revision of the horoscope based on the idea that the "houses of our psychological sky are no longer tenanted by rams, goats and crabs but by helicopters, cruise missiles and intra-uterine coils, and by the spectres of the psychiatric ward" (982). "Myths of the Near Future" and "News from the Sun" are dystopian tales about the aftermath of the Space Age and the PTSD experienced by people who had been affiliated with the space program.[7] "Theatre of War," a textual bricolage composed of quasi-scientific news flashes, reads like a television documentary with "all the dialogue except for the commentator's . . . taken from Viet Nam newsreel transcripts" ("Art" 194). Umberto Rossi discerns the uncanny atmosphere of the text, which "superimposes images of urban combat from the twentieth and twenty-first century taken from Stalingrad to Baghdad (and Beirut) . . . onto an urban landscape highly familiar to British readers and easily recognizable to most readers outside of Britain" ("Is the War" 158). In effect, Ballard dramatizes the Vietnam War on the stage of the British "theatre" and thus makes commentary about the turbulent sociopolitical state of affairs in his own country during the late 1970s.

Other stories thematize domestic space and gender relations, most notably "The Smile," a "wicked attack on modern domesticity where wives are fetishistic objects rather than real persons" (Brigg 84). A middle-aged malcontent who "belonged to a generation of men" detained by "a weary acceptance of militant feminism" and a "wounded masculinity" purchases a female mannequin from a curio shop and turns her into his concubine (864). As humorous as it is grave, the story ridicules male subjectivity and gender performativity yet problematizes and endorses them; no matter what we do, Ballard suggests, we can't escape the roles that the baton of social construction conducts us to play. "A Host of Furious Fancies" further explores this dynamic; in it, a hysterical girl with a Cinderella complex redirects her incestuous desires for her dead father onto the physician tasked with treating her physical symptoms.

"Having a Wonderful Time," "Motel Architecture," and "The Intensive Care Unit" deal with isolation, (re)mediation, and death. In the first, told through eleven postcards, a young husband and wife go on holiday to a resort in the Canary Islands. They enjoy themselves, but when they try to return home, their flight is repeatedly cancelled, until they realize that they have been exiled to the resort with other European "unemployables" by a nefarious government collective. The husband dies in the tenth postcard, leaving his widow, the author of the correspondence, alone with the rest of the outcasts. In "Motel Architecture" and "The Intensive Care Unit," social experience is mediated and pathologized by visual culture; Brigg says that these two stories are "much nastier extrapolations [than "Having a Wonderful Time"] that center around the intrusive presence of television in our lives" (79). Both operate in the tradition of classic science fiction and extrapolate technologies current to the decade into viable, tangible futures. Considering the effects of the internet and video gaming systems on human interaction and communication, these futures had already faded to black by the turn of the century, but in their historical context we see Ballard working expressly within the genre.

Myths of the Near Future also includes "The Dead Time," the pseudo-autobiographical germ for *Empire of the Sun*. Whereas the novel fictionalizes Ballard's experience on a grand scale before, during, and after World War II, the story recounts only the aftermath for a period of days. It is significant for being the first concentrated effort on his part to represent the psychological and actual trauma of his wartime boyhood, "organis[ing] some of his most repetitively inscribed images into a narrative that approximates the circumstances in which these scenes were initially encountered" (Crosthwaite).

WAR FEVER (1990)

War Fever • The Secret History of World War 3 • Dream Cargos • The Object of the Attack • Love in a Colder Climate • The Largest Theme Park in the World • Answers to a Questionnaire • The Air Disaster • Report on an Unidentified Space Station • The Man Who Walked on the Moon • The Enormous Space • Memories of the Space Age • Notes Towards a Mental Breakdown • The Index

Ballard's last collection assembles fourteen stories of various styles and themes. Some are naturalistic and conventional, some more playful than he had been since *The Atrocity Exhibition* was published twenty years earlier. In a 1991 review for the *New York Times*, Ursula K. Le Guin describes the science fictional properties:

> For readers who seek the self-referentiality of mid-20th-century film and fiction as a transcendence of what Mr. Ballard's characters call "human interest stories, of a banal and pointless kind, an enyclopaedia of mediocrity" or "that

everlasting provincial melodrama called ordinary life," the fantasies in *War Fever* offer a risk-free environment. Far more rigorous and fastidious than Jorge Luis Borges or Italo Calvino, Mr. Ballard keeps impeccably cool . . . [and] pursues the reversal of expectation and the extrapolation of trends—both mainstays of science fiction—with mercilessly linear logic, and often with dazzling humor. ("On the Verge")

The playful fiction is distinctly postmodern. Fragmented and self-reflexive, with elements of pastiche and metafiction, and fueled by an unreliable narrator, "Answers to a Questionnaire," for instance, is just that: one hundred short answers to unspecified questions, which compel readers to make sense out of the narrator and his environment based on responses such as "My greatest ambition is to turn into a TV programme" (1101), "Group sex" (1102), "Towards the constellation Orion" (1102), "He announced that Princess Diana was immortal" (1103), "The Kremlin" (1103), "The Second Coming" (1103), and, for the first and one-hundredth responses, "Yes" (1104). Whatever the data, readers linger on the cusp of the know, but never *in* the know, wondering about the interviewer's method and matter of inquiry. Obviously, the interviewee is a Ballardian, given the familiar people, places, and things he cites. For me, this experimental piece sees Ballard farcically looking backward and interviewing himself about the long career/stream of his (un)consciousness.

In the spirit of "Answers to a Questionnaire," "The Index" signifies its content via the title: an index of subjects, figures, and events listed from A to Z for an "unpublished and perhaps suppressed autobiography of a man [Henry Rhodes Hamilton] who may well have been one of the most remarkable figures of the 20th century" (940). "Notes Towards a Mental Breakdown" is a succession of eighteen footnotes, one for each of the words in this sentence: "A discharged Broadmoor patient compiles 'Notes Towards a Mental Breakdown,' recalling his wife's murder, his trial and exoneration" (849); Vladimir Nabokov's *Pale Fire* (1962), an experimental novel of footnotes to a 999-line poem, immediately leaps to mind and may have been a point of reference for this labor of whimsy.

A late story, "A Guide to Virtual Death," isn't in *War Fever*, but it's worth mentioning alongside "Answers to a Questionnaire," "The Index," and "Notes Towards a Mental Breakdown." Ballard arranges it in the form of a twenty-four-hour schedule of TV shows "transmitted to an unnamed city in the northern hemisphere on December 23, 1999," days before the extinction of "intelligent life on earth . . . in the closing hours of the 20th Century" (1173). The schedule begins with "Porno-Disco" at 6 A.M., peaks at noon with a newsflash wherein "networks promise either a new serial killer or a deadly food toxin" (1173), climaxes at 6 P.M. with a virtual-reality production of the Kennedy assassination, and ends at 5 A.M. with "The Charity Hour, [a] game show in which Third-World contestants beg for money" (1174). In all four stories, the presence of "the author" is palpable as Ballard invokes his favorite motifs: television, sexuality, celebrity culture, and media pathology.

Among the more straight-shooting stories in *War Fever* is "The Object of the Attack," the kernel for *Running Wild*, a Ballardification of Stephen King's "Children of the Corn" (1977) in which a group of children, possessed by "sanity," resort to the freedom of madness, massacring their parents and emancipating themselves from the cage of upper-middle-class order and materialism. "The Secret History of World War 3" and "The Largest Theme Park in the World" satirize, respectively, Cold War politics and the social ambulations of European vacation-goers. As in "Notes Towards a Mental Breakdown," a few stories revolve around the vicissitudes of pathology, like "The Enormous Space," an inner-spatial chronicle of a misanthrope who attempts to sever contact with the outside world by confining himself to a "haunted" house that incarnates his burgeoning psychosis. There are also a number of post–Space Age fictions: "Report on an Unidentified Space Station," "The Man Who Walked on the Moon," and "Memories of the Space Age," the latter strangely reprinted from the collection that preceded it.

Ballard builds "Dream Cargos" on the platform of Shakespeare's *The Tempest*, as he does with many of his novels (*The Drought*, *Concrete Island*, *The Unlimited Dream Company*, and *The Day of Creation*, for example). It was the last story to be published in a magazine (the Japanese *Shincho* in 1990) and collected in this volume. Thereafter he wrote a handful of stories published in *The Complete Stories of J. G. Ballard*, such as "The Secret Autobiography of J. G. B.," whose self-reflexive narrator, "B," possesses the same core desire of many Ballardian protagonists: to seek and discover the Garden of Solitude where he can "begin his true work" (1191). A fitting adieu.

NONFICTION

In light of the abundance of fiction he produced, it's easy to forget that Ballard was a prolific nonfiction writer, too, publishing articles, reviews, introductions, and other texts on diverse subjects over a period of more than thirty years. He wrote nonfiction mainly to supplement his income. He sold it to many venues, including science fiction magazines (such as *Ambit* and *New Worlds*), popular magazines (*Playboy* and *Drive* are two), newspapers (*Guardian* and *Sunday Times*, for example), literary anthologies, and catalogs for art exhibitions. As I mentioned earlier in the chapter, *A User's Guide to the Millennium* collects most of the nonfiction and is an important resource for serious Ballard scholars.

Book reviews dominate Ballard's nonfiction output. He began publishing them in *Chemistry and Industry* while serving as an editor between 1958 and 1964 and trying to jumpstart his fiction-writing career. Jeannette Baxter discusses his review method in an article that concentrates on the dissonant effects of reading his nonfiction. Citing Theodor Adorno's "The Essay as Form," she explains that the reviews are "less like closed accounts of discrete works and more like interventions which, in their 'mosaic-like' relation to other review essays, are provisional and resistant to the idea of origins and endings: they 'are neither deduced from any first principle nor do they come full circle and arrive at a final principle'" ("Uncanny" 53).

The books he reviewed are varied and sometimes eclectic. With a few exceptions (for instance, Kingsley Amis's *The Golden Age of Science Fiction*, John Clute and Peter Nicholls's *The Encyclopedia of Science Fiction*, and Brian Aldiss's *Billion Year Spree*), he did not review many science fiction texts, and he scarcely reviewed novels, preferring to write about nonfiction, especially biographies (of Marlon Brando, Mae West, Nancy Reagan, Edward James, Elvis Presley, Walt Disney, and others).[8] To say the least, Ballard went off on tangents when he reviewed books, often using them as springboards to comment on other matters both related and unrelated to the material under scrutiny, but always with flair, intuition, and wit. In a 1971 review of Lois and Stephen Rose's *The Shattered Ring: Science Fiction and the Quest for Meaning*, he mentions the book in only one sentence, denouncing its Christian m.o. and insisting that the authors "fail to realize . . . that science fiction is totally atheistic" ("Fictions" 206). Instead, Ballard expounds the state of science fiction as he saw it at the time and spins maxims that have become well known to fans and scholars of his work: "Everything is science fiction. . . . Science fiction is the most important fiction that has been written for the last hundred years. . . . The future is a better key to the present than the past" (205). Additionally, he jokes: "Science fiction is much more concerned with the significance of the gleam on an automobile instrument panel than on the deity's posterior—if Mother nature has anything in science fiction, it is VD" (206–7).

Ballard examines some science fiction films, such as *La Jetée* (1962), commending the "potent images" that inform its "inner landscapes of time" (Rev. of *La Jetée* 28), and in the essay "A User's Guide to the Millennium" he writes précis on ten films ranging from classic (*Forbidden Planet* [1956]) to cult (*Dark Star* [1974]) to blockbuster (*Close Encounters of the Third Kind* [1977]). In spite of ambivalent feelings about the banality of science fiction cinema, Ballard ultimately praises it: "Far from being a medium of escapist entertainment, the science-fiction film has always been a sensitive barometer of the cultural and political climate of the day" (17).

Certain figures stand out in the nonfiction, many of them associated with (post)modernism and the avant-garde, particularly Burroughs and Dali. His strongest nonfictions were on or related to science fiction, above all "Which Way to Inner Space?" but also "Time, Memory and Inner Space," "Cataclysms and Dooms," "The Future of the Future," "The Diary of a Mad Space-wife," "The Car, the Future," "Project for the Glossary of the Twentieth Century," "A New Metaphor for the Future," and "Fictions of Every Kind." Invariably short and succinct yet rich and revealing, these essays raise concerns that Ballard more fully unpacks in his fiction. In this sense, they were practice fields for him to scrimmage with ideas and engage in an "alternative form of storytelling" (Baxter, "Uncanny" 52), one that "is not innocent, but politically-motivated and partial" (58). More important, they had a tremendous impact on how the British New Wave was shaped and perceived, instigating controversy and debate in the genre about the direction that authors, editors, and publishers believed (or didn't believe) it should take.

Throughout the 1960s and 1970s, Ballard criticized science fiction for not reaching its true potential while insisting that "fictions of every kind" had become subject to it because, "[i]n essence, science fiction is a response to science and technology as perceived by the inhabitants of the consumer goods society" ("Fictions" 205). Late capitalism, he suggests, would ensure the science fictionalization of reality and thus literary representations of contemporary reality. Paradoxically, science fiction was lagging, not sufficiently recognizing and probing the affective dynamics of the mediascape. In "Images of the Future," written for the British fanzine *Fusion* in 1966, but unpublished until 1993 in the bulletin *JGB News*, he writes:

> Science fiction is distinguished from almost all other forms of literature by its prospective character, its interpretation of the present in terms of the future rather than the past. . . . [T]he future presents itself to us as a series of quantified images and relationships. To make any kind of fiction out of these elements demands techniques appropriate to them, and it is precisely here, I feel, that science fiction has failed. The principal literary technique of retrospective fiction, the sequential and consequential narrative, is wholly unsuited to analyse events that have not as yet taken place, let alone produce that free play and rapid association of ideas and images that is what we perceive of the future.

Comments of this nature didn't sit well with Old Wave fans and practitioners who believed that science fiction should look a certain way and essentially remain the same. Ballard expressed his disdain for this outlook in a speech he gave at a 1969 symposium in Brazil, called "Science Fiction Cannot Be Immune from Change," saying, "It distresses me when I see those who maintain the so-called grand tradition of modern American science fiction refusing to recognize the possibilities of any change at all. It strikes me as appalling in, for example, the American science-fiction magazines" (158).

Regarding the New Wave in particular, Ballard proclaimed to "absolutely detest" the term (157). "I think the notion of calling most of what has been written in science fiction over the last ten years, calling it 'new wave,' immediately puts a frame around a certain kind of writing done over the last five-to-ten years which isolates it" (ibid.). Still, he admitted to "identify[ing] with the new wave rather than the old wave at times. . . . I suppose," he said, "I'm identified with the so-called new wave; therefore a certain hostility is attributed to me against the older school of science fiction. . . . I get the impression that I am at times regarded as a kind of anti-Christ. In fact, I am the greatest possible defender of the traditional virtues of science fiction" (157).

By "traditional virtues" Ballard means the imaginative, visionary tactics and rudiments that distinguish science fiction from other genres and, in his opinion, make it "the greatest literature of the twentieth century" (157), investigating our relationship to advanced technology. He established himself as crusader and advocate of the genre, but not in its current form, lest it become a "literature of the past" (157). For him, an exploration of inner instead of outer space was the key—not sci-fi, per se, but *psy-fi*—and he appropriated modernist ideas and techniques to turn the key. While he did campaign to abandon the metaphor of the spaceship and interplanetary travel, he wasn't saying that other authors should replicate his exact methodology or subject matter. He just wanted them to push for the New by tapping the keg of modern culture, which, irradiated by the explosion of electronic media in the 1960s, had become a science fictional apparatus in itself, rich with creative possibilities. He may have hated the term "New Wave," but he loved what the authors and editors associated with the movement were trying to do.

Some of Ballard's essays, articles, and reviews unrelated to science fiction sparked debate, especially when he converged on political officials and media personalities. Throughout the years, for instance, practically everything he wrote about Margaret Thatcher, a "mysterious figure" he once compared to John Keats's "La Belle Dame Sans Merci—the merciless muse . . . [a]lso the archetype of the Medusa," was designed for aggravation, in spite of his "having always admired her enormously" ("JGB" 136, 134). In "Alphabets of Unreason," a 1969 review of *Mein Kampf*, Ballard made a case for the centrality of Hitler's pathology to the "lavish communication systems of the twentieth century" (223), and in a 1971 character study, "The Consumer Consumed," he speculated that Ralph Nader could be "the first dictator of the United States" (259). (A year earlier, Nader had factored as one of many celebrity punching bags in *The Atrocity Exhibition*.) In the mid-1990s, Ballard picked off several icons (new and old) in one shot for American music magazine *Spin*, the editors of which asked prominent writers, artists, and thinkers to answer this question: "Everybody talks about the end of the world, but we've actually asked the question: What will it be like?" Ballard responded:

> I dream of: Dying in a car crash with Madonna. Having sex with Hillary Clinton. Appearing in Zapruder frame 313 with Jackie Kennedy. Being transformed into a TV channel. Detonating a nuclear weapon over Disneyland. Having all the whores in Moscow call me on their mobile phones. Seeing time make a new beginning.

> Persuading Neil Armstrong to return to Earth. Meeting my younger selves on the virtual-reality highways of tomorrow. Being buried under the main runway at London's Heathrow Airport. (77)

Of course, Ballard didn't really want to do these things. He speaks the language of consumer-capitalist pathology, manifesting a persona constructed by the media torrent who implicates and indicts the icons of the torrent. What seem like personal attacks (whether Ballard meant them or not) are really satirical jabs at the system that inscribes us; he critiques the monster by becoming the monster. This is a common feature in the nonfiction. Maneuvering the voices of truth and reason, fiction and (con)fabulation, affectation and implosion, he slips in and out of characters mass-produced and brought to bear by the culture machine.

CHAPTER 3

DISASTER AREAS

The Natural Disaster Quartet

CONTEXTS

Ballard's first four novels all involve global cataclysms and fall into the apocalyptic subgenre of science fiction. Near the beginning of his third novel, *The Drought*, protagonist Charles Ransom makes a statement about the condition of his environment that corresponds with his subjectivity: "I've always thought of the whole of life as a kind of disaster area" (18). Ransom's world is undoubtedly disastrous. Poisoned by industrial dumping, the earth is drying up, cracking civilization like an egg and releasing the proverbial yolk of violence and pathology. The statement also reflects Ransom's perception of his world, which he "always" viewed through a glass darkly, even before the turning of the ecological worm. It could easily have been uttered by the protagonists of the novels that preceded and followed *The Drought*, both of whom, like Ransom, are scientists in search of their own identities through the vehicles of "insane" landscapes that hold the promise of demolition and rebirth.

The same might be said for Ballard himself, considering what he experienced as a child of war. In his fictional and nonfictional autobiographies alike, as well as in interviews, he conveys a sense of being drawn to and repelled by the blight and destruction that surrounded him. The prospect of war enlivens Jim in *Empire of the Sun*. He obsesses and dreams about it, not reveling in the spectacle of death but hanging on the knife's edge of its advent. These seemingly adverse feelings evoke Freud's concept of the drives, which he fully develops in *Beyond the Pleasure Principle*. As Dylan Evans explains: "Freud established a fundamental opposition between life drives (eros), conceived of as a tendency towards cohesion and unity, and the death drives, which operate in the opposite direction, undoing connections and destroying things. However, the life drives and the death drives are never found in a pure state, but always mixed / fused together in differing proportions" (32). This tension stands out in the thoughts, desires, and actions of the protagonists of *The Drowned World*, *The Drought* and *The Crystal World*, each of whom is a becoming-Adam seeking transcendence in his respective Garden of Ruin.[1]

Some reviewers called these novels cautionary tales that warned against anthropogenic activity. In fact, the environmental disasters were incidental to the characters, especially the psychic lives of the protagonists. In 1973 Ballard told Peter Linnett why he used and reused the disaster story:

> I wanted to deal with a large canvas. I was interested in events, if you like; systems, of a very large area. The entire biological kingdom viewed as a single organism, as a single continuing vast memory. In fact I've never thought of them as being disaster stories, because I don't see them as having unhappy endings. The hero follows the logic of his own mind; and I feel that anyone who does this is, in a sense, fulfilling himself. I regard all those novels as stories of psychic fulfillment. ("J. G. Ballard" 50)

The novels may not have unhappy endings, but they are disastrous in more ways than one. In "Cataclysms and Doom," Ballard campaigns for the liberation of the imagination in the face of potential oblivion: "I believe that the catastrophe story, whoever may tell it, represents a constructive and positive act by the imagination rather than a negative one, an attempt to confront a patently meaningless universe by challenging it at its own game" (208–9). This is the bedrock upon which he erects his oeuvre. After *The Crystal World*, only once did he return to an eco-apocalyptic setting—in *Hello America*—but the essence of what he does in these early novels recurs in nearly every major work: enframed by violence and the prospect of death, one or more characters bite into the forbidden fruit of pathology and aspire to unlock new realms of seeing and knowing within themselves. The Ballardian fruit is a far cry from the biblical fruit.

Many critical essays and book chapters have been devoted to the first four novels. *The Wind from Nowhere* has understandably received the least attention. The plot is formulaic. The prose isn't bad, but it lacks the geometric rhythm, detail, and stylishness of the novels that follow it, and it doesn't portray or explore the psychological effects of the environment—inner space plays no role. In short, *The Wind from Nowhere* isn't Ballardian, but it's much better than some critics (and Ballard himself) have said it was.

One thing *The Wind from Nowhere* does have in common with its natural-disaster siblings is a calculated use of science fiction clichés. Michel Delville has explained how the novels subscribe to popular conventions in the genre during and prior to the 1960s; however, whereas "it is clearly indebted to a tradition of British catastrophe stories that includes such apocalyptic 'classics' as John Wyndham's *Revolt of the Triffids* (1952) and John Christopher's *The Death of Grass* (1956), Ballard's early fiction differs from the plethora of disaster tales published at the time in various SF and pulp magazines, in that it focuses less on the disaster itself than on the characters' various mental and physical adjustments to it" (7). Even *The Wind from Nowhere* privileges character over catastrophe (without plumbing the psychic depths of character). In these four "examinations of human 'collaborations' with natural disasters" (Nichols and Pringle, "Disaster" 338), Ballard inscribes himself into a popular subgenre of science fiction while writing against it.

Throughout his career, Ballard has been accused of flat characterization. This is true in the charge of a certain rubric, as Jeannette Baxter and Roland Wymer, channeling Dan O'Hara, bring to light:

> Why is Ballard unable to draw convincing characters? O'Hara suggests that the critical consensus judges Ballard's fiction by the wrong formal and contextual criteria; Ballard's innovations cannot be fully appreciated if they are measured against the limited conventions of Realism. The active elements of Ballard's brand

> of anti-characterization—of gestures, roles and contexts—are systematically organized, O'Hara argues, and any meaning to be found in Ballard's characterization "resides in the formal system, not the individual agents." (9)

Ballard's characters can come off more like archetypes or dream-pieces than people, responding to stimuli in ways that don't synch with the usual flows of cause and effect. There are exceptions to the rule, such as Jim in *Empire of the Sun* and *Rushing to Paradise*'s Barbara Rafferty and Neil Dempsey, but a bird's-eye view of his canon does reveal a form of anti-characterization, one that is purposeful, symbolic, and metacritical.

In *The Drowned World*, *The Drought*, and *The Crystal World*, the most rounded and interesting (anti)characters—complete with detailed backstories—are arguably not people but *landscapes*. This is a result of Ballard's rich descriptive abilities and Surrealist convictions, which produce an uncanny quality in the geographies he brings to life. Baxter calls *The Drowned World* "the most painterly novel within Ballard's collection," making an insightful case for how it "incorporates Surrealist paintings . . . in order to access and mobilize the historical unconscious" (*Surrealist* 17). *The Drought* and *The Crystal World* also narrativize Surrealist artwork in such a way that landscapes often seem more alive and cognizant than many of the characters, who, pursuing complex desires for agency and self-discovery, interact with the landscapes in meaningful, "interpersonal" ways. In the scheme of Ballardian inner space, the landscapes are manifestations or externalizations of the protagonists' psyches. They also exhibit their own unique selves with more "personality" than many of Ballard's human(oid)s, who have been thoroughly criticized for being "so much dead wood," "mere spokespeople for Ballard's own views," and an assortment of postures and gestures (O'Hara, "Reading" 105).

Other science fiction writers have characterized landscapes. In his Mars trilogy,[2] for example, Kim Stanley Robinson charts the terraformation of the planet over hundreds of years, developing a massive cast of characters with respect to the changing environment, which matures and changes beneath their feet, supporting and imperiling them, bucking and kicking like a feral child en route to domestication. Based in California and fixated on the ecology, Robinson published his first novels in 1984 after receiving a doctorate in English, then went on to win all of the major science fiction awards several times over; he is probably the genre's best American literary author, and while he doesn't write in the vein of the definitively Ballardian, he was deeply inspired, he said, by Ballard's early work, especially *The Crystal World* (Robinson).

Prior to its release, the genre had not seen anything quite like *The Drowned World*. Reviews were mixed, but few could deny the power of the prose and the originality of the ideas that Ballard, confining himself to the same subgenre, continued to tweak and innovate throughout *The Drought* and *The Crystal World* before making a sharp, wild, postmodern segue to the catastrophes of celebrity culture and electronic media.

A MEANS TO A BEGINNING

The Wind from Nowhere (1962)

Shortly before writing his first novel, Ballard was at a crossroads. Since 1956, he had sold more than twenty stories, with a seven-story surge in 1961. He was deputy editor of *Chemistry and Industry*. Trying to balance the long commute to work from Shepperton into London with family life and three small children had worn him down. "The future looked extremely dismal, professionally speaking," said Ballard in 1973. "I needed a break. I didn't want to begin lowering my sights and begin churning out novels that were partly serious—you know, money-spinners" ("J. G. Ballard," Linnett 50). And yet he did just that. The caveat was not to waste too much time on it and think about the money-spinner as a way to ignite a full-time writing career. Prompted by Mary, he gave himself a two-week window, wrote six thousand words per day, and finished within ten working days. The product was *The Wind from Nowhere*. He sold the novel to American paperback publisher Berkley Books for $1,000 (roughly £300).[3] This allowed him to reduce his hours at *Chemistry and Industry* and eventually quit.

Ballard rarely discussed *Wind* in interviews. As I've mentioned, he badmouthed the novel when he did discuss it, rebuking it for what it was: a means to an end—or rather, a means to a beginning. He confessed to using a potpourri of generic science fiction clichés endemic to the English "cozy catastrophe."[4] Colin Greenland says that this type of story entails the following: "The world is destroyed by fire or plague, pollution or geophysical upheaval. The established order goes down with all hands. Clinging to the wreckage are a small group of survivors. The story commonly relates their attempts to resume human civilisation in a post-human environment" (93). Ballard services all of these earmarks, and for the plot, he uses the familiar technique of threading together several arcs. Two characters take precedence: American submarine captain Steven Lanyon and, principally, Dr. Donald Maitland, a watered-down version of Ballard's subsequent scientific protagonists—"clearly a man whose nature is in tune with a disaster. He has very little to live for, not even the excitement of experience, so he does not *mind* the events that are causing everyone else to panic. . . . [H]e comes close to a psychopathic lack of affectivity, of emotional involvement with the world around him" (Brigg 45–46).

The title refers to the novel's antagonist and its "origin." There is speculation that the despotic wind came from "somewhere"—oceanic drifts, cosmic radiation, "outraged Providence" (*Wind* 55)—but Ballard never explains it, and for all intents and purposes, the wind is the operative wheel around which Ballard spins his yarn. Once it starts, the wind gains momentum by five miles per hour each day until it reaches a velocity of over 350 miles per hour and then suddenly and inexplicably abates. During the rise and fall of the maelstrom, the narrative unfolds. It would be easy to say that the plot is disposable, with characters fleeing, taking shelter, trying to survive, going insane, fighting for their lives, and so on. These things certainly happen. But the book has more substance than many cozy catastrophe novels and the cinematic grandchildren of the subgenre, such as *Dante's Peak* (1997), *Armageddon* (1998), *The Day after Tomorrow* (2004), *2012* (2009), and *San Andreas* (2015).

The frame Ballard uses to start the novel, for instance, foreshadows Alfred Hitchcock's *The Birds* (1963). In this veritable disaster film, which takes place in a small Northern California town, Mitch Brenner's relationship with lovebird Melanie Daniels is jeopardized by his neurotic, controlling mother, who, like many of Hitchcock's matriarchs, wants him for herself. Without instigation, blackbirds attack the town, relentlessly, growing in numbers and hostility. Then, just as suddenly and inexplicably as the wind from nowhere dies down, the birds stop—although not without pecking Melanie half to death. Psychoanalytically, they are metaphorical byproducts of Brenner's mother's aggression, cathected primarily onto Melanie, but at the same time flying wild. No mother figure exists in Ballard's novel, but we can similarly read the wind as a product of a tension-fraught relationship between Maitland and his estranged wife, Susan, a "rich neurotic" and socialite uninterested in her husband's intellectual pursuits and "research into virus genetics" (10).

The first sentence of the *The Wind from Nowhere* denotes the initial effects of the impending gale: "The dust came first" (7). Thereafter Ballard reveals the dust of Maitland and Susan's relationship, how their seven-year marriage fell apart and Maitland transferred his research fellowship from a hospital in London to Vancouver, where he intends to relocate. In the opening pages, we get a firm sense of Maitland's mental state (cool, capable, troubled, obsessive), and even though he is not as nuanced as Kerans, Ransom, and Sanders in the succeeding natural-disaster novels, Ballard establishes a connection between interior and exterior, subjectivity and objectivity, the human mind and the untamed earth. In an exceptionally redolent scene, Susan, stubbornly unwilling to leave their apartment and take shelter underground, is caught by the wind through an open window and swept away before Maitland's eyes—death, as it were, by Psyche Unbound.

As Maitland assists the special British governmental unit responsible for intelligence and communications (the Central Operations Executive, or COE), Lanyon, accompanied by love interest and NBC News correspondent Patricia Olsen, travels across the Riviera to retrieve a prominent general from Nice, then returns to salvage his submarine, the *Terrapin*. Both parties experience their share of action and crises. In the end, Ballard brings them together in the pyramidal fortress erected by monomaniacal business tycoon, Hardoon, an effective Ahab for whom the wind functions as a white whale. With his private army, Hardoon wants to etch his name into the cornerstone of history by "challeng[ing] the wind [and] asserting Man's courage and determination to master nature" (165). Hardoon prefigures a host of other Ballardian monomaniacs—most of all, *Hello America*'s Charles Manson. His compensatory pathology certifies the novel's thesis (and the thesis of innumerable disaster stories): humanity is powerless against the brute whimsicality of nature.

In an essay on the Ballard archive,[5] Chris Beckett compares Hardoon to a Bond villain and describes how he "was originally a character in a draft story that never made it into *Vermilion Sands*. In that story, he is 'a shadowy eccentric millionaire . . . who has spent twenty-five years constructing a Cretan labyrinth (in which he dies) beside his opulent mansion on the edge of

Vermilion Sands. . . . Hardoon 'looks like a Francis Bacon executive,' calling to mind the tormented and mutilated figures that were often the subjects of Bacon's disturbing portraits" ("Progress"). In *Miracles of Life* we learn that the character derives from a Shanghai-based "Iraqi property tycoon who was told by a fortune-teller that if he ever stopped building he would die, and who then went on constructing elaborate pavilions all over Shanghai, many of them structures with no doors or interiors" (9). These manifestations of Hardoon form a Ballardian totem, drawing on the author's memories of childhood while signifying the surrealist impulses and ethics that would come to fruition in the next three novels.

Hardoon brags that his stronghold "will withstand ten-thousand-mile-an-hour gales, a hundred thousand, if you can imagine such a speed" (*Wind* 167). Of course, his hubris, his "moral stand against the hurricane" (170), sounds the death knell of the stronghold as the bunkers underneath it flood and the foundations cave in. Moments before our heroes perish, the wind lets up. And not half a page later the novel ends. The ending is so abrupt, it flirts with the metanarrational, as if Ballard were calling attention to the banality of the subgenre. Whatever the case, *The Wind from Nowhere* served its purpose. Now Ballard was in a position to write what he wanted.

LANDSCAPES OF DECLINE AND DESIRE

The Drowned World (1962) • *The Drought* (1964) • *The Crystal World* (1966)

As in *The Voices of Time*, Ballard foregrounds the theme of time in *The Drowned World*, *The Drought*, and *The Crystal World*, each of which takes place in a cataclysmic landscape of decline and desire. The novels deviate from the cozy catastrophe formula in two main ways: in a concentrated use of surrealist techniques and principles, and in the primacy of characters who do not fear or run from the catastrophe but rather crave and embrace it, seeking to reinvent themselves within the new wilderness.

Ballard manifested what he perceived to be at "the heart of science fiction": a "celebration of the possibilities of life" ("Cataclysms" 209). Some critics were distraught by the apparent pathology that drove his protagonists to pursue their obsessions despite the likelihood of death. Even today, readers have difficulty. In a 2014 review of *The Drought* on NPR, for example, Jason Heller refers to Ballard as "one of our bleakest writers" who offers "surrender as a way to cope with catastrophe." This small-minded deduction doesn't account for Ballard's conviction that with surrender comes hope and self-discovery, if not transcendence and downright happiness. Irving Wardle comes closer to the truth in a 1966 review of *The Crystal World*: "The purpose of the action is to show the characters gradually succumbing to the environment; and such is the force of the imagery . . . that one can share their view of it as an ancestral paradise" (27).

Ballard alludes to different forms of paradise in all three novels. The primary allusion is to the biblical book of Genesis and the Garden of Eden. As I stated earlier, each protagonist is a becoming-Adam, an alternative "original man" who aspires to forge a new identity out of a forsaken garden. In *The Drowned World*, Dr. Robert Kerans is "a second Adam searching for the forgotten paradises of the reborn sun" (175); in *The Drought*, Dr. Charles Ransom journeys through "a dusty Eden" (217); in *The Crystal World*, Dr. Edward Sanders is "some fugitive Adam chancing upon a forgotten gateway to the forbidden paradise" (79). Ballard turns the biblical story on end. His gardens are not safe but treacherous; his Adams don't stifle their desires, they chase them. Only under the aegis of Judeo-Christian mythology do his gardens entertain a Fall of Man. Beyond that aegis, they are sites of promise, fruition, power, and transcendence.[6]

Each novel deals with a specific time phase and focal element: for *The Drowned World*, the past and water; for *The Drought*, the future and sand; for *The Crystal World*, the present and crystal—or, as Ballard says, "the precious stone," a symbol of timelessness ("Interview," Uncredited 11). While all of them transpire in imagined futures, they are all about timelessness insofar as they put the nature and structure of time into question, exposing the socially and culturally constructed ways in which we perceive and experience time.

Synthesizing what Ballard accomplishes in these novels, Delville writes: "Together with a recurrent interest in the dialectics of time and space, the common denominator of Ballard's early works is an attempt to expand traditional science fiction plots and themes by merging the outer world of reality and the hidden life of the psyche" (18–19). In this manner, Ballard the science fiction author is a becoming-Adam, too, forging his own new identity out of the forsaken garden of the genre as the stuff of his experience increasingly became the mortar of his fiction.

Originally published in an abridged form in *Science Fiction Adventures*, *The Drowned World* was Ballard's breakout book and the first demonstrably Ballardian novel. In this "neuronic odyssey" (174), solar radiation has spiked the heat index and melted the polar ice caps, submerging the cities of Europe and America underwater. What remains of civilization is fractured at best, and the birth rate has declined to a terminal degree, as if "the genealogical tree of mankind was systematically pruning itself" (23). Set above the sunken vestiges of London, the novel depicts a primeval swamp in regression to the Triassic period. As the landscape regresses, so do the characters, retreating into the "archeopsychic past" (44) and repossessing "the time-codes carried in every chromosome and gene" that are the "organic memories" of Earth (43). Appropriately citing H. G. Wells, Dr. Alan Bodkin describes the process in greater detail:

> I am convinced that as we move back through geophysical time so we re-enter the amniotic corridor and move back through spinal and archaeopsychic time,[7] recollecting in our unconscious minds the landscapes of each epoch, each with a distinct geological terrain, its own unique flora and fauna, as recognisable to anyone else as they would be to a traveller in a Wellsian time machine. Except that this is no scenic railway, but a total reorientation of the personality. If we let these buried phantoms master us as they re-appear we'll be swept back helplessly in the flood-tide like pieces of flotsam. (44–45)

Bodkin is an associate of Kerans's. They work at a biological testing station with Beatrice Dahl. The station is towed from region to region so that they can perform research on flora and fauna and perfunctorily send data back to administrators at a camp in Northern Greenland who couldn't care less about their predictable findings; even in this devolved future, Kafkaesque bureaucratic machines loom in the shadows. Colonel Riggs and his military entourage supervise the station, but Kerans runs it and serves as its chief medical officer.

Dreams play an infectious and invigorating role in the characters' lives. "Superficial horrors" encroach on their sense of reality, imploding their psyches with increasing authority. For Kerans, the process of implosion compels his mind and body to merge with history and the dead, sweltering Earth. "Guided by his dreams, he [moved] backwards through the emergent past, through a succession of ever stranger landscapes, centered upon the lagoon, each of which . . . seemed to represent one of his own spinal levels" (83).[8]

At the outset of the novel, the forty-year-old Kerans has been living in a penthouse suite at a Ritz Carlton for the previous six months while performing his duties. The allure of his baroque, extravagantly furnished residence (a symbol of the civilized past) doesn't surpass his compulsion to abandon the station and go off by himself into the unknown (a symbol of the distant and uncivilized past—and his impending future). Lieutenant Hardman, second-in-command to Riggs, beats him to the punch, mysteriously disappearing and then escaping the search team that goes after him. Riggs and his men flee to more temperate weather in the north. Intoxicated by their dreams, their "biological pasts" (91), and a yearning for isolation, Kerans, Dahl, and Bodkin stay behind. Hardman's flight reifies and spurs Kerans's desires to go south toward the "unattainable shores of the amniotic paradise" (70), but before he can follow suit, an insidious albino pirate, Strangman, storms the lagoon with his congregation of African minions and mutant alligators.

Literary allusions pervade Ballard's fiction. In *The Drowned World*, Kerans is allied with the biblical Adam in addition to Daniel Defoe's Robinson Crusoe and his quest for self-alienation, an "inverted Crusoeism" (48). Strangman, in turn, points to Joseph Conrad's *Heart of Darkness*. Sebastian Groes calls him "a reincarnation of Conrad's Kurtz" and emblem of postcolonialism; regardless of the postcapitalist social order, he continues to savor a "Kurtzean lust for gold and treasure" (85).

Greedy for loot, Strangman drains the lagoon and exhumes the barnacled relics of London near Leicester Square. This maddens Kerans and Bodkin. They have developed a psychosymbiotic relationship with the lagoon, and Bodkin attempts to re-create it. Strangman kills him, takes Dahl as a concubine, and terrorizes Kerans. Before he can dispatch Kerans, Riggs returns and saves the day, but he will not re-flood the city. "If anybody tries," Riggs says, "I'll personally blow his head off. Reclaiming land, particularly an urban area like this right in the centre of a former capital city, is a Class A1 priority" (158). Bereft, Kerans disregards the threat, opens the floodgates, and drowns the world again, then takes flight, evading the wrath of Riggs. On the lam, he loses the security of the lagoon, which is repeatedly referred to as a womb, and determines more than ever to find "the paradises of the sun" (167). He encounters Hardman, who has been involved in his own "descent into the phantasmagoric forest" (169). The skeletal, wrecked, charred condition of the lieutenant foretells Kerans's prospective future and "Day of Judgement" (171), but we are left with a sense that death is a fair price to pay for rediscovery and the quest for newness.

The publisher of *The Drowned World* in the UK, Gollancz, debated whether to market the novel as science fiction, thinking it would sell better as mainstream fiction. Kingsley Amis, a fan of Ballard's writing and an advocate of the New Wave, convinced them to put the stamp of science fiction on the spine. He believed it would be good for the new novelist and the genre as a whole (Ballard, "Against" 207–8). With momentum from positive preliminary reviews and Ballard's own self-promotion,[9] *The Drowned World* sold well and created a buzz. Never would Ballard return to the prescriptions of *The Wind from Nowhere.*

In *The Drought*, he turns the universe of *The Drowned World* inside-out, projecting the desires of his characters into the future instead of the past, and sucking the water-logged landscape dry. Michael Moorcock praised this novel as "a kind of reversed *Drowned World* . . . filled with wonderful scenes of dried river beds, salt-flats, deserts, burning cities—like a series of beautiful surrealist landscapes. Baroque characters abound and the whole thing is beautifully written and described" ("Books" 118). It was first published in the US as *The Burning World*, a more resonant title in my opinion, one that linked it with the other two inner-spatial natural-disaster novels, each depicting a world (planetary and psychic) in a state of transformation. An expanded version was later published as *The Drought* in the UK.

Ballard lays on thick allusions to *The Tempest*. Among the players confined to a metaphorical island in his drama are the quixotic architect Richard Foster Lomax (Shakespeare's Prospero), his sister Miranda (Prospero's daughter), the deformed idiot-savant Quilter (Caliban) and the foster-child Philip Jordan (Ariel). Ballard starts and finishes the novel in the city of Mount Royal. "Industrial wastes discharged into the ocean basins during the previous fifty years" form an irremovable membrane on the ocean surfaces that prevents evaporation and cloud formation (36). This is the environmental catalyst of a worldwide drought that "functions as a [social and psychological] catalyst to bring out patterns of human behavior ranging from self-perception to bizarre personality traits and violence" (Brigg 49). As in *The Drowned World* and *The Crystal World*, we see these patterns through the perspective, presence, and peregrinations of the main character.

A general practitioner, Ransom worked at the Mount Royal hospital until it closed. In the first chapter we learn that his psyche and impulses are much like Kerans's. He has a penchant for solitude, and he is exhilarated by the transformation (in other words, the death) of the inland waters and the ensuing dystopian landscape, which has an oneiric quality: "The slopes of mud, covered with the bodies of dead birds and fish, stretched above him like the shores of a dream" (4). He joins a group that migrates to the coast in the beginning, spends ten years foraging for food and water while fending off the aggressions of other survivors, then returns to the womb of Mount Royal. Ransom is reborn and manifests his latent desire for complete solitude. Finally, he leaves the pack and ventures into the sandy depths of the scorched earth on his own.

The experience of inner space in *The Drought* is premised on the dissolution of time. The initial disappearance of the river, which once "played the part of an immense fluid clock . . . whose cumulative forward flow was as irrelevant and without meaning as the apparently linear motion of time itself" (8), creates a perceptual rift in the minds of the characters. The "erosion of all time and space beyond the flaccid sand and draining beaches" numbs Ransom (156). By the end, after Ransom takes leave of his companions at Mount Royal, time has halted for him to a point where "neither past nor future could change, only the mirror between them" (210). Bound to the landscape, he enters an eternal present in which "the sun seemed to be receding into the sky" and "he no longer cast any shadow on to the sand, as if he had at last completed his journey across the margins of the inner landscape he had carried in his mind for so many years" (233).

When Ransom returns to Mount Royal, Quilter, "the grotesque Caliban of all his nightmares" (79), has grown from a brusque, insidious child into a Kurtzian figure, one of many we encounter in Ballard's work.[10] Adorned in a robe of animal furs and a crown of feathers, he parades through the city on stilts and wields power over the villagers. Throughout the years, he and Miranda resorted to cannibalism and spawned three children, "perfect replicas" of their parents with "their swollen heads and puckish faces" (208). The family represents an endpoint for the old order of civilization on the threshold of timelessness, of a land and life of virtual permanence and immutability. Hence Ballard's reference to Quilter and Miranda as "a last Eve and Adam waiting for time's end" (221). Ransom is the new Adam, his former identity drained like the lakes and rivers of space and time. The last sentence of the novel punctuates his (be)coming: "It was some time later that he failed to notice it had started to rain" (233). Baptized by the world that (re)produced him, Ransom's lone pilgrimage into the dunes is a rebirth into a new and uncertain Eden.

There has been less literary criticism written on *The Drought* than on *The Drowned World* and *The Crystal World*, both of which contain heavier doses of surreality and are perhaps more thought provoking and thematically complex. In 1976 Ballard recalled that he didn't like *The Drought* very much when he wrote it. "There was something rather too arid—something of the aridity of the landscape spilled over into the novel, and it didn't take off for me. I still don't care for it that much" ("Interview," Goddard and Pringle 23). *The Drought* is an incubator for the ideas that Ballard would cultivate and unbridle in *The Atrocity Exhibition* and *Crash*. Images of cars and other everyday technologies, for instance, figure prominently throughout the novel. In one scene, a pavilion made from technological detritus is equated with a place of worship: "It had been constructed from assorted pieces of chromium and enameled metal—the radiator grilles of cars, reflectors of electric heaters, radio cabinets and so on—fitted together with remarkable ingenuity to form what appeared at a distance to be a bejewelled temple" (213). More generally, *The Drought* includes the key motifs of "quantified image, isolated object, and emotion detached from any human context" that form the basic narrative architecture for *The Atrocity Exhibition* ("Interview," Goddard and Pringle 23).

Earlier I mentioned that the landscapes in these novels may be viewed as (anti)characters. I would say this is least pronounced in *The Drought*, but there are definitely passages where the desiccated earth is "brought to life," probing the human characters' bodies and minds like an alien invader. Ballard's descriptions of the environment abide by the laws of the Freudian uncanny and tap into human experience and perception; they are both familiar and foreign, inviting and dread inducing. Ballard cultivates this dynamic with relish in *The Drowned World*. In *The Crystal World*, he brings it to complete fruition and imagines a landscape that literally infects the bodies (and pathologizes the minds) of people who come into contact with it. The novel concerns an area in Africa's Cameroon jungle whose flora and fauna are being systematically crystallized by a virus that works like leprosy, although the process of crystallization entails debilitating and healing properties alike. "Visual and verbal geographies function in *The Crystal World* to alert the reader to the 'inner space' of Ballard's postcolonial Africa" (Baxter, *Surrealist* 46). For readers, the geography is a beacon; for characters, it is a gateway.

By the mid-1960s, Ballard's fan base had grown considerably. At the time of the publication of *The Crystal World* in 1966, LSD, popularized by Timothy Leary, was all the rave. The novel's trippy, psychedelic imagery made many readers think it had been composed on acid. It hadn't, as Ballard confirmed years later:

> A lot of people who knew I had taken acid thought I had written the book on the basis of that. I wrote the book in '64, I think, but I didn't take LSD until 1967 or '68. The curious thing is that the book does convincingly, in my experience, describe what an LSD vision is like; particularly the effects of light and time. And it made me feel that in fact the imagination can reach those visions that LSD elicits—you can systematically assemble into the critical imagination those visions that LSD elicits biochemically. ("Interview," Juno and Vale 25)

Even so, Ballard didn't have a lot to go on: his personal experience with LSD was limited to one "classic bad trip" that "opened a little Trojan horse inside [his] mind" and flooded him with nightmarish visions and paranoid delusions. As a result, he quit smoking (cigarettes and marijuana) and even claimed to be wary of taking aspirin, restricting himself to "the alcohol standard firmly forever" (24).

Delville notes that all three novels involve "literal and metaphorical devolution" (10). Likewise does a temporal oddity inform their environmental crises. In *The Crystal World*, "anti-time" incites the transformation of the rainforest. Sanders explains in a letter to a colleague:

> The recent discovery of anti-matter in the universe inevitably involves the conception of anti-time as the fourth side of this negatively charged continuum.

> Where anti-particle and particle collide they not only destroy their own physical identities, but their opposing time-values eliminate each other, subtracting from the universe another quantum from its total store of time. . . . As more and more time "leaks" away, the process of super-saturation continues, the original atoms and molecules producing spatial replicas of themselves, substance without mass, in an attempt to increase their foot-hold upon existence. (85)

Crystallization is compensatory, a means of trying to restore balance. And yet it is entropic. Sanders theorizes that the natural product of the process will be the expiration of time and the crystallization of the entire universe, "a macrocosmic zero beyond the wildest dreams of Plato and Democritus" (85). Once again, Ballard science fictionalizes time, extrapolating it from known science, but more captivatingly than ever before, and surely with more innovation and "believability" than most of his predecessors and contemporaries, even in the New Wave.

Like the protagonists of *The Drought*, *The Drowned World*, and *The Wind from Nowhere*, *The Crystal World*'s Sanders, an assistant director at a leper hospital in Fort Isabelle, has a troubled relationship with a woman. Former colleagues Max Claire and his spouse Suzanne have relocated to a leprosy treatment clinic near Mont Royal. Sanders had an affair with Suzanne that he attributes to the "dark side of the psyche" and his "attempt to come to terms with himself and his own ambiguous motives," which center on his interest in "the idea of leprosy, and whatever it unconsciously represented," more than the treatment of the disease (19). Compelled by the dark side (of the Ballardian Force), he decides to pursue Suzanne. He gets sidetracked on multiple occasions and incrementally discovers more about the crystallization of *the body of the jungle*, which resembles the way leprosy spreads in the human body. Both processes involve a pathological component, too, metaphorically connecting the landscape to the psyche. The emerging crystal world can be read as an inner-spatial projection of Sanders's "ambiguous motives."

The major characters he encounters en route to Mont Royal and the Claires can be read as different expressions of his persona and desires, or both—a prelude to the T-men of *The Atrocity Exhibition*.[11] Notable are Louise Peret (a journalist who becomes Sanders's lover and Suzanne's double), Thorensen (director of a diamond mine), Father Balthus (a lapsed priest),

Ventress (a fanatical Belgian architect), and Serena (Ventress's tubercular wife and Thorensen's lover). Ventress is an important figure. Obsessive and menacing, he may be a prototype for *Crash*'s Vaughan, Ballard's ultimate desiring-machine; he also reminisces Strangman from *The Drowned World* "with his skeletal face and white suit" (25). This is brought out most emphatically in his dispute with Thorensen over Serena. When she initially left him, "Ventress had gone berserk and spent some time as a voluntary patient at an asylum. . . . Thorensen seemed convinced that Ventress's morbid and lunatic presence was responsible for Serena's lingering malaise" (110). Sanders gets caught in the middle of Ventress's attempt to steal Serena back from Thorensen, who has been keeping her alive at a summer house in the forest.

As in his relationships with other characters, Sanders comes to be a passive observer, and we view the various (re)actions to the leprotic aggression of the crystals through him. Like many of Ballard's protagonists, he is a hinge on which other storylines and characters swing, yet his role increasingly favors the perceptual over the interactive. It could be argued that Sanders is the true prototype for Vaughan in light of his predilection for corporeal (and psychological) deformity. Suzanne's contraction of leprosy, for example, invigorates him and "increase[s] his need to remain with her" (137). His need intensifies when he witnesses her lead a troupe of crystallizing lepers into "their new-found paradise" (165). In a sense, *Crash* is *The Crystal World*, extrapolating it from the jungle to the city, from uncultured nature to technological culture.

We never learn the actual function of the crystals. We know they slow the clockwork of organic bodies and show the effects of cryopreservation. As such, they become religious insignia and sources of spiritual agency, even as they expand across and consume the flesh like a parasitic exoskeleton. Given the biblical motifs that run throughout these novels, it is appropriate that one of the last scenes in *The Crystal World* takes place in a church where Father Balthus, once an apostate, rediscovers the divine through the vehicle of the crystal world. "In the forest we see the final celebration of the Eucharist of Christ's body," he tells Sanders. "Here everything is transfigured and illuminated, joined together in the last marriage of space and time" (162).

Sanders, whose arm had become crystallized, stumbled upon the church by chance. Earlier we are told that jewels have the ability to reverse "the process of crystallization . . . by some optical or electromagnetic freak [where] the intense focus of light within the stones simultaneously proved a compression of time" (148). A jeweled cross deliquesces Sanders's arm and allows him to escape the forest without falling prey to the crystals. He uses the cross to free a small, crystallizing child along the way. The equivalence of Sanders and Jesus is, of course, crystal clear—an unspoken pun on Ballard's part.

The theme of rebirth is central to the plot. We don't really know what the crystals do to the body or if they might deliver people into some sort of eternity or oblivion. Sanders thinks of himself in terms of Jesus, "re-animating the lost children he passed like a deity on his day of creation" (172), but the novel concludes with him in the role of a new Adam en route to a reanimated Eden. A loss of identity accompanies his escape from the jungle: "Somewhere in the crystalline streets of Mont Royal were the missing fragments of himself, living on in their own prismatic medium" (174). With thoughts of Suzanne, an imagined new Eve, Sanders returns from the last page to the first, on a river boat, moving up the channels of desire. His fate is as uncertain as that of Kerans and Ransom. But there is an air of hope and fulfillment that borders on the utopian. At the closing of *The Crystal World* as well as *The Drought* and *The Drowned World*, Ballard paints a light on the wall at the end of the dystopian tunnel.

This is more than we can say for his next installment of books. Published between 1970 and 1975, they include the experimental novel *The Atrocity Exhibition* and the trilogy *Crash*, *Concrete Island* and *High-Rise*. Supercharged desiring-machines run rampant through these books, and even though they don't plunge into nihilism—in fact, a twisted optimism empowers some of their inner workings—they exhibit a much darker, nuanced, and fearsome charisma. And somehow they are both more surreal yet more real than the novels that preceded them. The death of Ballard's wife in 1964 had something to do with it; in a retrospective footnote to the condensed novel "Cinecity," he writes: "[C]learly, my younger self was hoping to understand his wife's meaningless death" (*Atrocity* 125). But the content, it seems, is the real culprit—not the effects of *nature* on the psyche, but the effects of *culture* on the psyche.

CHAPTER 4

PSYCHOPATHOLOGIES OF EVERYDAY LIFE

The Atrocity Exhibition and the Cultural Disaster Trilogy

A POSTMODERN TURN

The Atrocity Exhibition (1970)

At the turn of the twentieth century, Steven Best and Douglas Kellner identified an emergent paradigm in the trajectory of aesthetics, science, and culture that suggests we are somewhere between modernism and postmodernism rather than firmly situated in the latter camp. They call this liminal space "the postmodern turn," a transitory point "between a modernist past and a future struggling to define itself."[1] Ballard's fiction signifies this turn, grappling with historical forces while mapping new ontological territory and digging innovative reservoirs of desire. Some of that fiction can be quantified in terms of a more general definition of postmodernism as a literary form. Nowhere else in his canon is this more the case than in *The Atrocity Exhibition*, an anomaly unlike anything else he ever wrote.

Many critics regard *Atrocity* as Ballard's masterwork. Strange, dark, labyrinthine, disjointed, elusive, and beautiful, the book is a testament to his stylistic talent and dynamism. It began as a series of collage illustrations that he referred to as "Project for a New Novel." In "Desperate Measures: A History of *The Atrocity Exhibition*," a meticulous account of the text's origins and evolution, Mike Holliday explains how this prototype was "a series of spreads using magazine-style layouts and headlines, accompanied by largely meaningless text. The intention was for the titles and layout to provide the imaginative content, as is the case with an advertising hoarding" (105). Ballard failed to find a publisher and reverted to straight prose. The narrative itself was far from straight.[2] In 1970 it was published in the UK by Jonathan Cape and in the US by Doubleday. That same year, Doubleday took it out of print, worried about being sued by the politicians, movie stars, and other media figures Ballard lampooned, roasted, and eroticized. Grove Press picked it up two years later in 1972 and published it as *Love and Napalm: Export USA*, a title selected against Ballard's advice. He believed it would lend the book an anti-American vibe and tie it too intimately to the Vietnam War (*Atrocity* 151–52).

The British magazine *Impulse* (formerly *Science Fantasy*) published the earliest iteration of *Atrocity* in 1966 as *You and Me and the Continuum*, the title of one of the chapters (just as "Love and Napalm: USA" and "The Atrocity Exhibition" are chapter titles); later that same year, a version of the titular chapter was printed in *New Worlds*. As a whole, it is by far Ballard's most experimental book, a compendium of what he labeled "condensed novels" that together amount to an aggressive antinovel, breaking the conventions of traditional narrative inside and outside of the science fiction genre in the vein of William S. Burroughs's cut-up novel *Naked Lunch* (1959) and the techno-surreal trilogy *The Soft Machine* (1961), *The Ticket That Exploded* (1962), and *Nova Express* (1964). Ballard had allegedly not read Burroughs's books before he composed it, but there are striking similarities. In today's literary climate, *Atrocity* is not terribly shocking or out of bounds. Consider the schizophrenic *normalcy* of contemporary media technologies and, for example, the tsunami of porn available at the tap of a finger. In its historical context, however, the book was quite radical and a massive departure from Ballard's natural-disaster novels, chasing the fine wine that was *The Crystal World* like a shot of kamikaze tequila. He caught readers off guard.

Chris Beckett provides a concise description of *Atrocity*'s source materials:

> amongst them, Surrealism, varieties of Pop Art from Richard Hamilton and Eduardo Paolozzi to Andy Warhol, the prose of William Burroughs, French New Wave cinema . . . and the spatial and object-driven narratives of Alain Robbe-Grillet. The dream-like and deadpan collision of disparate prose registers—the disorienting, and frequently humorous, hallmark of the work—was partially generated by the incorporation of material derived from scientific and medical reports that Ballard plundered, spliced and parodied. ("Progress")

Another profound influence was *This Is Tomorrow*, an exhibition at the Whitechapel Art Gallery in London that is widely considered to have given birth to pop art (Sellars, Introduction 36). Ballard attended in 1956, the year he sold his first story. Piqued by artists' fetishization of American popular culture and pulp science fiction,[3] he had an epiphany. Not only did the exhibition convince him that "science fiction was far closer to reality than the conventional realist novel of the day" (*Miracles* 171), it exposed him to the vast creative potential of mass media. In 2003 Ballard reflected: "At the time I didn't see *This Is Tomorrow* as an aesthetic event. For me it wasn't primarily an art show, just as I didn't see exhibitions of Francis Bacon, Max Ernst, Magritte and Dali as displays of paintings. I saw them as among the most radical statements of the human imagination ever made, on a par with radical discoveries in neuroscience or nuclear physics. *This Is Tomorrow* showed how the world could be reperceived and remade" ("Nothing" 385). This is what he set out to do in *Atrocity*, reperceiving and remaking his own style, technique, and method of narration. He engendered a new line of flight in science fiction.

For the most part, Ballard did not consider *Atrocity* (or anything that came after it) to be a work of science fiction. In 1991 he said: "By the time I got to *The Atrocity Exhibition* in the late sixties, and then went on to *Crash*, *Concrete Island* and *High-Rise*, and then at the end of the seventies *The Unlimited Dream Company*, I had left science fiction behind completely. Nobody, in fact, ever called *Empire of the Sun* a science fiction novel, but other novels of mine that were not are termed SF (*Crash* is still referred to as a science fiction novel—which is silly, of course)" ("Interview," Lewis 257).[4]

Ballard's stance is problematic. *Empire of the Sun* is a work of realist fiction, and most of the books that followed *The Crystal World* did not fit comfortably in any science fiction subgenre, let alone the genre at large. But they are unequivocally science fictional inasmuch as they explore the relationship between technology and humanity, cognitively estrange readers, and effectuate novums. The novum in *Atrocity* is predominantly linguistic and gave incentive to the cyberpunks' new romance (or, as William Gibson might say, *neuromance*) with language in the 1980s. Ballard even suggests it. In a subchapter of "You and Me and the Continuum," where the novel's resident pseudo-scientist, Dr. Nathan, tries to make sense out of the torrent of media and "irreconcilable data" that barrages him, he poses the question: "What language could embrace all these, or at least provide a key: computer codes, origami, dental formulae?" (134).

At its core, *The Atrocity Exhibition* exhibits the atrocity—at once terrifying and rapturous—of the emerging electronic media landscape. In order to define the social, cultural, and somatic contours of this landscape, Ballard developed a mediatized language and narrative edifice that, in addition to the stimuli itemized by Beckett, seems indebted to Marshall McLuhan's media theories. In fact, reading McLuhan's *Understanding Media: The Extensions of Man* can be uncannily like reading an interpretation (or "extension") of *Atrocity*—and vice versa.[5]

In *Modernism and Science Fiction*, Paul March-Russell calls *Atrocity* a "cybernetic masterwork" (131). If only because of the prefix, science fiction readers often associate "cybernetic" with the body implants and prosthetics, futique bling, genetic mad scientism, technofetishism, and the overall surreality of classic 1980s cyberpunk fiction. We don't find any console cowboys, implant addicts, Panther moderns, or schizophrenic AIs in Ballard's cyberfiction, but it does contain the genetic code of the cyberpunk novels and stories inspired by him. Schizophrenia is a normative condition, and as Bruce Sterling expounds in his legendary preface to the definitive cyberpunk anthology, *Mirrorshades* (1986), "technology is visceral . . . pervasive, utterly intimate. Not outside of us, but next to us. Under our skin; often, inside our minds" (xiii). In *Atrocity*, it is always inside our minds, or rather inside the mind of the "protean T, presumably a psychiatrist who has suffered a mental breakdown, and is confined to an asylum where he performs bizarre behavioral experiments with the inmates, and is in turn observed by the clinician Dr. Nathan" (March-Russell 131). The asylum is a germane setting for the theme of media explosion and implosion that *characterizes* the novel. Just as the natural landscapes function as (anti)characters in *The Drowned World*, *The Drought*, and *The Crystal World*, so do the cultural landscapes of *Atrocity*. I will talk about the vicissitudes of the protagonist in a moment. First I want to say a few words about the title of this chapter and Ballard's rhizomatic methodology.

"Psychopathologies of Everyday Life" signals Freud's famous study and his persistent impact on Ballard's writing, especially in the novels under discussion here. Samuel Francis classifies them as "insane modernities" (52). In *The Psychopathology of Everyday Life*, Freud hypothesizes that divergences from "ordinary" conduct (for example, rhetorical forgetfulness, mysterious anxieties, inscrutable behavior) originate in the unconscious and are "motivated by repression" (17). In *Atrocity*, Ballard plunges into the maelstrom of the unconscious, exploring the effects of cultural pathology *from the inside*, from the very heart of inner space (the only time he dives all the way in), whereas in *Crash*, *Concrete Island*, and *High-Rise*, he zooms out and foregrounds the pathological architectures of autogeddon and urbanity that inscribe us, although we must keep in mind that "it is quite a distinct question whether the modern urban realities pictured in the trilogy are created by the psyches of those who live in them or whether they are in some way created by the worlds around them" (Brigg 67). Once again, Ballard's variety of inner space finds solace in the fold of ambiguity as he waxes the psychopathology of everyday (mediatized) life in four different contexts.

The narrator of *Atrocity* mentions a "conceptualized pathology" that is intimately linked with "technology and its instrument, the machine," leading him to conclude that "Freud's classic distinction between the manifest and latent content of the inner world of the psyche now has to be applied to the outer world of reality" (Ballard, *Atrocity* 156). Images of the helicopter, "with its unstable, insect-like obsessiveness" (38), permeate the book. So do images of the automobile, a literal and metaphorical vehicle of desire. It debuts in "Crash!," the "chromosome that contains the main themes of the subsequent novel" ("J. G. Ballard's Cinema" 371): "An understanding of this identity can be found in a study of the automobile, which dominates the vectors of speed, aggression, violence, and desire. In particular the automobile crash contains a crucial image of the machine as conceptualized pathology" (Ballard, *Atrocity* 156).

Cars preoccupy Ballard, but they are one of many machines (soft and hard) that populate the narrative and expose the production of subjectivity by machinic forces. All this is reified by the machinic composition of *Atrocity*. The book smacks of automatic writing[6] and displays many thematic and stylistic traits of literary postmodernism and cybernetic fiction.[7] As in Burroughs's cut-ups, Ballard has "constructed a physics of the human nervous system or more accurately the human nervous system defines the physics [he has] constructed" (Burroughs, *Nova* 86). He admits that "the nervous systems of the characters have been externalized, as part of the reversal of the interior and exterior worlds. Highways, office blocks, faces and street signs are perceived as if they were elements in a malfunctioning nervous system" (Ballard, *Atrocity* 76n). But *Atrocity* is not a cut-up. Ballard's word hordes are far more organized, methodical, polished, and well-oiled than Burroughs's.

Readers still found themselves at a loss. In an author's note written in 2001, Ballard says that the structure of *Atrocity* is much simpler than it initially appears. Victor Sage discusses the problem of reading and making sense of it:

> [It] takes the form of an encyclopaedia of conceits about postwar history and politics from Hiroshima to Vietnam, about psychohistory and psychopathology, art, sex, technology and particularly Science—hard science, not just computer science. Its 15 sections form a romance of documentation, its narrative conveyed in a style of paragraphing which plays between encyclopaedia entries (each paragraph in the entire book is headed in bold type) and the kind of 'objectivist' poetic style of the immediate postwar French novel of Alain Robbe-Grillet. There are also lurches into recycled surrealist motifs from painting and drama (Marcel DuChamp, Max Ernst, Salvador Dali, Alfred Jarry). We do not know therefore whether we should be reading in a linear fashion and connecting up paragraphs, or whether the relationship between them is random and we always have to start again. It is a strange mixture of the two, which wrong-foots the reader all the time: conventional linear narrative does not survive this process of defamiliarization. (41)

From the standpoint of postmodern theory, *Atrocity* is a rhizome akin to Gilles Deleuze and Félix Guattari's cybernetic writings on capitalism and schizophrenia.[8] In *Anti-Oedipus* and its sequel, *A Thousand Plateaus*, Deleuze the philosopher and Guattari the psychiatrist map a "schizosophy" of desire, the body, subjectivity, and the socius in the late capitalist era. Clinically, they oppose the stringent, reactionary, fascist tendencies of Freudian psychoanalysis; as an alternative, they propose schizoanalysis. "In both psychoanalysis and its object, there is always a general, always a leader (General Freud). Schizoanalysis, on the other hand, treats the unconscious as an acentered system, in other words, as a machinic network of finite automata (a rhizome), and thus arrives at an entirely different state of the unconscious" (18). This state of acenteredness extends to writing and reading. They encourage readers to enter the architecture of their narrative from any doorway, since the rooms they lead into are all interrelated: "We call a 'plateau' any multiplicity connected to other multiplicities by superficial underground stems in such a way as to form or extend a rhizome. We are writing this book as a rhizome. It is composed of plateaus. We have given it a circular form. . . . Each plateau can be read starting anywhere and can be related to any other plateau" (*Thousand* 22).

Ballard wasn't familiar with Deleuze and Guattari when he composed *Atrocity*. He didn't like literary criticism or theory and may never have read them. Their books on capitalism and schizophrenia were published in French in 1972 and 1980 and didn't appear in English until 1977 and 1987. Still, *Atrocity* has the properties of the deleuzoguattarian rhizome. Ballard even prompts readers to approach it like a multiplicity of plateaus in his author's note: "Rather than start at the beginning of each chapter, as in a conventional novel, simply turn the pages until a paragraph catches your eye. If the ideas or images seem interesting, scan the nearby paragraphs for anything that resonates in an intriguing way. Fairly soon, I hope, the fog will clear, and the underlying narrative will reveal itself. In effect, you will be reading the book in the way it was written" (vi).

Atrocity has been reprinted many times over. The 2006 edition (Fourth Estate) contains extensive, insightful annotations written by Ballard for each chapter that provide background information and commentary on the subject material as well as a schematic of his authorial motives. They were written some twenty years after the printing of the first UK edition for Andrea Juno and V. Vale's 1990 RE / Search Publication edition, which also features a revised, expanded version of the text with illustrations. This is the definitive version of *Atrocity*, even if the annotations, while edifying and useful for scholarship, dilute the experience of reading the book from its ideal perch of *immersive pathology*, hurling readers into the verbomaniacal media torrent and forcing them to navigate it. Then again, much of the book's content and cultural context will be lost to contemporary readers, such as the role of Ralph Nader, a media star in the 1960s and today relatively unknown.[9] The annotations give us an idea of what Ballard thought of the book from the perspective of a future in which electronic media had become normative, if not banal.

Atrocity implicates readers, who, like the book's many characters, are pathologized by the flailing tentacles of mass media. The core pathology belongs to Ballard's protean T. There are several faces: Travis, Talbot, Tallis, Trabert, Talbert, and Travers. The central identity is Traven. Ballard took the name "consciously from B. Traven, a writer I've always admired for his extreme reclusiveness—so completely at odds with the logic of our own age, when even the concept of privacy is constructed from publicly circulating materials. It is now almost impossible to be ourselves except on the world's terms" (36n). He first used Traven in the short story "The Terminal Beach" as a pilot marooned on Eniwetok who suffers a schizophrenic breach (see chapter 3). The thematic catalyst in the story for this breach is the nuclear bomb and the Atomic Age. In *Atrocity* it is the information bomb and the Media Age: Ballard jacks Traven into the matrix of blip culture where the "human organism is an atrocity exhibition at which he is an unwilling spectator" (9).

On television the juxtaposition of violent, sensationalized clips from, for example, the Vietnam War and the Kennedy assassination with cereal commercials and movie previews indicated an emergent *force of culture* that desensitized viewers and reduced death and destruction to the level of cornflakes. This is emphasized from the beginning: "Entering the exhibition, Travis sees the atrocities of Vietnam and the Congo mimetized in the 'alternate' death of Elizabeth Taylor; he tends to the dying film star, eroticizing her punctured bronchus in the over-ventilated verandas of the London Hilton; he dreams of Max Ernst, superior of the birds; 'Europe after the Rain'; the human race—Caliban asleep across a mirror smeared with vomit" (12). Ballard exhales war, celebrity, art, and Shakespeare in one breath. Confronted by the surreality of it all, Traven and his doppelgängers are de facto mad men in a default mad world.

The protean T is an archetypal blip subject—"ephemeral, electronically processed, unreal" (Bukatman 33)—manufactured by the "implosion of the media age: the reduction of all the things in the world to blips, to data, to the message units contained within the brain and its adjunct, the computer" (70). A more domineering media-father than the computer is the television, an instrument of desire that is the most consequential, affective instrument in all of Ballardian iconography, even trumping the automobile and aircraft. As numerous postmodern texts demonstrate, effectively representing the blip subject can entail untraditional, unorthodox characterization. For Ballard, it entails various intersections and meltdowns of personality:

> I don't see them as 'characters' in the conventional sense of the term; they are aspects of certain character situations. They haven't got the same name, but they have variations of the same name. . . . All these characters operate on a number of levels. I feel that the fictional elements in experience are now multiplying to such a point that it is almost impossible to distinguish between the real and the false, that one has many layers, many levels of experience going on at the same time. On one level one might have the world of public events. Cape Kennedy, Vietnam, political life . . . on another level the immediate personal environment, the rooms we occupy, the postures we assume. On a third level, the inner world of the mind. All these levels are, as far as I can see them, equally fictional, and it is where these levels interact that one gets the only kind of valid reality that in fact exists nowadays. ("New," Macbeth 53–54)

In other words: *fiction is a gateway to reality*. Even better (and riffing on Lacanian theory): *fiction is the structure of reality.* This idée fixe runs throughout *Atrocity* and manifests to a lesser degree in all Ballard's novels, even *Empire of the Sun*, where Jamie's technological fantasies about flying and war scaffold his identity and actions in the real, objective world.

As the T-men scurry like vermin through the warren of the mediascape, Dr. Nathan monitors them. Like Burroughs's Dr. Benway in *Naked Lunch* and *Nova Express*, the recurrent psychiatrist cares less about the welfare of the T-men than about making quixotic diagnoses and observations, "operating" as an impartial spectator; even when it is clear somebody will perish, he never intercedes, like a newscaster covering a story and reflecting on events.[10]

Nathan is a foil for the protagonist(s), a voice of reason that contrasts with and irradiates what they represent: the flows of desire, imagination, and the unconscious. There are a few recurrent female characters, the most important of which is the protagonist(s)'s wife, Catherine Austin (also the wife of "Ballard" in *Crash*), and Karen Novotny, who often dies brutally at the end of one chapter, only to be rebooted like a computer in another chapter. Holliday implies that she may be a terminal recapitulation of the senseless death of Ballard's actual wife ("Desperate" 107). Jeannette Baxter contends that Novotny is a "serial victim of sadistic and stylized scenarios in which the male protagonist dismembers her compulsively in a bid to gain access to 'truth, to a heightened sense of reality—a surreality'" (*Surrealist* 76).

"Alternate deaths" pervade *Atrocity*. Nobody suffers more than Novotny. Ballard clarifies: "By [alternate deaths] I mean the re-enactment of various tragedies staged by Traven and his many selves. They take place partly in his own mind and partly in the external world, and represent his attempt to make sense of these unhappy events and attribute to them a moral dimension and even, perhaps, a measure of hope" (90n). Overall, women subordinate the plight of the T-men. This is a patriarchal space subject to the male gaze and masculine, machinic desire. Ballard's entire oeuvre occupies the same space, but he doesn't necessarily endorse it. He critiques and satirizes masculinity and patriarchy as much as he validates them.

Besides trying to make sense out of Mary's death, Ballard said that *Atrocity* was an attempt to extricate the 1963 Kennedy assassination in Dallas, Texas. "The mass media created the Kennedy we know, and his death represented a tectonic shift in the communications landscape, sending fissures deep into the popular psyche" (53n). Ballard fictionalizes (and thus *realizes*) JFK in absurdist states of unrest, as he does with other political figures and celebrities, including Marilyn Monroe, Mae West, James Dean, and, infamously, Ronald Reagan. Controversy ensued. The book received the greatest attention for one of its shortest chapters, "Why I Want to Fuck Ronald Reagan," which focused on, among other "posture concepts" (167), "powerful erotic fantasies of an anal-sadistic character [that] surrounded the image of the Presidential contender" (165). The former Hollywood movie star was ripe fruit for Ballard, signifying a troubling conflation of celebrity and politician, a media cyborg whose image and body language far outshone the Orwellian doublespeak that constituted his rhetoric.[11] The chapter was originally published as a chapbook by Brighton's Unicorn Bookshop in January 1968. On the day it came out, police raided the store and seized three copies of the chapbook along with thousands of other books and magazines that were deemed inappropriate or obscene; later that year, the owner of the store, American poet Bill Butler, stood trial on behalf of Ballard's "dirty and diseased mind."[12]

Other chapters caught flak for satirizing American icons, such as "The Assassination of John Fitzgerald Kennedy Considered as a Downhill Motor Race," a spoof-of-a-spoof that reimagines Alfred Jarry's "The Crucifixion Considered as an Uphill Bike Race," and three "appendices" that appeared in the RE/Search edition, all of which have to do with plastic surgery and the toxicity of image-culture: "Princess Margaret's Face Lift: An Intersection of Fiction and Reality," "Mae West's Reduction Mammoplasty," and "Queen Elizabeth's Rhinoplasty." "Plan for the Assassination of Jacqueline Kennedy," a mock scientific study of the potential sexual reactions of the former first lady and other female luminaries, was publicly derided by Winston Churchill's son Randolph. It first appeared in *Ambit* in 1967. Churchill petitioned the Arts Council that funded the magazine to retract its grant, "all this at a time when the ordeal of Mrs. Kennedy and her courtship by Aristotle Onassis were ruthlessly exploited by the tabloid newspapers, the real target of my satire" (*Miracles* 188). Like many of *Atrocity*'s readers, Churchill didn't understand it—he couldn't make sense out of Ballard's surrealist efforts to make sense. All he saw were famous people put in compromising positions with hypersexualized, ultraviolent rhetoric. In a sense, the book's readers were (and remain) T-men themselves, blip subjects lost in the vortex of mass media.

Ballard's use of specific names vitalizes his portrayal and scrutiny of American society and culture. Some chapters "name names" more than others. "The Generations of America" is an eruption of names—a literal, machine-gun litany that plays on how generations of families are listed in the Bible. It even begins with a biblical prompt: "These are the generations of America" (159). Then there is a chain reaction of people getting shot and shooting other people: "Sirhan Sirhan shot Robert F. Kennedy. And Ethel M. Kennedy shot Judith Birnbaum. And Judith Birnbaum shot Elizabeth Bochnak. And Elizabeth Bochnak shot Andrew Witwer. And Andrew Witwer shot John Burlingame. And John Burlingame shot Edward R. Darlington" (ibid.). And so on. Most of the people listed didn't actually shoot one another; Ballard took the names from the mastheads of *Look*, *Life*, and *Time*, prominent American magazines in the 1960s that he read dutifully and "helped to create the media landscape at the heart of *The Atrocity Exhibition*" (163n). Originally published in *New Worlds* in 1968, "The Generations of America" was among the tamest and least provocative chapters. Today it might be the most relevant, considering the excessive gun violence that harrows twenty-first-century America.

Atrocity received bad reviews and sold poorly in the US. In Europe, it was warmly received, and reviewers in Denmark, Germany, and Holland grasped and appreciated what Ballard was trying to do, even if English reviewers didn't care for his style or subject matter ("J. G. Ballard," Linnett 53). He returned to a conventional writing style with his next novel, *Crash*, the so-called "psychopathic hymn" whose subject matter was far from conventional (Self 369). It is the book most frequently associated with his signature, in part due to David Cronenberg's film adaptation and the controversies surrounding it. I think it has to do primarily with the sheer oddity of the book. Nobody had written a novel about "symphorophilia"[13] like that before. Certainly nobody had written about it in such a compelling way, causing one reviewer to say: "The author of this book is beyond psychiatric help" ("Interview," Revell 49).[14]

TECHNOLOGIES OF THE PRESENT

Crash (1973) • *Concrete Island* (1974) • *High-Rise* (1975)

Atrocity brought Ballard's fiction into the dark and machinic "realities" of the present in 1970. He stayed in the present until the 1980s. Unlike, say, the novels of contemporary British authors Graham Greene and Anthony Burgess, both of whom Ballard admired, he focused on the hard technologies of metal, motors, and concrete, of the vehicles and architectures that inscribe us, and of the dreams and desires that our products *produce* in our minds and on our bodies. Ballard dived like a sailor, head first, into the seas of late capitalism and consumer culture, and he never looked back.

Critics normally refer to *The Drowned World*, *The Drought*, and *The Crystal World* as the natural-disaster trilogy, and *Crash*, *Concrete Island*, and *High-Rise* as the urban-disaster trilogy. For the latter, I prefer the *cultural*-disaster trilogy, "culture" being the technological foil for "nature." Ballard distinguishes between them: "My earliest three or four novels, which are more explicitly science fiction, are all heavily influenced by the surrealists (Max Ernst, Dali), and also the symbolist painters like Gustave Moreau. Once you get to *The Atrocity*

Exhibition, *Crash*, *High-Rise* and so on, they're sort of *technological* books set in the present day—you've got all the imagery that the titles themselves are about" ("Interview," Juno and Vale 32).

Like the natural-disaster trilogy, the cultural-disaster trilogy involves physical landscapes that affect (or are affectations of) psychological landscapes, broadening the scope of inner space. Earlier I mentioned that Ballard didn't think the cultural-disaster trilogy was science fiction. Regardless of the vitality and imaginative might of *Crash*'s prose, none of the novels are cyberfictions in the mold of *Atrocity*, but it seems that whenever Ballard references science fiction, he means the conventional guidelines and trappings of genre science fiction, which he spent the first part of his career writing against. Whatever the case, his texts consistently destablize the genre. *Crash*, *Concrete Island*, and *High-Rise* are different novels than, for instance, Arthur C. Clarke's *Rendezvous with Rama* (1973), Joe Haldeman's *The Forever War* (1974), and Cordwainer Smith's *Norstrilia* (1975), published the same respective years as the cultural-disaster trilogy. By Ballard's own admission, however, they are novels about technology. More important, they represent a dawning science fictionalization of his present-day reality, one that began to take shape with the ascension of media technologies in the 1960s.

The media, transit, and structural environments in these books would have belonged to science fiction of the past. A good example is Edward Bellamy's *Looking Backward* (1888), even though the term "science fiction" didn't exist at the time of its publication and was retroactively applied to it. The environments of Bellamy's future 2000 A.D. are less futuristic than those of Ballard's present 1970s. Most of all, they estrange readers by way of their presentation, by the "geometry" of Ballard's inner-spatial milieus, *modes de vie*, and zones of terror, wonder, and jouissance. It is this trait more than anything else that follows Ballard throughout his career and binds him to the apparatus of science fiction.

There is an immensity of criticism pertaining to the novels in the cultural-disaster trilogy. Some scholarship couples *Crash* with *Atrocity* and treats *Concrete Island* and *High-Rise* as individual symptoms or aftershocks of "the coming autogeddon" instigated by *Atrocity* (*Crash* 106). A number of critics lump the latter three novels together, and Ballard himself once referred to them as "a kind of trilogy" ("Interview," Goddard and Pringle 31). Between *The Drowned World* and *High-Rise*, Ballard moves his uncozy catastrophes from the actual jungle to the concrete jungle through the way station of a postmodern experiment.

Peter Brigg persuasively compares and contrasts this transition. In the "kind of trilogy," he argues, Ballard looks at the effects of complex technologies on urban capitalist subjects with a "cool amorality" that is the books' strongest and most recognizable feature; hence the novels "are cautionary insofar as they suggest that technology together could lead to violence and inhumane attitudes," but they "lack the 'what if' quality of predictive science fiction" (75). This is a viable claim, and Ballard labeled *Crash* "cautionary" years after he wrote it, comparing it to the pokerfaced method of Jonathan Swift's *A Modest Proposal* (1929).[15] Given Ballard's fondness for cultivating ambiguity, an equally viable claim can be made that *Crash*, *Concrete Island*, and *High-Rise* are mere depictions of the contemporary technological human condition removed from the gavel of any judgment or moral dictum.

In "The Texture of Modernity" Sebastian Groes treats the novels in the cultural-disaster trilogy as late capitalist allegories, contending that "the dominating technology of concrete reshapes social structures and relationships in monstrous, dehumanized and Americanized ways. As Ballard puts it in *High-Rise*, 'this was an environment built, not for man, but for man's absence'" (124). Groes examines the "death of affect," a phrase coined by Ballard that harks back to Georg Simmel's influential ideas about human development in "The Metropolis and Mental Life" at the turn of the twentieth century. Simmel conjectures that people lose the ability to respond emotionally to the sensory stimuli of city life and risk being "swallowed up in the social-technological mechanism" (409). For Ballard, the death of affect can lead to a triumph of the imagination. Urbanity and technology may be flawed, but they are also modes of agency, spawning flows of desire that are thanatonic, therapeutic, and transcendent.

The cultural-disaster trilogy sacrifices the rational in the name of the irrational and gives primacy to the creative forces of the unconscious. From this standpoint, Colin Greenland offers a model definition: "These three contemporary 'catastrophes' are detailed studies in the latent violence of the urban landscape. They comprise a triptych illustrating the thesis presented in

Atrocity that modern technology satisfies the irrational urges of the human mind more than the rational purposes for which it was apparently designed" (120).

Crash is the pole star of Ballard's canon—his most "extreme" novel and the one most readily associated with his name, not by devout or even casual science fiction readers but by general audiences. *Empire of the Sun* is a close second because of Spielberg's film. Cronenberg's adaptation of *Crash* facilitated its popularity, but to a lesser extent, and while the novelistic and cinematic versions of *Empire* are only three years apart, for *Crash* they are separated by more than twenty years. The book became a phenomenon long before the movie came to pass, whereas Spielberg's movie drew more attention to the novel on which it was based.

Stylistically, *Crash* isn't an experimental novel, but it is as unique as *Atrocity*, and Ballard wrote nothing like it before or after. This has been something of a detriment to scholarship. Recently the current has changed, but for years, much criticism wrongly totalized his canon with *Crash* and *Atrocity*, reducing it to the designs and themes of these novels. They can't be ignored, but in spite of their striking features, the novels do not necessarily represent Ballard's most compelling work, and the tendency to focus on them has led to a distorted view of the author as a postmodern, hypersexual, technofetishistic, ultraviolent, and literary auteur, when in fact what Martin Amis classifies as the "brutalist period" represents a small, short-lived window in his career (xii).

David Pringle describes *Crash* as "perhaps the best example of 'pornographic' sf" ("Ballard, J. G."). Ballard didn't think it was a science fiction novel, but he did call it "the first pornographic novel based on technology" in an introduction to the 1974 French edition ("Crash"). I'm not the only one to disagree with the author. Jean Baudrillard famously and divisively wrote about *Crash* in science fictional terms.[16] In *Simulacra and Simulation*, he puts it on a pedestal and differentiates it from other kinds of science fiction,

> which most of the time still revolves around the old couple function/dysfunction, which it projects in the future along the same lines of force and the same finalities that are those of the normal universe. . . . In *Crash*, everything is hyperfunctional, since traffic and accident, technology and death, sex and simulation are like a single, large synchronous machine. . . . There fiction surpasses reality

> (or the opposite), but according to the same rules of the game. In *Crash*, no more fiction or reality, it is hyperreality that abolishes both. (118)

He concludes that it is "the first great novel of the universe of simulation" (119). Francis criticizes Baudrillard, saying his analysis of *Crash* is persuasive yet hindered by an antipsychological approach that ignores the novel's Freudian connotations (107). He makes a good point. Baudrillard's reading nonetheless accurately locates the novel within the technological, media-saturated cultural climate of its composition—even if, as Nicholas Ruddick and others have suggested, he misinterprets it.[17] Ballard searingly denounced postmodern criticism of science fiction and the "dismal jargon" of the "over-professionalized" academics who write it,[18] but he felt an affinity with Baudrillard, and he loved *America*, a travel narrative about American hyperreality that he said was one of his favorite books alongside *Naked Lunch* and *The Secret Life of Salvador Dali*.[19] As for Ballard's response to Baudrillard's vision of *Crash*, he simply stated: "I have not really wanted to understand [it]" (qtd. in Ruddick 355).

As a work of "unauthorized" science fiction, *Crash* lands somewhere between Baudrillard and Freud, hyperreality and psychoanalysis, what pulses on the surface and what begs to be unburied. Both read like science fiction, one exploring the matrix of electronic consumer culture, the other the matrix of the machinic unconscious. But *Crash* is at its most science fictional on the plateau of language. A linguistic novum reinforces the architecture of Ballard's prose. It is not the same "unique vocabulary and grammar of late-20th-century life . . . whose psychology [Ballard] tried to describe" in *Atrocity* (128n), but it is cut from the same cloth, as Baudrillard implies in a comment on Ballard's choice of sexual terminology: "Here, all the erotic terms are technical. No ass, no dick, no cunt but: the anus, the rectum, the vulva, the penis, coitus. No slang, that is to say no intimacy or sexual violence, but a functional language: the adequation of chrome and mucous as of one form to another. The same goes for the correspondence of death and sex: it is more as if they are covered together in a sort of technical superseding than articulated according to pleasure" (116).

Crash may be set in London, but it addresses a distinctly American phenomenon, a torrid romance between the human and the automobile, the dynamics of which illustrate collective desires, insecurities, bodies, and perceptions. The specter of Hollywood plays a crucial role. Not only does *Crash* fetishize the object par excellence of American affection and affectation, it fetishizes the image of the celebrity and the ratchet of capitalist cinema that produces the celebrity as *objet petit a*—in Lacanian discourse, the unobtainable object of desire. Vaughan is the indubitable antihero of this "amazing story," which is far more amazing than anything ever dreamed up in a science fiction pulp magazine (and, incidentally, far more dreamlike). Scarred physically and psychologically in a motorcycle accident, the "hoodlum scientist" cum sex-and-violence messiah, a technological version of the Burroughsian junkie, yearns to die in a headlong collision with Elizabeth Taylor. Vaughn is *the seminal vehicle*. He introduces new ways of seeing and thinking by fusing together the car, the movie star, and sexuality, "the codes of a new marriage of sensation and possibility" (106). And a masculine ethos inscribes these codes. *Crash*, after all, is a novel about the phallus—its empowerment, its fluidity, its assertion/insertion, and its "automutilation."

Ballard fixates on Vaughan's damaged face, an emblem of his transformed identity and transformative abilities. Fittingly, we encounter him for the first time in *Atrocity* in the chapter "Tolerances of the Human Face." Outside the casualty ward, Travers is taken aback by "the flame-like scars on his knuckles, residues of an appalling act of violence. . . . The dented plates of his forehead and the sallow jaws were features as anonymous as any police suspect's. The musculature of his mouth was clamped together in a rictus of aggression, as if he were about to commit a crude and unsavoury crime" (105). Vaughan has a tactile presence and an aura of danger and excitement, but he appears only in a few brief scenes. In *Crash*, Ballard develops him into a centripetal force.

The narrator and protagonist, "James Ballard," is the first major instance of self-reflexivity in his writing and another reason the novel came under attack. Some readers mistook it as an autobiographical statement of the author's own desires and actions when the use of his name is a literary technique that blurs the lines between fact and fiction, reality and fantasy, logic and absurdity. The name advances the theme of implosion that dominates *Crash*. "Ballard" teaches us how, between conscious and unconscious realms, we never quite know who we are or what we want.

Crash takes after classic narratives of exploration and discovery, only instead of deep sea or outer space, Ballard navigates the media environment and, in Simmel's words, the "social-technological mechanism." A forty-year-old television commercial producer, the narrator and his wife Catherine are defined by a lack of affect they continually try to fill with sex. Catherine has relationships with multiple men and women. "Ballard" has a mistress and partakes in their open marriage, but not with the same conviction. Television is the primary catalyst and agent of the media. Shortly after the car accident that sets the plot in motion, "Ballard" lays injured in a hospital bed and describes his condition(ing) as a blip subject:

> I was already becoming a kind of emotional cassette, taking my place with all those scenes of pain and violence that illuminated the margins of our lives—television newsreels of wars and student riots, natural disasters and police brutality which we vaguely watched on the colour TV set in our bedroom as we masturbated each other. This violence experienced at so many removes had become intimately associated with our sex acts. The beatings and burnings married in our minds with the delicious tremors of our erectile tissues, the spilt blood of students with the genital fluids that irrigated our fingers and mouths . . . [E]ven the vagal flushes that seized at my chest seemed extensions of that real world of violence calmed and tamed within our television programmes and the pages of news magazines. (37)

Sex in itself doesn't suffice. They must link it with "the elements of new technologies" (32). Vaughan is the harbinger. He sanctions them with a "benevolent psychopathology" that holds the key to sensitization (138). Ironically, the liberating technology of Vaughan—what he does and what he represents—frees them from the encroaching technologies of late capitalist life. The relationship between "Ballard" and Vaughan literally and figuratively climaxes in their LSD-fueled sex act in Vaughan's Lincoln convertible, the same kind of car that Kennedy was assassinated in. As a pornographic narrative, everything that happens in *Crash* can be viewed as foreplay for this surreal climactic scene, a representation of the *Frankenstein*-like fusion of technology and humanity.

Before Vaughan, "Ballard" develops a bond with Dr. Helen Remington, whom he crashes into at the novel's outset, sliding into oncoming traffic when his car hydroplanes in the rain, killing her husband. The crash is the "only real experience" "Ballard" has had in years (39). It exhilarates him. Remington is traumatized and stirred by the accident. "Ballard" says: "A powerful sense of eroticism had sprung up between me and this bereaved young woman, almost as if I unconsciously wished to re-conceive her dead husband in her womb" (44). Here and elsewhere, we can never be certain about the objective situation. "Ballard" may or may not be an unreliable narrator; everything filters through his perception, subjectivity, and inner space.

Helen and "Ballard" have sex only in his car because he can't achieve an erection anywhere else (82), but both of them experience a heightened sexual awareness and sensitivity from this multivalent vehicle in which they "recapitulated her husband's death" (83). A nexus of death, sex, and technology (e)merges for "Ballard," setting in motion the birth of affect that is later enflamed by Vaughan, "nightmare angel of the expressways" (84). The novel commences with a reflection on Vaughan's death, then reverts to the primal collision with Helen and progresses forward to his death again. After meeting in the hospital, "Ballard" befriends Vaughan, falls in with his cadre of thrill seekers, and eventually becomes his chauffeur, "giving him money to pay the prostitutes and part-time whores who hung about the airport and its hotels" and voyeuristically watching him "explore every byway of sex and the automobile. For Vaughan the motor-car was the sexual act's greatest and only true locus" (171). "Ballard" comes to realize that he wants to fuck Vaughan, but homophobic anxiety delays him. In part, Ballard the author was writing from the perspective of 1970s culture where homosexuality remained widely stigmatized and taboo. More than that, he demonstrates how his protagonist transcends the limits of sex, gender, and the human body in favor of the techno-corporeality epitomized by Vaughan.

At first, Vaughan excites a "homosexual impulse" in "Ballard" (117), but only within the confines of his car. While making love to Catherine, he fantasizes about being "in an act of sodomy with Vaughan, as if this act alone could solve the codes of a deviant technology" (194). The fantasy becomes flesh one night in the Lincoln, which he parks beneath an airport overpass in a virtual cocoon of technology. "In the screen of the rear-view mirror I watched the cars climbing the access ramp on to the motorway behind us, eager arrivals at this aerial carnival. They sailed along the road surface above our heads to join the aircraft Vaughan had watched for so many months.

. . . I could see that everywhere these metabolized creatures were soaring through the sunlight, ascending from the traffic jams that had locked them together" (199). "Ballard" likens the spectacle of technology that surrounds them to godliness, and sex with Vaughan, fueled by LSD, becomes a stairway to heaven. Afterward "Ballard" recognizes that "this sex act between us had been devoid of all sexuality" (212). What mattered was the *idea* of the "erotic delirium of the car-crash" (16); gay or straight, man or woman—these binaries collapse and cease to possess meaning or resonance.

Vaughan attempts to run over "Ballard" after they come down off the acid. Later he stalks him and Catherine like a vengeful ghost. They take it in stride and realize that he is extending his fetishistic death wish to its natural conclusion; "Ballard" always suspected that Vaughan would try to kill him "in a final display of his casual love for me" (210). On one hand, his apathy has precedence if we consider that sex with Vaughan produced an intensity of sensitization that he feels like he will never be able to attain or match again. On the other hand, the apathy suggests that we may have entered his inner space, as he implies in the final chapter: "Increasingly I was convinced that Vaughan was a projection of my own fantasies and obsessions" (220). And in the final sentences, "Ballard" professes to be a becoming-Vaughan, "designing the elements of my own car-crash" (224). Once again, Ballard the author injects the venom of ambiguity and problematizes the already questionable identity of his main character.

Previously I referred to Vaughan as Ballard's ultimate desiring-machine. Simon Sellars lends more insight in a review of *Crash*, saying that he is "the first appearance of Ballard's fully blown 'catalyst figure' . . . an archetype Ballard seems to refine in every one of his latter-day novels: the dark, mysterious urban professional liberating the middle-classes by feeding their deepest, darkest psychopathological fantasies." Among these protean Vs, however, nobody triangulates the coordinates of death, sex, and technology like Vaughan does.

In addition to being extrapolated from *Atrocity* and the idea that "we need to invent a series of imaginary sexual perversions just to keep our feelings alive" (95), *Crash* arose from an exhibition of demolished cars at the New Arts Laboratory in London that Ballard hosted in 1969.[20] It lasted a month. He wanted to gauge the reactions of attendants; supposedly, they often became drunk and violent as a result of witnessing the mechanical carnage. Ballard said that he didn't care about cars themselves. "It's technology that interests me. . . . I really believe we've created a technological landscape which is not just around us but it's actually beginning to enter our minds. I don't want to sound too pretentious but we're getting a sort of marriage between sex and technology. And the car-crash represents the psychopathology of this system" ("J. G. Ballard *Repsychling* Interview" 36, 35).

At the time of its publication, many critics responded positively to what *Crash* was trying to do, but in general, it rubbed them the wrong way, or they disliked it altogether. Pringle, one of Ballard's most devoted and knowledgeable scholars, panned it as tedious, disappointing, and "relatively plotless and sloppy" ("Incredible" 74). Peter Linnett, in a review of *Concrete Island*, went so far as to call it a failure (73). These sentiments may have to do with Ballard not following the rules (of science fiction or any kind of writing) with such wild abandon, along with the sex, of course, which is explicit, excessive, and weird.

Curiously, pornography and science fiction are not so dissimilar, as Pringle indicates: "Both create worlds of fantasy; neither has much patience for reality. A pornography of the machine has always been implicit in SF" ("Honest" 63). Puzzled by the scarcity of sex in the genre, Ballard puts it in the spotlight, believing that "sex will play the same role in science fiction that used to be played by outer space, and that the sexual organs will become the starships and planets of inner space" ("Everything" 29). This has yet to happen. In fact, the genre continues to vegetate in sexual infancy. Many authors have written what qualifies as science fiction erotica or soft porn, but nothing has approached the singular hardcore aesthetic of *Crash*.

The follow-up to *Crash* retains the technology, landscape, and spirit of autogeddon. It also begins with a car accident. In style, execution, and substance, however, *Concrete Island* is a very different novel, even though critics have branded it a sequel or near-sequel. At first glance, it reads like it could have been written by somebody else, but familiar themes, uses of language, and character traits quickly rise to the surface. Still, Ballard distances himself from the aesthetics of *Atrocity* and *Crash*, irking some readers and relieving others. For instance, Ian Watson observes in an early review that *Concrete Island* "seems to be *Crash* in a minor key; a limp passive cadenza to the furious concerto of the former book" ("Greening" 67). Conversely, Linnet says it "takes up where *Crash* left off, and is a far better book" (71).

The narrative simplicity of *Concrete Island* stands apart from anything else Ballard wrote, yet it is among his most literary novels. Drawing on William Golding, Samuel Beckett, Shakespeare, John Donne, and Daniel Defoe, Ballard modernizes *Robinson Crusoe*, a kind of ur-text that, like *The Tempest*, he returns to and recycles with tenacity.[21] In a 1994 introduction, he explains that *Concrete Island* has the same schema as the other cultural-disaster novels: "Modern technology, as I tried to show in *Crash* and *High-Rise*, offers an endless field-day to any deviant strains in our personalities. Marooned in an office block or on a traffic island, we can tyrannise ourselves, test our strengths and weaknesses, perhaps come to terms with aspects of our characters to which we have always closed our eyes" (4).

Ballard returned to a sheer linear mode of storytelling that he never veered from again in his novels. *Crash* and *Atrocity* brought him so much attention that he suddenly found himself being pigeonholed as an experimentalist despite that the vast majority of his work had been written in a conventional format. As he related in 1973, "subject matter comes first. The style and technique serve the subject matter" ("J. G. Ballard," Linnett 54). Story reigned supreme for Ballard. Even if he preferred style over story, he knew better than to turn exclusively (or even moderately) to a nonlinear practice, which would sound a death knell for the careers of most professional authors.

The titular location of *Concrete Island* is "a small traffic island, some two hundred yards long and triangular in shape, that lay in the waste ground between three converging motorway routes. . . . Supported on massive concrete pillars, its six lanes of traffic were sealed from view by the corrugated metal splash-guards installed to protect the vehicles below" (11–12). The island itself isn't concrete; the architecture of transportation that encloses it like a prison is. And it becomes a prison (of the body and the mind) for the protagonist, thirty-five-year-old architect Robert Maitland, who loses control of his Jaguar in central London on the Westway interchange near Shepherd's Bush and plummets off the road. Unlike "Ballard"'s inaugural crash, which was a genuine accident, Maitland's is deliberate. Beleaguered by juggling a relationship with his mistress (another doctor) and wife (another Catherine) as well as an existential discontent with the modern world, he derails his car (and life) on purpose, although he doesn't realize it until later, and he never entirely owns up to it.

The size and complexity of motorways captivated Ballard. In contrast to *Crash*, *Concrete Island* has little if anything to do with cars as sources of agency or affect. Rather, it concerns the motorways themselves—how the superstructures dominate much of the urban landscape and, metaphorically, how they function as externalizations of the human psyche and nervous system. There is a fundamental lack of humanity to these human-made, human-powered systems of transportation. "It always struck me," said Ballard, "driving around these complex interchanges, what would happen if someone stood by the wayside and tried to flag you down? Of course, nobody would stop. You can't stop—you'd just have a multiple pile-up. You'd be dead if you tried to stop" ("Interview," Goddard and Pringle 34). Maitland feels the brunt of this simple fact of life when he unsuccessfully tries to flag down passersby, and when he tries to cross the road and escape, he causes a car accident and is flung back onto the island, injured and despondent.

Usually scholarship acknowledges three main characters in *Concrete Island*. I like to think there are four: the stranded Maitland, the two "castaways" he encounters on the island, and the island itself, a topographic outcrop of his inner space.

The first half of the novel is devoted entirely to Maitland and his struggle to come to terms with his predicament. Like the hero of *Robinson Crusoe*, he must deal with the minutiae of survival. He tends to his wounds and forages for food, nursing a case of wine from the trunk of his car and fighting off fever. Ballard revisits the quest for solitude that Kerans, Ransom, and Sanders pursued in the natural-disaster trilogy, but Maitland doesn't know he wants solitude until he "dominates" the island and all of its inhabitants. His "will to survive, to dominate the island and harness its limited resources" eventually supersedes his desire to escape (65). But what if the island is himself? At first, "parts of his mind seemed to be detaching themselves from the centre of his consciousness" (63). Then, "more and more, the island was becoming an exact model of his head. His movement across this forgotten terrain was a journey not merely through the island's past but through his own" (69–70), a linkage that reminisces Kerans's relationship with the "archeopsychic past" of *The Drowned World*. Finally, Maitland reaches epiphany: "I am the island" (71).

The utterance is an actualization of his surname: to *mate* with the *land*, to become one with the landscape. It immediately summons a literary counter-response from John Donne in a familiar passage from "Meditation XVII": "No man is an *Iland*, intire in itselfe; every man is a peace of the *Continent*, a part of the *maine*. If a *Clod* be washed away by the *Sea*, *Europe* is the lesse, as well as if a *Promontorie* were, as well as if a *Mannor* of thy *friends*, or of *thine owne* were: Any Mans *death* diminishes *me*, because I am involved in *Mankinde*; And therefore never send to know for whom the *bell* tolls; It tolls for *thee*" (126).

Larded with irony, Maitland refutes Donne's notion that humans are negatively affected by isolation and alienation, making a claim to the island with the stake of his individuality and will. Then again, the bell that tolls for Donne is a social issue—a matter of community and the body. For Maitland, it is psychological. When he calls himself the island, he doesn't only mean that he possesses the strength to survive and prosper in the absence of other human beings. He means that he perceives the island as himself, which is to say, as an articulation of his mind that has escaped the prison of his body. Maitland experiences psychic implosion. By dominating the island, he dominates himself, colonizing his inner space like Crusoe on his tropical island and taking charge of his life, which had been spinning out of control, and which reached a symbolic crescendo when his Jaguar spun out of control. As Ballard indicated on numerous occasions, this is the plight of many of his protagonists: to survive, adapt to, control, and dominate a strange or altered landscape.

Ballard never confirms whether or not the island is a mental incarnation. As usual, he invites multiple interpretations. If it is an incarnation, the characters Maitland encounters could be psychic offspring or byproducts of his "mating with the land" that must in turn be dominated and ousted (or exorcized?) before he can fully embody the dominion of his selfhood. Proctor is a former circus acrobat who suffered brain damage in a fall from a trapeze; strong and volatile, he has "the natural dignity of a large, simple animal" (123). Jane Sheppard is a dissident and "neurotic runaway" who suffers from a "classic" bourgeois upbringing (137, 95); she takes refuge on the island to "get away from all these moral attitudes. . . . People are never happier than when they're inventing new vices" (115). Both are outcasts, ejected from society by the technologies of capitalism, Proctor by circumstance, Jane by "half-baked ideals" (95) and possibly psychosis (it is suggested that she escaped from an insane asylum). Together they form a "conspiracy of the grotesque" (125), confining Maitland to the basement of an abandoned cinema.

Jane's role seems particularly fixed in Maitland's inner space given how much she purports to know about the flows of his desire, even if he likes to tell himself that she just "needed someone to be angry with" (101). On several occasions she makes light of his "dangerous" impulses. "Do you think you crashed on this island deliberately?" she inquires. "Self-destruction is something I know about" (96). Most evocatively, she later deduces: "You've been on the island long before you got here" (141). This occurs after he has turned the tides on his fellow castaways and captors. He degrades, humiliates, and fucks Jane in a huff of alpha maleness. Proctor—the island's savage, a caricature of *Robinson Crusoe*'s Friday and *The Tempest*'s Caliban—is put in check when Maitland gets him drunk and pisses on him, then treats him like a horse, patrolling the island on his back and beating him. Maitland fights the grotesque by turning himself into a grotesque who remakes self-pity into cruelty (139). These aggressions permit him to negotiate his feelings about his personal history and future *on the island* and *in his head*. He craves "to be freed from his past, from his childhood, his wife and friends, with all their affections and demands, and to rove forever within the empty city of his own mind" (142).

Proctor dies helping Maitland escape, as if the gods of his psyche forbid it, and Jane, worried about being discovered by the police, flees the island. She encourages Maitland to come with her, but he defers and makes excuses, saying, "I just want to leave in my own way. . . . I'll do it in my own time" (174). While he has lingering thoughts of being reunited with his wife and son, he feels "no real need to leave the island, and this alone confirmed that he had established his dominion over it" (176).

Earlier Maitland suspected that Jane knew a secret pathway off the island. It turns out that coming and going was much simpler; he could have left anytime. As David Paddy elucidates, this "urban space is fully connected to the rest of the city, but it feels as if it is thoroughly isolated and disconnected. It is this very feeling of disconnection that appeals to Maitland. This space is not an island, but Maitland *wants* to think of it as such because he desires the sense of isolation and control that would come of it" (142). Not by accident is Maitland an architect: he builds his own reality whether we are inside or outside his head. *Concrete Island* entertains delusions of agency—of escaping (the self as subject) by not escaping (the self as world). Again, in terms of desire, we confront the same man in this novel as in the novels of the natural-disaster trilogy, only Maitland is not a victim of nature, but culture, subjected by and subject to the highways of modern technology that tower over his body and constellate his mind.

Ballard wrote a screenplay for *Concrete Island* commissioned by Cadence Productions in 1972. The manuscript was never published but is now available at the British Library.[22] In it, Maitland, a New Yorker residing in London, isn't just any architect. He designs high-rise apartment buildings—a gesture toward Ballard's third and final novel in the cultural-disaster trilogy about the social breakdown of the bourgeois occupants of an ultramodern, self-sustaining, forty-story tower block located just outside London. Equipped with the services and facilities needed for everyday life (supermarkets, banks, hairdressing salons, gyms, schools, and the like), "the apartment block [is] a small vertical city, its two-thousand inhabitants boxed up into the sky" (9). *High-Rise* foreshadows the gated communities of Ballard's later novels. Provisionally titled *The Towers, The High Life*, and *Up*, it is another iteration of Ballard's "new conceptualisation of psychopathology, where you're getting a real liberation of the apparently deviant, but merely an expression of certain sorts of universal quirks" induced by modern technology ("J. G. Ballard," Savage 119).

High-Rise is a novel about machines. "Variously described as a spaceship," according to Rick McGrath, the building is a machine that processes and (de)constructs human bodies and minds, "coddling a community, yet still catering to each individual's every whim" ("Reconstructing"). The narrator describes it as "a huge machine designed to serve, not the collective body of tenets, but the individual resident in isolation" (10). This "environment built, not for man, but for man's absence" signposts the proverbial cold inhumanity of the science fictional machine, which produces more machines: "A new social type was being created by the apartment building, a cool, unemotional personality impervious to the psychological pressures of high-rise life, with minimal needs for privacy, who thrived like an advanced species of machine in the natural atmosphere" (35). This is an operational deleuzoguattarian plateau. The tenants fall prey to desiring-production and devolve into raw desiring-machines. But do they devolve, or evolve? An element of freedom and liberation accompanies their general transformation from civilized yuppies to tribal enclaves to transcendent mongrels. As with Deleuze and Guattari's desiring-machines, the tenants' breakdown is also a breakthrough to a new form of thinking and being. Hence the novel's working hypothesis: "In many ways, the high-rise was a model of all that technology had done to make possible the expression of a truly 'free' psychopathology" (36).

In *Concrete Island* Ballard limits himself to one uncomplicated plotline. In *High-Rise* three plotlines intersect. Each concerns one of three protagonists. Furthermore, like Maitland's island, the high-rise is a kind of character. One tenant thinks of it as a "huge animate presence. . . . There was something in this feeling—the elevators pumping up and down the long shafts resembled the pistons of a heart. The residents moving along the corridors were the cells in a network of arteries, the lights in their apartments the neuroses of a brain" (40). Ballard equates the technological machine with the soft machinery of the human body. The high-rise feels like a living being. And it contains hundreds of other, smaller high-rises, each of which harbors its own technological desires and designs.

The dissolution of the high-rise takes place over several months. Anthony Royal mans the helm of this postmodern ship of fools. An elitist, patriarchal, eccentric architect, he is a mad (social) scientist, and the high-rise is his monster and laboratory. He lives with his young, melancholy wife Anne in a penthouse on the top floor and represents upper-class snobbery and insecurity, "detest[ing] the orthodoxy of the intelligent" (81). Royal channels Doctor Moreau more than Victor Frankenstein; collectively the tenants are his experiment in social vivisection. Once determined to design his own zoo, he unknowingly makes the high-rise into "a gigantic vertical zoo, its hundreds of cages stacked above each other. All the events of the past few months made sense if one realized that these brilliant and exotic creatures had learned to open doors" (134).

Years ago, Royal damaged his legs in a car crash and sustained injuries that fascinate his wife—a retroactive nod to *Crash* and that novel's mad scientist, Vaughan. "His scarred forehead and chromium cane, the white jacket which he affected and wore like a target, together seemed to be the elements of a code that concealed the real relationship between the architect of this huge building and its uneasy tenants" (73). A hybrid stunt driver, lab technician, and zookeeper, Royal may have produced the machine, but like everybody in *High-Rise*, he is a product of the machine.

Richard Wilder is a foil for Royal. He drowns a dog in the tenth-floor pool during a power outage and ignites the chaos of the ensuing breakdown/breakthrough. "A thick-set, pugnacious man who had once been a professional rugby player" (14), Wilder is a television producer and lives with his wife Helen and two sons on the "proletariat" second floor. Proles include "film technicians, air-hostesses and the like" who reside beneath the tenth-floor shopping mall, which forms a borderline with the "middle class," "doctors and lawyers, accountants and tax specialists who worked, not for themselves, but for medical institutes and large corporations"; the "aristocracy" occupies the upper five floors, a "discreet oligarchy of minor tycoons and entrepreneurs, television actresses and careerist academics" (53).

Confined by marriage and fatherhood, aggravated by class divisions, and propelled by artistic as well as libidinal and primal energies, Wilder, recalling Maitland, aspires to "dominate" the high-rise in order to "come to terms with the building" and "meet the physical challenge it presented to him" (48). He travels to the roof while shooting a documentary of the violent goings-on, armed with a cine-camera in one hand and a gun in the other. His ascent is a point of action that allows us to see the different castes of residents. Moving upward, Wilder becomes more animalistic and, as such, free, no longer inhibited by "the whole system of juvenile restraints that he had been trying to shake off since his adolescence" (118). Early in the novel, Royal and his "lunatic troupe" of jumpsuit-clad thugs—hilariously consisting of "a stockbroker, two pediatricians and three senior academics" (66)—catch him in the act, beat him up, and send him back to the starting line of the first-floor lobby, like a pawn in the board game *Monopoly*. By the end, though, he makes it to the roof and puts a bullet in Royal.

The third protagonist is Dr. Robert Laing, an archetypal Ballardian desiring-machine and a neutral vertex between the social extremes of Royal and Wilder. The surname alludes to "anti-psychiatrist" R. D. Laing, whose work focused on mental illness and psychosis, and whose "vision of alienation as the normative condition of modern man" and "argument for insanity as potential liberation" seem tailor-made for Ballard (Francis 120, 171).[23] Many critics have suggested that Laing emulates the author. He is far closer to the real Ballard than the "Ballard" of *Crash* and even the "Jim" of *The Kindness of Women*. A divorced medical doctor, he craves solitude and moves to the high-rise on the advice of his elder sister, Alice Frobisher. The building's services give Laing the privacy he so desires, and the social atmosphere forms "the perfect background into which [he] could merge invisibly" (10). And for much of the novel, he is more or less an invisible man, observing the activities and antagonisms around him. "He had come to the high-rise to get away from all relationships" (13), and in "the security of the high-rise" where it feels as if "he had travelled forward fifty years in time," his life "was as self-contained as the building itself" (9).

As the novel progresses, Laing's pathological impulses come to the fore. He doesn't act on these impulses with the hostility of Royal and Wilder, but he does become an androcentric like them, secluding himself with Alice and TV critic Eleanor Powell. They become his female minions and objects of *affect*. "He needed to be alone with Alice and Eleanor, to be as aggressive and self-reliant, as passive and submissive as he wished. . . . He was satisfied by his self-reliance, his ability to cope with the tasks of survival. . . . Above all, he was pleased with his good sense in giving rein to those impulses that involved him with Eleanor and his sister, perversities created by the limitless possibilities of the high-rise" (154). In the final pages, he looks forward to addicting them to morphine and binding them to their polygamous, incestuous family unit. He foresees himself lording over them with measures of generosity and ferocity. "It no longer mattered how he behaved, what wayward impulses he gave way to, or which perverse pathways he chose to follow" (172). Laing moves beyond good and evil and completes his transformation.

The gender dynamics of *High-Rise* are markedly Darwinian and heterosexual. Rape supplements the objectification, exploitation, and domination of women by the emergent classes of alpha male ape-men. The role of women symptomatizes the building's register of technologically generated hypermasculinity. Circumstances aside, they don't all turn out like Alice and Eleanor. In a short, conclusive scene, Ballard introduces a new breed of female subject forged by the machine. United she stands in opposition to the novel's greatest ape-man, Wilder, who at one point is even described in simian terms, "patting one armpit in an almost animal way . . . directly involved at last in the struggle for territory and womenfolk. His shirt was open to the waist, exposing a barrel-like chest that he showed off with some pride" (89).

After shooting Royal through the chest, Wilder goes onto the roof and finds a sculpture garden populated by women and children. It is another Ballardian Garden of Eden—inverted and perverted. Allegorically it belongs to Lilith, the primal Eve/Evil. In Hebrew mythology, God banished Lilith from Eden because she wouldn't lie in the recumbent position during sex with Adam, the superior male; thus, the creation of the second, submissive Eve. She didn't work out for Adam either, but she let him be on top, and her story, unlike Lilith's, made it into the Christian Bible. The women on the roof of the high-rise include Charlotte Melville (Wilder's mistress), Anne Royal, Jane Sheridan (Royal's mistress), and Wilder's wife, Helen, whom he misrecognizes as "Judith" (167). Pathologized in his own right, Wilder struts forward in hopes that the women will notice him. They seem "to belong to another century and another landscape, except for their sunglasses, whose dark shades stood out against the blood-notched concrete of the roof terrace" (167). They encircle him and remove knives from their aprons as the children in the background play with bones. In spite of the threat, it feeds Wilder's longing to be a boy again. "Shy but happy now, Wilder tottered across the roof to meet his new mothers" (168). We don't know what happens to him. Ballard suggests that the violence of the father has been appropriated and will be exerted by "mother nature," a stronger, post-Stepford species of matriarch much wilder than Wilder.

As always, inner space informs the lives of the protagonists, each of whom perceives the high-rise as a materialization of his psyche. For Laing, it is "as if this huge building existed solely in his mind and would vanish if he stopped thinking about it" (34), and when he leaves the building to go to work, he feels "that he was leaving part of his mind behind him" (35). Royal and Wilder experience a similar, if subtler, awareness. For all of the protagonists, the "real duel would be resolved among the deserted corridors and abandoned apartments of the building inside their heads" (92). The machinery of the high-rise references and sensitizes the mind as much as the body.

Wilder and Laing both end up "happy" while Royal awaits death beside a drained swimming pool, now a gutter for "the skulls, bones and dismembered limbs of dozens of corpses. Tangled together where they had been flung, they lay about like the tenants of a crowded beach visited by a sudden holocaust" (170). Assisted to the poolside by Laing, who rues Royal's demise (but not enough to abandon his new identity), the mad scientist bleeds out next to the remnants of his failed creation. McGrath has a theory about the three protagonists that links them to the human body and to characters that Ballard develops in future novels:

> Wilder is the genitals, Laing the heart and Royal the brain. Interestingly, all is well until the final component (the heart) arrives to initiate the "critical mass" that precipitates the ensuing mayhem. All three are, however, damaged organs. As the story progresses they influence the "animate presence"; as Wilder attempts to rise from the unthinking passion of the basement, Laing stays close to the building's internal organs, and Royal loses his position of dominance and control as his thinking deteriorates. The body of the building essentially starves itself—much like Ballard's characters in *Empire of the Sun*—and in many ways sets the stage for the equally self-destructive homeowners in *Millennium People*, who choose to change their community publicly in comparison to the inner upheavals of the *High-Rise*. (Re: "HR")

Presaging the bourgeois estrangements and exploits of *Millennium People* as well as *Cocaine Nights*, *Super-Cannes*, and *Kingdom Come*, *High-Rise* is the last novel in which Ballard fetishizes how "modern technology makes possible the expression of a guilt free psychopathology," something he strongly believed that humanity was progressing toward (107). The ontological influence of technology didn't disappear from his writing. High-tech media and the implosive authority of television became key fixtures. After *High-Rise*, however, he wanted to do something different. Asked in 1975 if he would continue his "series on the 'technological landscape,'" Ballard replied: "No. I don't have an idea for a novel, but I'd very much like to write several stories that I haven't had the time to write these last few years. And it's been a long time since I've written anything in the way of imaginative narratives, romances" ("Interview," Hupp 80). Four years and fifteen or so stories later, he published his next novel, *The Unlimited Dream Company*, the first concerted venture into the realm of his personal experience and history.

CHAPTER 5

EMPIRES OF THE SELF

Autobiographical Novels

OVERVIEW

So far, I have discussed Ballard's novels in chronological order of publication. This is because of their tidy thematic progression and grouping (a starter novel, a trilogy, an experimental novel, and another trilogy). After *High-Rise,* Ballard becomes less systematized until we arrive at the final quartet of "crime" novels. Between 1979 and 1994, he published six novels and one novella. Three of them form another trilogy that fictionalizes Ballard's life and are the subject of this chapter: *The Unlimited Dream Company*, *Empire of the Sun*, and *The Kindness of Women*. The latter two follow Ballard's life from childhood to adulthood in his fifties. They are among his most realistic novels. *Unlimited* is his most oneiric, fantastical novel, yet it is set in Shepperton and extremely personal, shedding light on his place of residence and narrative fixations; Jordi Costa calls it "a sort of perverse gospel, which describes the passion, death and resurrection—not necessarily in that order—of an apostle of the febrile imagination who seeks to be deciphered as an extreme metaphor of Ballard himself" (170).

Critics don't usually consider *Unlimited* to be a work of Ballardian autobiographika, and it doesn't pretend to do the same things as *Empire* and *Kindness*. But they are all intimate expressions of Ballard's life. *Unlimited* is particularly interesting if we think of it as an expression of his own inner space—an adventure through the unconscious suburb of the "real" man.

In *Grave New World*, Dominika Oramus proposes that Ballard's entire canon can be viewed as an effort in self-fashioning and the creation of his own image. His "quasi-autobiographies, numerous articles and memories . . . present a persona or rather a number of personas that he constructed in different moments of his life" (13), as do the becoming-Adams of the natural-disaster trilogy, the protean T of *The Atrocity Exhibition*, the "Ballard" of *Crash*, the fish-out-of-water "detectives" of his later novels, and so on. Together these extrapolations form a certain idea about the "real" Ballard. Oramus warns that the idea is just that—not the real, and not an ideal, but the imagined—and it shouldn't be mistaken as historical or personal truth.

Ballard enjoyed playing with readers' assumptions about himself as well as the role of the author, but he was relatively adamant about how his various "Ballards" were fictions conjured from his internal and external experiences. Still, some readers and critics have "accused" the "Ballards" of being Ballard, perhaps because he wrote them so well, perhaps because, deep down, people wanted them to be real, embracing their own psychopathies in a kind of vicarious projection. It just wasn't the case, and in daily life, Ballard was thoroughly un-"Ballard."

His autobiographical novels adhere to the postmodern rule of thumb that, because we are products of the media environment, our names should be enclosed in quotes. Modern capitalist technologies render identity a terminal fiction—this thesis has its roots in *The Atrocity Exhibition* and thereafter continues to grow and mature, culminating in his final novel, *Kingdom Come*. Subjected to aggressive mediascapes, Ballard's characters jeopardize the concept of a fixed identity on multiple levels. Scott Bukatman writes: "His characters are without ego, and they become only a part of the landscape, and the landscape becomes a schizophrenic projection of a de-psychologized, but fully colonized, consciousness. As in melodrama and surrealism, everything becomes at once objective and subjective" (41). I take issue with the notion that the characters lack ego. Technically they are *pure ego*, compulsively trying and retrying to assert and define themselves, and unable to get over or outside of their own hang-ups, crises, passions, needs, imaginings, and inhibitions. They are clinical psychopaths in this respect, subjugated and liberated, yet in search of fixity, of achieving some kind of negotiation between objective and subjective worlds and escaping the hammer of implosion. I can't speak concretely for Ballard the man. But his protagonists suggest that he was engaged in a constant effort to find (and fix) himself. We see this engagement most intensely in the autobiographical novels.

Ballard has visibly integrated his personal experience into his writing more than most science fiction authors. Kurt Vonnegut is an exception. Peter Brigg says that *Empire* and *Slaughterhouse-Five* (1969), for instance, "rise out of the personal experiences of their authors in wartime and, in both cases, an argument will be made that the authors worked through a series of science fiction novels to develop the style to express the almost inexpressible aspects of their own experiences" (106). More autobiographical than Vonnegut is Philip K. Dick, who, born two years before Ballard in 1928, had published almost ten novels and scores of stories prior to the release of *The Wind from Nowhere*.

Dick wove his involvements with drugs, paranoia, and spirituality into the fabric of his books, most famously in *A Scanner Darkly* (1977) and the VALIS novels.[1] In *The Divine Madness of Philip K. Dick*, psychologist Kyle Arnold says that Dick's "process was *overincorporative*, in that his imagination consumed the details of his life and transformed them into science fiction narrative" (54). He was an American counterpart to Ballard in some ways, not just by fictionalizing his social and psychological life, but by exploring many of the same themes, especially media pathology and technologized desire. Dick produced a semi-autobiographical work in the form of an eight-thousand-page diary about his mystical experiences. In 2011 an abridged version was published as *The Exegesis of Philip K. Dick* (2011). He never wrote anything like *Miracles of Life*. Nor did he so closely represent himself as Ballard did in *Empire* and *Kindness*. I would argue that no other science fiction writer has autobiographed themselves as Ballard has. Such self-writing occurs more frequently in literary fiction, and whereas some science fiction can be categorized as "literary," most of it is decidedly not. Along with authors like Samuel R. Delany, Kim Stanley Robinson, William S. Burroughs, Ray Bradbury, and H. G. Wells, Ballard writes with poise, evocation, and artfulness, deploying literary techniques onto the playing field of waxed, finely tuned prose.

Empire is Ballard's first truly mainstream novel. He doesn't set it in an alternate reality or near-future but in the present day of his childhood. In the aftermath of *Empire*, there is a certain recession of "concrete" deterministic technologies of influence and affect (the machinic building of *High-Rise*, the artificial atoll and motorways of *Concrete Island*, the automobiles of *Crash*, the media-flows of *Atrocity*, and so on). As Pippa Tandy suggests, however, Ballard's entire oeuvre "charts the delivery of a new, technologically constituted subject" (179), and his characters variably manifest as "psychic maps of the encounter between the central nervous system and the technological landscape" (181). Tandy even argues that *Empire* "is explicitly science fiction. . . . Ballard textualizes the connection between the technological future and his own experience of World War II. That is to say, in Ballard's terms, it is 'a response to science and technology as perceived by the inhabitants of the consumer goods society'" (271). We could say the same for the later novels, all of which take place in techno-capitalist near-futures.

In "Mind Is the Battlefield," Umberto Rossi analyzes the interface of fact and fiction in Ballard's life trilogy in the context of war literature. Instead of *Unlimited*, he includes *Miracles*, maintaining that the autobiography contains omissions that destabilize its nonfictional label.

> While the book casts light on, or one might say even *de-fictionalizes*, some aspects of the author's life (such as the death of his wife, Mary, who died from pneumonia while holidaying in Spain), *Miracles* conspicuously ignores other aspects of the author's private and public lives. . . . Shanghai may well be seen as a projection of Ballard's obsessions . . . but, at the same time, the young J. G. Ballard is also possessed by the mythology of Shanghai, the "bright but bloody kaleidoscope" which was infinitely produced, circulated and transformed by the media during his childhood. (68)

His point is that *Miracles* doesn't paint the definitive portrait of the real Ballard's life. Fair enough. For my part, I consider the book more of a self-reflection in which Ballard, from the traumatic perch of a dying man, revisits places in his life that he had already extrapolated in his fiction as a younger, healthier man. *Miracles* was not an effort by Ballard to produce a fictional work. *Unlimited*, *Empire*, and *Kindness* are all fictionalized accounts based on or connected to real events. Rossi's central outlook remains viable: "J. G. Ballard's exposure to the heinous physical and psychological realities of the Second World War left such deep traces in his mind so as to inform everything he has written since the publication of his first short story" (67).

Much of Ballard's writing concerns postwar English society and culture. The fictional autobiographies extrapolate his Chinese origins and his adult life as an English citizen. Andrzej Gasiorek acknowledges the problem of situating Ballard in the tradition of British fiction "because his work engages in an idiosyncratic 'mapping' process of its own; Ballard's oeuvre insists that neither the history of the twentieth century nor the significant features of the contemporary landscape can properly be grasped in terms of conventional narrative forms" (2). The mapping in which he partakes is diverse and multivalent, ranging from the cognitive, corporeal, and social to the narrational, topographical, and geopolitical. Like most Ballard scholars, David Paddy agrees with Gasiorek, saying that "Ballard's work is not *exclusively* about the British empire but about many others as well" (22).

Foremost among them is the empire of the *self* wherein Ballard interpellates his own experience amid the clashes and intersections of other forms of empire. His navigation of this terrain is at once playful and serious, fabricating a surreal version of the author and the man. Jeannette Baxter suggests that one way to read *Empire* and *Kindness* "is to see them as experiments within the Surrealist tradition of convulsive autobiography, a form of life-writing which, through strategies of invention, rewriting and dissemblance, was concerned with rescuing subjectivity, history and memory from the 'confines of rationality or temporal chronology'" (*Surrealist* 138). *Unlimited* may be an even better candidate for such an enquiry. All three novels possess (or are possessed by) a symptomatic lack and traumatic kernel of desire. Ballard's childhood was forsaken by war, and he did seem to have a vested interest in "rescuing" himself. At the very least, the autobiographical novels show him disentangling memories of conflict, complication, and compliance.

JACK-OF-ALL-BALLARDS

The Unlimited Dream Company (1979)

As in *Crash*, Ballard uses first-person, unreliable narration for the protagonist of *Unlimited*. Paddy says that his name, Blake, "seems hardly coincidental and certainly evokes the image of the poetic bard as eccentric outsider who follows his own vision and develops his own mythology against current social norms" (305), and in an early review, Malcolm Bradbury says he "opens the doors of perception and evokes apocalyptic mirages of heaven and hell." Like Maitland in *Concrete Island*, Ballard also casts him in the role of *The Tempest*'s Prospero, which manifests in his aspiration to dominate and thereby free the "island aquarium" and reality studio of Shepperton, a projection of himself (*Unlimited* 41).

Blake's desires and perspectives waffle and transform throughout his struggle to come to terms with a dreamlike realm where he can fly, shapeshift, and heal the sick. Bradbury rightly calls the Shepperton of the novel "a world that is like a surrealist painting." In this painting, Blake is part angel, part demon, part superman (in comic book and Nietzchean senses). A failed medical student, mercenary pilot, Jesuit novice, and pornographic writer, he exhibits many of the characteristics of the real Ballard in an exacerbated form, including a love for human-powered flight, his "only formal education [coming] from in-flight movies," a strained relationship with his father, and "everything touch[ing] off [his] imagination in strange ways" (12). Additionally, he exhibits the qualities of many characters and extrapolations that precede him: disfigurement in a car crash, "compulsive role-playing" (11), recurrent bouts of megalomania and solipsism, employment at a zoo, a Freudian desire to fuse sex and death, and a determination to "be true to [his] obsessions" (122).[2]

Blake is a Jack-of-all-Ballards—more "Ballard"/Ballard than any of his precursors. Working at the zoo, he fell prey to a "Pied Piper complex, and genuinely believed that [he] could lead . . . twenty children and their startled mothers, the few passing dogs and even the dripping flowers away to a paradise" (13). In spite of Blake's many failures, he keeps faith in himself, "a messiah as yet without a message who would one day assemble a unique identity out of this defective jigsaw" (13). And once he finds a message and assembles an identity, he fulfills his destiny as a messianic Pied Piper who leads the blip, blasé subjects that populate Shepperton up, up, and away from their suburban existence, exhuming affect from the grave.

In this bildungsroman, Blake transforms from delinquent everyman into all-powerful deity. Shepperton emerges as yet another Ballardian Garden of Eden. Anybody can remake themselves (146), although the real powers of creation belong to the protagonist, and all the characters he encounters, as well as the landscape of Shepperton, may very well belong to the diegesis of his own mind (another likeness to Maitland).

Blake is a technological, mimetized being, an assemblage deterritorialized by consumer-capitalism and the media torrent. Drawn to the literal and figurative machinery of flight, a formative trait for Jim in *Empire*, he frequently perceives the world through the lens of film. At the outset, he steals a Cessna airplane[3] and crashes it into the Thames after a knee-jerk attempt to murder his fiancé "without the slightest hate or anger" (14). His first impression of "the placid town" of Shepperton and its residents is cinematic, "as if all these apparently unhurried suburbanites were in fact actors recruited from the film studios to play their roles in an elaborate conspiracy" (26). This perspective intensifies throughout the novel as Blake matures and evolves into the director of an oneiric reality show.

At first, he wants to escape Shepperton, which, "known only for its film studios, seemed to be the everywhere of suburbia, the paradigm of nowhere. . . . Anyone who came within its clutches was unconsciously assumed to have died" (35). Unsure if he is dead or alive, sane or insane, awake or dreaming, he tries and fails to get away (yet again: Maitland). Soon he develops an affection for the suburbanites that blossoms into a messianic compulsion to save them from themselves, instilling in them the supremacy of the imagination, turning them into the best actors they can be, and liberating them from their dull, meaningless, small-minded lives. He becomes a god intent on "remak[ing] Shepperton," he says, "in my own image" (124). He "greet[s] the sun as an equal" (125), and he wants everybody "to discover their powers." "If they existed within me, they existed also within themselves. Each of them had the power to conjure a miniature Eden from the ground at his feet" (136). Eventually he asks himself: "Could I feed on the people of this town, use their eyes and tongues, their minds and sexes to construct a flying machine that would carry me away? I was almost sure now that my powers were limitless, that I was capable of anything I wished to imagine" (154). Gestures toward altruism are almost always balanced by egoism—a seminal Ballardian attribute.

Fantastical happenings accompany Blake's spiritual "conversion" into a god who vacillates between paganism and Christianity. Ultimately he is Nietzschean, resolved to shed the skin of conventional morality and manifest a guilt-free pathology. Hence this epiphany: "I was certain now that vice in this world was a metaphor for virtue in the next, and that only through the most extreme of those metaphors would I make my escape" (166). Conditional to his escape is a synthesis with the natural world, a counterattack against the cultural world of consumer-capitalist suburbia. Birds are ubiquitous. Flora and fauna pulse with transcendentalist energy. Blake morphs into different wild animals, namely a whale and a stag, both phalluses that complement the chapter titled "The Remaking of Shepperton," where he "scatter[s] [his] semen on this dawn circuit of the town" (127) in an act of deculturalization, usurping suburbia under the authority of his new "nature."

"Egged on by the rising sun, which had at last caught up with me," says Blake, "I moved in and out of the empty streets, a pagan gardener recruiting the air and the light to stock this reconditioned Eden. Everywhere a dense tropical vegetation overran the immaculate privet hedges and repressed lawns, date palms and tamarinds transformed Shepperton into a jungle suburb" (128). A hypersexual urge and "sinister paedophiliac drive" supplement his new nature (108). This progresses into a full-blown polysexuality and need to copulate with every living creature, which he believes will contribute to the rebuilding of himself. "I knew then that I would stay in this small town until I had mated with everyone there—the women, men and children, their dogs and cats, the cage-birds in their front parlours, the cattle in the water-meadow, the deer in the park, the flies in this bedroom—and fused us together into a new being" (64).

Blake literally interacts with all of Shepperton's residents. Flying over the suburb, he assimilates them one by one into his body. Following a sacrificial gesture that caricatures the death, rebirth, and ascension into heaven of Jesus, he allows himself to enter their bodies and becomes "their mother and father, they had passed through me, born from my aerial flesh" (205). Besides

Blake, only a few characters have any real presence; the rest are cardboard cutouts, extras on a movie set going through the motions of life among "these television sets and kitchen appliances" (164). The two most important auxiliary characters are Father Wingate, a priest, and Miriam St. Cloud, a young doctor, both stereotypes with little personality, the priest serving as a father figure to Blake, the doctor as his desideratum and bride. When he meets Miriam, he lies about being a stunt pilot. He lies again about being a flying-school instructor, then reneges and says that "in a way" he is in fact a stunt pilot. Figuratively he's being truthful: prior to crashing the Cessna, he had been flying dangerously and headlong through life.[4]

Blake's violent arrival transfixes the natives who witness it; they stand dumbly on the shore "like actors waiting for a director's cue" (18).[5] By the end, he transmogrifies into that director and cues everybody to follow him in an "immense aerial congregation" (208) away from Shepperton like "children returning to their earlier selves" (206–07). En route to their own new natures, they pay homage to the technologies that they will leave behind and that sustained them for so long: "We gave thanks to the appliance islands and the bedroom suites, to the fuel pumps in the filling-station and to the rusting car which had once sheltered me" (208).

Blake, like Moses, can't go with them to the Promised Land. He returns to Shepperton to discover his physical body in the cockpit of the Cessna. "This drowned flier was my former self, left behind when I escaped from the Cessna. Half-submerged, as if between two worlds, he sat at the controls" (214). One implication is that his disembodied spirit has been trapped in limbo where he had to atone for his wrongdoings in order to open the gates of heaven. In the final, titular chapter, Blake instructs the only remaining resident, Miriam, to fly away, then sends the dead and every last living creature into the sky. He stays there, alone, waiting for Miriam to come back to him after she merges with the divine so that together they can "set off, with the inhabitants of all the other towns in the valley of the Thames, and the world beyond . . . celebrating the last marriage of the animate and inanimate, of the living and the dead" (220).

We still don't know for certain what sort of ontological or psychological ground the novel takes place on. *Unlimited* begs a question that Philip K. Dick fielded in scores of novels and stories: What is reality? Blake's constant speculation about whether he's dead or alive or dreaming recollects Dick's *Ubik* (1969). In this novel, the protagonist, Joe Chip, slowly realizes that he may have been killed in an explosion and exists in a realm called half-life or cold-pac, a state of cryopreservation in which the dead can communicate with the living. The diegesis of Chip's world contains overt genre science fictional themes and devices (psi powers, space travel, time slips, futique clothing, and architecture). Blake's world, on the contrary, is aggressively surreal and punctuated only by the media technologies of late capitalism (another prominent theme in *Ubik*, as is solipsism and the idea of the supreme god/director in the form of Glen Runciter, Chip's boss). *Unlimited* is far more estranging and uncanny, representing ideologies, desires, behavior, and a locale that are at once familiar and unfamiliar.

Although he yearned to be a mainstream, literary writer, Dick, unlike Ballard, was not known for the dynamism of his prose. Nonetheless, *Ubik* is a science fiction classic and widely considered to be one of Dick's strongest novels; it has been and will continue to be praised and remembered far more than *Unlimited*, which is a novel for Ballardians, or at least a novel best appreciated by Ballardians. Above all, *Unlimited* is a novel for and about Ballard himself, as self-indulgent and subjective as it is self-critical, satirical, and exploratory.

In an interview published the year of *Unlimited*'s release, Ballard said:

> Although I don't want to make too much of it, I think [*The Unlimited Dream Company*] *is* my autobiography. If for flying you substitute writing fiction, or using the imagination, the book has all the elements of an autobiography. I fell into this place, as it were, and into the predicament of ordinary life, some twenty years ago, and have used my imagination for those twenty years to try to give that ordinary life some sort of meaning. But all this just occurs to me with the benefit of hindsight; it didn't occur to me at the time because there are no correspondences between me and the character—or just very minor ones that aren't important. ("Unlimited" 8)

Blake seems to be more than a minor correspondence, in light of what Ballard has said in other interviews, reminisced in *Miracles*, and extrapolated in *Empire* and *Kindness*. A cursory reading of the second chapter of *Unlimited* alone reveals striking analogies as Ballard recounts Blake's backstory. To a greater extent, *Unlimited* confirms how profoundly Ballard felt trapped—regionally (in postwar Shepperton) and mnemonically (in wartime China)—and sought agency in the creative act of fictionalizing himself, sometimes discreetly, sometimes to the hilt. In an introduction to *Queer* (1985), William S. Burroughs wrote that the traumatic memory of the accidental shooting of his wife through the head left him "no choice but to write my way out" (18). Perhaps Ballard was involved in a similar project, compelled to interpolate pieces of himself because of his own internal battles, not only as a child of war but as a widower and single father stuck in English suburbia.

Removed from Ballard, *Unlimited* is almost entirely humorless, despite its surreality and absurdism; it could be taken broadly as a serious novel about life, death, and desire in the consumer-capitalist world. Readers acquainted with Ballard, however, may find it comedic if we read Blake as a personification of the author who is by default a "household god" in the universe of his narrative (122). Viewed this way, Ballard takes potshots at himself, waxing the spleen of megalomania and misanthropy. In Blake's eyes, the inhabitants of Shepperton are all beneath him—a great irony given his shady past—and they need him to wake them up and show them how to be *übermenschen*. Not only do they come to worship him, he comes to worship himself, and even after he has remade Shepperton in his image, incarnated Jesus, and consumed and spit out the populace, he wants more. Shepperton isn't enough. The world isn't enough. He wants to "save" the entire cosmos. Of course, the novel is heavily filtered through Blake's subjectivity, and what might seem like saving to him could be extinguishing or voiding to somebody else (just as vice and virtue could be interchangeable). To absurdly, hedonistically bask in his authorial glory—with this extreme metaphor, Ballard metafictionalizes his personal role as a writer and makes satirical commentary on the postmodern nature of authorship in general.

Unlimited points to the thesis of "The Death of the Author" in which Roland Barthes stipulates that authorial intentionality and biographical context are unrelated and unimportant to the text under scrutiny. What matters is the text itself and how we interpret it. As a rule, I follow this line of postmodern thinking, but I must admit that Ballard's life compels me to read his work through a biographical lens, even as a critic, deepening my analyses and unearthing nuances and connections that would otherwise elude me. That said, *Unlimited* works perfectly fine as a stand-alone, dead-author novel, as do all texts in this theoretical light. I'm not saying that Ballard consciously deployed Barthes. If he had even read Barthes's work, he probably wouldn't have liked it. The point is, he plays with his authorial persona in *Unlimited* more than in any other novel.

In his biography, John Baxter wants us to believe that Ballard was an egoist with an inflated sense of self. He wasn't—not as an author, not as a man. He was probably modest at best, especially considering the grave lesson he learned as a child during the war, a lesson he returned to in many interviews and autobiographical texts that is most plainly articulated in *Empire* as Jim marvels at the American air raids over Lunghua: "He welcomed the air raids, the noise of the Mustangs as they swept over the camp, the smell of oil and cordite, the deaths of the pilots and even the likelihood of his own death. In spite of everything, he knew he was worth nothing" (152).

Ballard confessed that *Unlimited* could be read as a fictional autobiography. He didn't perceive it as science fiction, but as of 1979, he continued to see himself working in the genre.

> I still call myself a science fiction writer although, being realistic, of my total output I imagine that, even by my elastic definition of the term, at least a third of it isn't SF but is fantasy. Is *The Unlimited Dream Company* SF? I'd say no. I think I could make a claim for something like *Crash*, or even *High-Rise*, being SF because their subject-matter and their points of view are inspired by changes in our world brought about by science and technology, and their perspective on these changes—my approach—is rather analytical. And I use the scientific vocabulary, on the whole. But I think of my total output as being largely homogeneous, even though some of it is clearly SF and some clearly not, and for that reason I feel that my imagination belongs within what is loosely called "the realm of science fiction" rather than to so-called mainstream fiction. I've always felt that. That's why I began writing within the SF field, and why I've always thought of myself as an SF writer. ("Unlimited" 6)

Ballard both allies and distances himself from the genre in this passage. Essentially, he claims to operate on the periphery of science fiction in his own self-contained escape pod, deterritorializing the codes and flows of conventional practice and formulas. This may be the most accurate definition he ever made of his writing. As for *Unlimited*, it is an undeniable fantasy, but that fantasy hinges on the capitalist media technologies that define everyday life and construct the postindustrial human condition. The same goes for his later novels. Variously called *Fury* and *The Stunt Pilot*, the final title even suggests it. The Blakes and "Ballards" of the world may have the capacity for unlimited dreams, but only under the thumb of the "company." At the same time, the company represents the tableau of characters Blake sees in his "vision" of Shepperton, all of whom can be read as protean Bs (in other words, different shades of Blake / "Ballard") and all of whom are pregnant with the fetuses of techno-capitalism.

EMPIRES OF THE SON

Empire of the Sun (1984) • *The Kindness of Women* (1991)

A scene in *Empire* harks back to *Unlimited*, linking Blake (a semblance of the adult Ballard) to Jim (a semblance of the young Ballard). Jim has been captured and imprisoned by the Japanese in a temporary detention center. Food is in short supply, but he is "happy" there, no longer forced to roam the streets of Shanghai fending for his life. As always, he takes comfort in the warm bed of his imagination and reveries of the sky: "When he was hungry or missed his parents, he often dreamed of aircraft. During one of his fevers he had even seen a flight of American bombers in the sky above the detention center" (84). For better and for worse, Blake is the pilot of Jim's dreams. Or, in the world of *Unlimited*, Jim is the bruised sapling of Blake's desire for transcendence and escape. Ballard once said that the protagonist of *The Day of Creation*, Dr. Mallory, is a grownup Jim, but many of his adult characters can be traced back to the conduct and desires of *Empire*'s young hero, a proto-Adam subjected to a Garden of Death, Destruction, and Wonderment. He builds Jim and Blake with the bricks of his own experiences, one premised on the technology of violence and war, the other on the technology of late capitalism.

Blake and Jim both have messiah complexes. Spawned by the trauma of a broken past, Blake's complex becomes a reality as he reenacts the death and rebirth of Jesus, shoulders the "sins" of the people of Shepperton, and delivers them from "evil." Clinching his martyrial status, he states: "They were waiting for me to die and set them free. I remembered the holocaust I had seen as I stepped from the aircraft, a vision of my own death under the bonfire sky. Despite all my efforts to prove myself, I was not a corpse propped in its tomb. . . . Despairing at last, I decided to die" (197). The vision looks forward to Ballard looking backward. In *Empire*, Jim sees the nuclear bomb dropped on Nagasaki explode in the distance (Ballard himself never witnessed it). The godlike "great big flash" in the sky triggers the messiah complex that gains momentum throughout his internment (218). It culminates at the end of the war, which renders him nonmessianic and existentially anxious; part of him wants the war to continue—or a new war to begin—so that he can retain his "power" and the comfort it gave him.

Michael Delville writes: "At the end of the novel, after his apparent 'resurrection' of a dead Japanese pilot whom he regards as his 'imaginary twin,' Jim even sees himself as the Saviour of the millions of people who have died during the war" (70).[6] Delville notes that the episode recalls "a similar dream fantasy of global regeneration" in "The Dead Time" (70). Released from a prison camp after the Japanese surrender, the young protagonist of this story must drive a load of dead bodies to a Shanghai graveyard. He "later identifies with the corpses and, out of a sense of loyalty to the dead, pledges himself to revitalize and repopulate the land, becoming 'the instrument of the new order which [he] had been delegated by them to bring to the world'" (71).[7] This sentiment relates to Jim as much as to Blake, the latter of whom becomes the instrument of a new order in Shepperton, whereas Jim must cut off his wings and strap himself back into the cockpit of banal mortality.

Empire is a turning point for Ballard. The quasi-autobiography deviates from speculative fiction into the mainstream while retaining the concept of inner space in a more diluted, transparent form compared with previous books. It sets the stage for the second half of his career, during which he published almost as many novels as in the first half, if we use *Empire* as a midpoint. Temporally it is exactly a midpoint for the novels—there are twenty-two years between the publication of *The Wind from Nowhere* and *The Drowned World* in 1962 and *Empire* in 1984, and twenty-two years between *Empire* and *Kingdom Come* in 2006. Ballard had no idea how long his career would last, of course, but it's fitting that he would reach back so intimately and candidly into his actual past at this mean time.

Grounded in realism (the antithesis of *Unlimited*), *Empire* represents the charisma, perseverance, and pathology of a young boy under harsh circumstances. In addition to pathology, he makes use of many stock themes and tropes, predominantly technologized desire and the mediatization of reality and subjectivity. In interviews, he emphasizes that the novel extrapolates and fictionalizes his experiences, but in *Miracles*, he says, "My entire fiction is the dissection of a deep pathology that I had witnessed in Shanghai and later in the post-war world, from the threat of nuclear war to the assassination of President Kennedy, from the death of my wife to the violence that underpinned the entertainment culture of the last decades of the century" (131–32).

The novels Ballard wrote after *Empire* are more realistic than surrealistic, yet they all contain varying degrees of science fictional riggings, techniques, and modalities, and *Empire* lays the asphalt for their impetus and composition. The title is multivalent and references numerous depths of experience. I indicated that *empire* refers to different regions and cultural powers (Japan, England, and China) as well as Ballard's historical and mnemonic exploration of his own identity. Ballard adds: "The title *Empire of the Sun* does refer both to the empire of Japan with its rising sun flag and to the empire or domain in which we all exist under the sign of the atom bomb: the nuclear age" ("Interview: Psychoanalyst," Pringle 9). *Sun* can be read in multiple ways, too, most conspicuously as Japan's naval ensign and the name of the country, pronounced *Nihon* or *Nippon*, literally meaning "the sun's origin" and often translated into English as "land of the rising sun." From this angle, the empire of the sun denotes the powers that uprooted and redefined Jim's life—or, if we view Jim via other protagonists, that *dominated* his life and forced him into a state of psychological self-domination.

There is a more resonant meaning if we consider *sun* in the homophonic form of *son*. Jim has many fathers in the novel: the American sailor Basie, who grants him occasional kindnesses but is driven by self-interest; Dr. Ransome, whom Jim initially distrusts but comes to admire; the Japanese military, whose strength and capacity for destruction he respects, and with whose willpower and ethics he empathizes far more than that of the Chinese; American media in the form of magazines and books, which constantly foster his imagination and the agency it offers him; and his own father, who affects Jim by being *absent*, compelling him to fill that lack in his psyche. The most powerful and affective father is war itself—its technology, its violence, and its spectacle. War cultivates Jim and leaves behind a scar garden that he must cultivate in his own right. We could say the same for Ballard: he harvests his science fiction from the dirt of his wartime past.

Ballard frames *Empire* with electronic media, establishing and then reifying Jim as a mediatized subject and desiring-machine. The novel opens with exposition on how he "had begun to dream of wars. At night the same silent films seemed to flicker against the wall of his bedroom on Amherst Avenue, and transformed his sleeping mind into a deserted newsreel theater" (3). In many texts, Ballard describes the garish image-culture that animated prewar Shanghai. Jim is a product of that urban environment and feels like the entire city is "turning into a newsreel leaking from the inside of his head" (5). He worries that he has seen too many war movies and that they have negatively affected his mind. But he claims to know what is real and what is fantasy—a claim that foreshadows the slow implosion of reality and fantasy that he experiences during the war. In the first chapter, Ballard illustrates how the technology of media has invaded Jim's unconscious, the repository of desire, and made him anxious about his sense of perception and self.

He comes full circle over three years later in the final chapter. Dog-eared from the brutalities of war and imprisonment, he reunites with his parents on Amherst Avenue. He also reunites with the media that Ballard initially used to depict him. In Lunghua, he could only play it on his mind's screen, fueled in part by consumer magazines like *Life* and *Collier's* "that Jim needed as much as the extra sweet potatoes. The magazines fed a desperate imagination" (177). He fantasizes about appearing in *Life*, posing beside tanks, soldiers, admirals, and generals.

Back in the city, he returns to the original source of his fantasies. "Dominating this panorama of the Shanghai night were three cinema screens which had been set up on scaffolding along the Bund . . . in order to give the population of Shanghai a glimpse of the world war that had recently ended" (275). Playing on the screens are *sturm und drang* newsreels of Allied powers trouncing the Axis forces and reveling in victory. Looming above the populace, these sequences convey an "imposed truth" that mythologizes the war (275). Jim goes to the reopened theaters in Shanghai on a regular basis. The Hollywood movies enthrall him, and he views the world through imploded eyes, even "the unreal house [on] Amherst Avenue, which had once been his home but now seemed as much an illusion as the sets of the Shanghai film studios" (276).

Remembering the final weeks of the war, Jim acknowledges that "everything had become a little muddled. He had been starving and gone slightly mad" (277). He remains convinced that he saw the sunflash of the atom bomb detonating over Nagasaki. In his mind, it is also a newsflash signaling the dawn of World War III validated by the superscreens over Shanghai. "The crowds watching the newsreels on the Bund had failed to grasp that these were the trailers for a war that had already started. One day there would be no more newsreels" (277). Still, he craves the womb of Lunghua and the flights of fancy that World War II drove him to entertain. *Kindness* divulges that he continues to crave it well into adulthood, which is one of the reasons Jim joins the RAF: "A career as a military pilot offered an even more direct entry to the realm of violence for which [I] hungered" (99).

This compulsion can be traced back to the beginning of the war, when he was separated from his parents and killed time watching Japanese planes soar overhead while waiting for his parents' return; additionally, he made an effort to build a "man-flying kite" (*Empire* 46), and during the war he increasingly obsessed over a Japanese pilot who he imagined was his twin and would someday fly away with him. As with most acts of violence, however, watching aerial dogfights and dive-bombers on screen captivates Jim more than the reality of such things. The lukewarm real doesn't compare to the stylized image. More provocatively, the suggestion that newsreels will cease to exist indicates Jim's deep connection to and identification with media technology. For him—for his machinic unconscious, at least—the true apocalypse would be contingent upon a destruction of media technology.

During the first stages of war and then his later internment, Jim endures loneliness, alienation, disease, starvation, physical and mental beat-downs and deterioration, and the recurrent spectacle of violence and death, not to mention the smaller details, like the steady swarms of flies that buzz and crawl around his head and body. Ballard's use of a child's perspective evokes sympathy and compassion. That perspective also allows him to view the war more objectively. "Jim has a boy's amoral, unformed judgments and is immune in the egotism of boyhood from the suffering of others and even from most of his own pain" (Briggs 107).

Ballard endured similar hardships, as do many of his other protagonists, but he avows that Jim is more fiction than fact. "The picture I give of my twelve, thirteen, fourteen year old hero is really myself at that age: all that is invented. I was in that camp but I was with my parents and of course that was a huge difference. The bulk of the book, seen from the narrative point of view, is an invention" ("Writers"). Moreover, he based Jim not so much on himself as on a boy he had been friends with at Lunghua. The boy was "separated from his parents who were trapped in North China. He was virtually orphaned by the war and he spent the war in this room with a family . . . in circumstances rather like Jim's in the book. So it's an amalgam of experiences but it's basically a fiction" (ibid.). Why did Ballard choose this method to recount his story? Why write a fictitious account instead of a straight autobiography? No autobiography is universally truthful; the subjective nature of autobiographical construction (along with the instability of memory and historical records) prohibits it. But *Empire* and *Kindness* are different animals from (and with different ends than) *Miracles*.

The reason echoes something Ursula K. Le Guin said in an introduction to *The Left Hand of Darkness* (1969) regarding the nature of science fiction as a form of personal expression: "The only truth I can understand or express is, logically defined, a lie. Psychologically defined, a symbol. Aesthetically defined, a metaphor" (xv). Le Guin argues that science fiction allegorizes the present more than the future, and truth (not fact) is a byproduct of consciousness and cognition, a naturally creative process. She concludes: "[T]ruth is a matter of the imagination" (xvi). Ballard's intentions align with this apothegm. Questioned about why he chose the form of fictional rather than nonfictional autobiography to tell *Empire*, he answered:

> Because I think in fiction you can reach the psychological truth or the imaginative truth of a set of events in a way that you can't in an autobiography. Autobiographies, particularly if they are written in later life, tend to be retrospective, they tend to be written with the advantage of later and more mature reflection on an experience of life, and they tend to impose on earlier events the benefit of hindsight. It is difficult

> to dramatize events as they occurred with the same sort of vividness that you can when you are writing fiction. ("In Conversation" 84)

On the issue of "psychological truth," he cites the example of his parents being with him in the camp where he nevertheless felt very much alone. Creating a protagonist with parents in absentia came closer to the psychological truth—that which he experienced cognitively and emotionally—than the reality of his situation. Likewise in *Kindness*. Jim grows up and traces the pathway of the real Ballard's life, ending with the production and release of Spielberg's adaptation of *Empire* in 1987, when Ballard was in his late fifties, but he takes significant liberties in the interest of representing the psychological truth of actual events.

Reviewers and critics acclaimed *Empire*. It was short-listed for the Booker O'Connell and Man Booker Prizes. It won Britain's oldest literary award, the James Tait Black Memorial Prize, for best novel of 1984, tying with Angela Carter's *Night at the Circus*, and it won *The Guardian* newspaper's prize for best novel. Sales of Ballard's books were spurred by the buzz in Britain but not in America until it caught the attention of Hollywood. Ballard collected $250,000 in film rights, a sum that exceeded the combined earnings of his entire career. The cash injection changed next to nothing. He continued to write and publish at the same speed. Shortly before the film's release, Nick Kimberly said that the success of *Empire* had to do with British enthusiasm for war novels, no matter how conventional or esoteric (88), but Spielberg really put Ballard in lights. Encouraged by the film, Ballard set out to write a followup novel.

Between *Empire* and *Kindness*, Ballard published another novel, *The Day of Creation*, a fascinating hybrid recreation of *Moby-Dick* and *Heart of Darkness* with distinctive autobiographical symbolism, and one novella, *Running Wild*, the embryo for his final four novels. *Kindness* came out seven years after *Empire* the novel and four years after the film. It didn't receive the same approbation or award nominations. In places, it comes off as overly self-indulgent, too, and not having the energy and invention of *Unlimited*. The writing is strong, though, invigorating some of the more mundane, trivial episodes. It was marketed as a sequel, yet it revises and deviates from the original in meaningful ways, as if making an effort to reinterpret young Jim and the author who created him.

Set between the outbreak of the Second Sino-Japanese War in 1937 and 1987, *Kindness* covers a fifty-year span in a series of long vignettes that trace Ballard's life in Shepperton with his children, wife, friends, and girlfriends. There is some overlap with *Empire* in the first three chapters. Then Ballard moves away from China. He doesn't return until the end—on the set of Spielberg's adaptation, which recreates Shanghai in Shepperton. It is a suitable conclusion given the dominant trope of media technology and affectation that galvanized *Empire*. The real Ballard actually did return to Shanghai in the BBC documentary released the same year as *Kindness*, which I discuss in chapter 1, but the fictional Jim returns only through the vehicle of cinema, solidifying Ballard's thematic chant *in verba* a postmodern Shakespeare: *All the world's a film studio.*

Like *Empire*, *Kindness* is a bildungsroman, but of a different type. Jim grows into adulthood negotiating the trauma of war and then the sudden death of his wife Miriam (based on Mary). As the years pass, these stressors push him in tenuous, sometimes hazardous directions, and he relies on the "kindness of women" to help him through the mire of his past while catering to his needs in the present. Many of these needs are sexual. *Empire*'s young Jim has little interest in sex. *Kindness*'s adult Jim fixates on sex. As with so many of Ballard's protagonists, Jim wants to escape a double-reefed island. One reef is mnemonic and psychological. The other belongs to Shepperton, where he, like the real Ballard, feels stranded and, after Miriam dies, forlorn and helpless to raise his children by himself. *Kindness* may be mainstream, but it is also a work of erotica, detailing Jim's coming-of-(middle)-age and the development of his sexuality and perspective through the fog of emotional turmoil. In the end, the fog clears and he finds solace:

> The war had postponed my childhood. . . . The time of desperate stratagems was over, the car crashes and hallucinogens, the deviant sex ransacked like a library of extreme metaphors. Miriam and all the murdered dead of a world war had made their peace. The happiness I had found had been waiting for me within the modest reach of my own arms, in my children and the women I had loved, and in the friends who had made their own way through the craze years. (342)

The sex scenes primarily feature Miriam, Cleo Churchill (based on Claire Walsh), and Sally Mumford (possibly based on Emma Tennent). Ballard articulates their relations with Jim in forensic, techno-erotic language that recalls

Crash. One reviewer was taken aback by Jim's sexuality yet seems to recognize that it erupts from a place of distress and damage.

> A compulsive womanizer, Jim jumps the bones of virtually every female who crosses his field of vision in a series of couplings Mr. Ballard describes with a somewhat quizzical, almost clinical specificity. In some of these pairings there are hints of affection or even the possibility of love, but on other occasions Jim is remote, all the more impersonal for the details he adduces, and his exertions have about the same moral weight as those of a strenuous game of handball. Finally, this is what the novel is about: the way in which the boy Jim of *Empire of the Sun* was hurt, crippled and deformed by the things he witnessed and experienced in Shanghai and in the Japanese internment camp at Lunghua during World War II. (Slavitt)

Less discerning is John Baxter's evaluation of Jim's sexuality, which he attributes to the real Ballard being a sleazebag at heart. "The promotional blitz for *Kindness* included numerous magazines and newspaper profiles, TV and radio interviews, almost none of which commented on the fact that, in coming clean about his life, the genial Jim Ballard had elected to talk dirty" (298). In fact, sex scenes constitute a small percentage of *Kindness*, so if he really wanted to "talk dirty" with more frequency, what was stopping him? After *Crash*, why didn't he write more pornographic novels and stories, if only under a pseudonym?

Ballard published over a million words throughout his career. Few of them—I would say fewer than ten thousand words, maybe five thousand—describe sexual activity, and most of them appear in *Crash* and *Kindness*. Furthermore, *Kindness* revolves around the axis of Miriam's death, Jim's response to it, and the conscious and unconscious connections he makes between her death and the trauma he experienced as a child of war. "Take it from me, the death of a wife is all about sex" (167)—Jim's proclamation is the Freudian bedrock of the sexual dynamic; the totem of sex and the life instinct (*Eros*) wards off the death instinct (*Thanatos*) that Miriam's demise shifts into high gear. Baxter's argument that the novel is "before everything else . . . a sexual memoir" is off the mark and rooted in juvenile insecurities regarding sexuality (296). The technology of media takes thematic precedence over sex, structuring Jim's relations and worldviews. Sex may be "the last great frontier"

(*Kindness* 260), but only under the fizzling spotlights of the reality studio. More than anything, *Kindness* represents and works through a technological trauma that began with the 1960s media explosion and congealed into the realm of simulation in the 1980s.

In contrast to *Empire*, Ballard returns to a first-person point of view, saying, "My alter ego for the narrative is an adult, and I can easily get into my own adult mind" ("In Conversation" 83). This usage creates a greater sense of intimacy, but not necessarily greater than what the young, third-person Jim elicits (then again, despite perspective, the suffering of children normally trumps the suffering of adults). He divides the novel into three parts. The first, "A Season for Assassins," (re)tells young Jim's story. The second and longest part, "The Craze Years," accounts for most of Jim's life and covers the key events of studying in medical school, serving in the RAF, working as an editor, becoming a father and husband in Shepperton, dabbling in hippie and drug culture, staging a car-crash exhibition, and attending a film festival—all of which the real Ballard experienced.[8]

There is little discussion of his writing career; nevertheless, *Kindness* takes us behind the scenes. As the years unfold and we wander through the hallways of Ballard's quasi-past, Jim develops several key relationships, the most important with Miriam, Sally, and Cleo, but also with David Hunter (likely an amalgam of Ballard's male friends with strong hints of *Crash*'s Vaughan) and psychology professor cum media personality Dick Sutherland (based on computer scientist Chris Evans, one of Ballard's closest male friends[9]). Jim's three kids have lesser roles, but they are crucial; during his time of grief, "it was the children who were bringing [him] up. They had come to terms with the past far more quickly than their father" (*Kindness* 168).

In the titular chapter that appears halfway through part 2, Jim states: "The kindness of women and the affection of my children steered me safely through those first long months" after Miriam died from injuries sustained falling down a staircase (155).[10] For a while, Sally serves Jim as a partner and mother to his kids, as well as a sort of tour guide to the "new world" of the 1960s (184). Fashioned by "the volatile landscape of the mid-sixties, which made a virtue of psychic damage" (177), she grows unstable, and Cleo takes the reins, becoming Jim's lover and lifetime partner. Jim has other brief relationships with women, such as Peggy Gardner, his oldest friend from Lunghua, and Olga Ulianova, his prewar nanny. Whoever it is, she is as much a mother figure as a sexual object, and her kindness resides in her capacity to attend to the needs of his mind and body.

If most of the novel involves the kindness of women, it ends with the pathology of men. In the final chapter of part 2, David is legally institutionalized after a deadly car accident. Then, in part 3, "After the War," which is less a reference to World War II than to the mnemonic war activated in Jim's psyche by World War II and Miriam's death, Dick contracts cancer and turns his demise into a reality show, filming it as a documentary. These men clinch Jim's development. Through their destruction—coupled with the *construction* of women—he harnesses the clarity and stamina to rebuild himself at last.

Looking back, Jim wonders how responsible he had been for everybody's finales: "When I thought of David Hunter, of Dick and Sally, I sometimes wondered what part I had played in plotting the course of their lives, steering them towards goals that I had set many years earlier. I had never consciously manipulated them, but they had accepted their assigned roles like actors recruited to play their parts in a drama whose script they had never seen" (262–63). Ballard gives a metanarrational nod to his authorship—everybody is an actor in *Kindness*, and Ballard is a director manipulating their strings. In broader terms, the novel operates as a metanarrative by ironically marginalizing his professional writing life in favor of a semi-fictionalized "extracurricular" life even as Ballard engages in the project of professional writing by conceiving of, composing, and publishing *Kindness*. In other words, from behind the scenes he writes about that which takes place behind the scenes. More significant, this conclusive reflection confirms the forces of media pathology and implosion that preoccupy Jim for most of the novel and that Dick epitomizes in his "final programme" (293).

The 1960s shaped Ballard's science fiction and Jim's identity more than any other decade by turning "the tables on reality. The media landscape had sealed a Technicolor umbrella around the planet and then redefined reality as itself" (180). Marshall McLuhan theorized that this umbrella constitutes the "extensions of man," a projection of our new, electronically charged desires onto the sphere of culture, which in turn projects itself back onto us, endlessly reproducing us as machinic beings. Like most Ballardian protagonists, Jim feels a distinct ambivalence about media technology, enlivened and remade by it on one hand, beset by existential dread on the other. Jim equates the 1960s with mad scientism:

> In this overlit realm ruled by images of the space race and the Vietnam War, the Kennedy assassination, and the suicide of Marilyn Monroe, a unique alchemy of the imagination was taking place. In many ways the media landscape of the 1960s was a laboratory designed specifically to cure me of all my obsessions. Violence and pornography provided a kit of desperate measures that might give some meaning both to Miriam's death and to the unnumbered victims of the war in China. The demise of feeling and emotion, the death of affect, presided like a morbid sun over the playground of that ominous decade, to which Sally seemed to hold a key. The brutalising newsreels of civil wars and assassinations, the stylisation of televised violence into an anthology of design statements, were matched by a pornography of science that took its materials, not from nature, but from the deviant curiosity of the scientist. (185)

This passage reveals the profound influence of the era. Many of the telltale themes, figures, and events he uses and reuses are visible: Vietnam, JFK, Monroe, imagination, obsession, death, pornography, China, television, affect, violence, science—all of it fermented by Ballard in the science fictional crucible of techno-culture's "deviant curiosity." His science fiction derives straight from the 1960s, even after the decade had long passed away. An argument could be made that his fiction traces the movement of an alternate reality that accounts for some capitalist and technological developments but remains in the media environment of the 1960s. After *Unlimited*, the governing technologies in his novels and stories belong to television and filmmaking, and it is no surprise that, as Iain Sinclair says in his book on *Crash*, the fiction reads "like storyboards for unmakeable films" (8).[11]

Ballard appropriately stages the conclusion of his second fictional autobiography on the set of *Empire*. "This is the right way to go back to Shanghai, inside a film," says Jim. "In a sense they started shooting it fifty years ago" (*Kindness* 333). Even in his "real" autobiography, one of the last things he writes about is his perception of how cinema bolsters reality. During his return to Shanghai in 1991 he glimpses an old homeless man in the street squatting on a stool with a bowl of rice. At first he sympathizes with him, wondering if it will be the man's last meal. Then he realizes that the stool is made from a stack of Arnold Schwarzenegger videos. The man exudes confidence, as if the movie star was flexing his muscles and lending him strength.

On the set of *Empire*, Jim observes that all the people working on the film participate in the construction of a simulacra of Shanghai, a hyperreality that is "more real than real" (Baudrillard, *Simulacra* 81), or, as Jim says, "a more convincing reality than the original I had known as a child" (*Kindness* 328), which isn't the actual original, but a mnemonic vestige. Jim sees everything through the lens of a camera. Visits from his children seem "eerily like cast reunions" (*Kindness* 277); he uncannily senses the reel in the real, and he epiphanizes that "images of ourselves formed the real walls of our lives" (317). He makes this closing diagnosis: "I could almost believe that my memories of Shanghai had always been a film, endlessly played inside my head during my years in England after the war" (341). Jim has obtained zen-cybernetic enlightenment, understanding the transcendent truth of what he is and how the factories of technology and media culture have manufactured him. As such, Ballard once again demonstrates "his ability to interrogate the slippages between fiction and reality, [which] makes him 'a true televisionary'" (Baxter and Wymer 3). In terms of his cultural production and technological identity, the Jim of both *Empire* and *Kindness*, Ballard's least science fictional novels, may be his most science fictional protagonists.

Chris Beckett says that reviewers of *Empire* and *Kindness* "welcomed the interpretive promise of their candour: the books appeared to supply a biographical route map that signposted the psychological and biographical origins of the author's more opaque fantasies and dystopias. It was a reductive perspective that Ballard endorsed, in interviews and in the subsequent autobiography *Miracles of Life*" ("The Progress"). Readers who might have been uneasy with the weird, graphic direction Ballard took after the natural disaster quartet (for example, the experimental schiz-flows of *Atrocity*, the hardcore pornography of *Crash*, the extreme violence of *High-Rise*, the excessive psychedelia of *Unlimited*) could take solace in *Empire* and *Kindness*, which allowed them to "make sense" out of Ballard's lines of flight. As Rossi points out, however, "the more recent critical tendency has been to warn against reading *Empire* and *Kindness* as semi-autobiographical texts which not only 'decode the bizarre and perverse aberrations that had gone before' but also claim a transparent and coherent identity 'between J. G. Ballard and the Jamie/Jim figure in the texts'" (67).[12]

This postmodern inclination to distrust the novels has validity. And yet there remains a critical resolve to "trust" them, or at least to separate the real from the fictional, as if Ballard's intricately misshapen trees are impossible to bear in the absence of clear-cut roots. Whatever the stance, *Empire* and *Kindness* echo and advance the theme of technological subjectivity and affect that informs all his major works. These mainstream novels are definitive illustrations of Ballard's belief in the science fictionalization of reality, and they deliver the governing principles for the final phase of his career.

CHAPTER 6

THE ROAD TO CULTURE
Later Novels

ON THE DEATH OF FUTURITY

In this final chapter, I examine the novels Ballard published between 1981 and 2006, except for the fictional biographies covered in chapter 5. These novels exhibit a variety of tropes, settings, and storylines that reach back to his early work, push forward into new territory, and fixate on the stimuli and affects of culture. By the early 1980s, critics widely agreed that Ballard had forsaken the science fiction genre. The path he took was more in line with that of William Gibson, who, in the 1990s, started telling interviewers that the world of science fiction had already become the world of the present, so a true science fiction author would naturally have to shift his or her attention to writing about the present. This is what he did throughout the early 2000s in his Blue Ant trilogy,[1] explorations of the "alien present" where "the future is right here, right now" ("William"). Gibson stated in 2010: "In the 1960s I think that in some sense the present was actually about three or four years long, because in three or four years relatively little would change. Now the present is the length of a news cycle some days" (ibid.).

Ballard made a similar argument much earlier. In 1987 he reported: "The future had *arrived* by the mid-1960s, so it seemed to me that the main subject matter for the science fiction writer was about the present day. And I think I was right. We were *in* tomorrow, and I felt that I had to write about it" ("J. G. Ballard," Platt 94). He's justifying the style and subject matter of *The Atrocity Exhibition* here, but the idea can be extended to the end of his career and the postcapitalist, hyperreal environments of his so-called crime thrillers. Ballard sets them in near futures or alternate presents, flirting so heavily with the actual present that the distinction between them implodes.

Typically, these novels are not associated with science fiction, but they fall into the spectrum of the genre. In *100 Must Read Science Fiction Novels*, Stephen E. Andrews and Nick Rennison say that *Hello America* is Ballard's only "pure science fiction novel since the late sixties," but they include *Super-Cannes* among their picks, calling it a "masterful speculation in social science that can arguably be claimed for the genre. . . . Ballard has done more to make us consider how (post)modernity has altered our consciousness" (7). David Pringle endorses the science fictional properties of the later work, too. Referring to *Super-Cannes* as "near-sf," he writes: "Ballard may no longer be writing what the world regards as sf, but it's clear, in novels such as this and his last, *Rushing to Paradise*, that his is still a fiction which operates on the utopian-dystopian axis which is at the heart of sf" ("Books" 64).

In theory and practice, Ballard didn't do anything that different at the end of his career than he did at the beginning of it. Notwithstanding *The Wind from Nowhere*, he flouts science fictional conventions with as much acuity in *The Drowned World* as in *Kingdom Come* while using the genre's tackle for his own furnishings and finishings. Ignited by the electronic culture of the 1960s, Ballard foresaw the headlong absorption of science fiction into everyday life. He declared in 1971 that "everything is becoming science fiction" ("Fictions" 205), and his writing reflected this stance. By the 2000s, he was writing from the stance that everything *had become* science fiction, a prodigal literature that, according to Ballard, had usurped the law of the father, "reseeding itself in the mainstream novel" ("In Conversation" 82). Certainly, arguments can be waged against this outlook even as the second decade of the twenty-first century rushes to a close. My suggestion is that, in the last two decades of his life, Ballard was writing science fiction in the form of a culturally science fictionalized being, not as a projectionist of novums and futures, but as an author and a man living in a technologically advanced and dependent present that had been anticipated in many of his older stories and novels.

I have divided this chapter into two sections. The first deals with novels in which Ballard returns to the landscapes of decline and desire in his natural-disaster trilogy; they were published over a thirteen-year period with several interruptions, namely *Empire of the Sun* and *The Kindness of Women*. In the second section, I focus on his last four novels, which, like his first four novels, were published in sequence and are located in "disaster areas" that feature interrelated architectures of space, psyche, and havoc.

SPECTERS OF CULTURE IN NATURE

Hello America (1981) • *The Day of Creation* (1987) • *Rushing to Paradise* (1994)

The Day of Creation is a good segue from chapter 5. It's not a fictional autobiography, but it does contain key autobiographical traits, depicting the fevered journey of World Health Organization doctor Mallory to the source of a river in central Africa that he accidentally creates ("authorizes") and then names after himself. The creation of the river has nothing to do with him; it results from natural causes, but he stakes a claim to it "in an act of extreme self-identification" (Paddy 218).

Torn between altruism and egoism, Mallory must cross terrestrial, psychological, allegorical, and metanarrational thresholds. He is yet another "Ballard" / Adam driven and determined by obsession. As he eludes the aggressions of rival guerrilla factions and the eccentric, vengeful madam of a "floating brothel" (249), he debates whether he should "kill" the river or encourage its growth, irrigating the Sahara Desert with this potential third Nile and turning the region into an "Edenic paradise" (159). Ultimately it symbolizes a part of himself he abhors, and he decides to engineer its demise. Ballard relentlessly equates the body of water with the body and mind of Mallory and his emerging "riverine" self (47). It becomes a stream of consciousness *for* him and *of* him. Gazing into its waters, he gazes into himself, his psyche and the machinery of his drives, as if, he says, "my own imagination was inventing the river as we moved along its course" on a stolen ferryboat called the *Salammbo*, the seagoing version of the "Ballard" / Adam's stolen *Cessna* in *The Unlimited Dream Company* (117).

As he closes on the source, delirious with malaria, the lightning of epiphany strikes: "I had become so obsessed by myself that I had seen the Mallory as a rival, and measured its current against my own ambition. . . . I had been wounding myself, and my attempt to kill the river was no more than a surrogate suicide" (259–60). Finally, at the source, beyond the lost Eden of a primeval lake, he watches the last drops of the Mallory die between his fingers in a sun-dried basin. His identity follows the river into obscurity. Tabula rasa.

The Day of Creation revisits the physical and psychological topography of *The Drowned World*, *The Drought*, and *The Crystal World* where one man desires to "merge" with a poisoned, proliferating landscape as a means of transcendence. In addition to familiar allusions and yokings,[2] the novel retells *Heart of Darkness*. Ballard casts Mallory in the role of Marlow, who circumnavigates a treacherous stream of consciousness in search of the Kurtzian sublime. Unlike Marlow, however, Mallory does not quest for a man, or rather, the idea of a man. He quests for the source of the river, an idea of *himself* that represents the heart of his own consciousness, imagination, identity and, as the title of the final chapter indicates, "memory and desire" (284).[3]

The tides of Mallory's inner space constitute Kurtz, a double-sided "horror-horror" that invokes euphoria in equal measure with terror. In both novels, the "moral" is the same: Kurtz resides in all of us. To a lesser degree, *The Day of Creation* bears likeness to *Moby-Dick*, with Mallory as Ahab in pursuit of the white whale (in other words, Kurtz, or his own demons) and constantly asking himself: "Is Ahab, Ahab? Is it I, God, or who, that lifts this arm?" (Melville 406). Deprived of his patients by guerrilla warfare, Mallory echoes the classic monomaniac, losing sight of his identity in an oneiric conflation of himself as God (the creator), Jesus (the healer), Adam (the fallen, pathological man) and the Devil (the voice of temptation and desire).

Not coincidentally did warfare deprive the real Ballard of his life circumstances. Just as Mallory seeks the source (of himself), so does Ballard draw on a source (of himself, his literature, and his authorship). In a 1988 interview,

Michelle Field paraphrases Ballard: "The boy in *Empire of the Sun* . . . grows up to be Dr. Mallory in *The Day of Creation*—not a science fiction writer in Shepperton. . . . It is the story of *Empire of the Sun* turned inside-out." In his own words, Ballard tells her: "The circumstances in *Empire of the Sun* completely enclose the boy and shape him; in *The Day of Creation* it is Mallory himself who creates the landscapes in the book, and he imposes himself on the landscapes, not the other way around" ("J. G. Ballard Discusses"). Moreover, Field speculates that "the rich descriptions of plants and watercourses in the . . . novel may stem in part from young Jim's childhood on the margins of the Yangtze and Whangpoo rivers in Shanghai, as well as the older Ballard's trip on the Nile and his impressions of the rain forest that encroaches on Rio de Janeiro" (ibid.). In terms of his canon, the production of *The Day of Creation* can be viewed as a river, originating in the natural-disaster novels, channeling through *Empire*, and emerging onto new ground where the old is inverted and transfixed into the new. Mallory, then, is "Ballard" as well as Ballard, the author of *The Day of Creation*, a book that can be traced back to the "source" of his literary imagination.

Near the beginning of the novel, Mallory finds a bucket of memorabilia that contains film strips, a syringe, a cine-camera, a magazine, and a bullet shell—all resonant symbols and features in Ballard's life and fiction. "Together these objects formed a record of my life," he utters, "an inventory that summed up all [my] adventures" (9). More specific to Ballard's writing career, Mallory is accused of "always hav[ing] to find the extreme position" (13), and his general backstory, like *Unlimited*'s Blake, extrapolates events that contributed to Ballard's professional and psychological growth on paper and in reality. Extracted from memories of the vast lagoon world of Shanghai,[4] *The Day of Creation* is a natural extension of *Empire*. The two novels have the same "psychological thrust . . . embedded in a quest in which the hero clings desperately to his dreams" (Adachi B4). Published between *Empire* and *Kindness*, *The Day of Creation* functions as a kind of bridge between Ballard's fictional youth and adulthood. It may not be a thoroughbred autobiographical fiction, but during the time of its composition, Ballard seemed to be in an autobiographical mode.

If Mallory is the God of Creation, the world he makes is as much an environmental as a social and psychological dystopia. All of the main characters are variably antagonistic. The supreme antagonist is Mallory (the river and the shifting concept of the man it reflects). Subsidiary antagonists include Captain Kagwa, the Mercedes-obsessed police chief of Port-la-Nouvelle; General Harare, leader of the guerrilla rebels and Kagwa's rival for territorial control; Nora Warrender, a veterinarian, misandrist, and lordess of a ship of nurses and prostitutes who pursue Mallory and dispatch vagrant soldiers;[5] Noon, a child soldier; and Professor Sanger, a pseudo-biologist, reality-TV persona, and documentarian. Kagwa, Harare, and Warrender are nuanced characters but mainly sources of peril for Mallory. Noon and Sanger, on the other hand, facilitate his development and embody the central theme of media technology, construction, and affectation. All of them possess a dualistic nature with the capacity for "good," but the longer and stronger the Mallory flows, the more it siphons the "bad" from their stores of morality.

Mallory understands Sanger's adman persona, but Noon perplexes him. From their first to their last encounter, he can't figure her out: "Her motives were as unreadable as my own" (101). Like the river, Mallory names her, branding and thus possessing her. At the end, he wonders if she may have been "a figment born from a river itself sprung from my imagination" (286). She preoccupies him more than any other character and serves him as a metaphysical guide and evolving object of sexual desire. In *The Empires of J. G. Ballard*, David Paddy underscores her "thoroughly literary role":

> This young black African girl accompanies Mallory on most of his long treks and, due in part to a language barrier, she seems to function throughout as a cipher on which he projects roles and symbolic identities, from Eve to girl Friday. Together they evoke a strange variation of Mark Twain's Huckleberry Finn and Jim going down the river on their boat, or, perhaps more appropriately, Kipling's Kim and Lama. While Mallory at times wants to conceive of Noon as an innocent figure, a virginal Eve for his new Eden, this impression is undermined by her experience as a young guerrilla fighter and by Mallory's paedophiliac desires for her. Perhaps this makes her even more symbolic of Africa than he is aware. Either way, she works less as the novel's representative of an authentic African than as the figure upon which European ideas of Africa are projected. (219)

Paddy concentrates on the orientalist aspects of Noon and other characters. He uses Freudian and Lacanian theory to explore their subject-positions.

These are viable concerns, but I am more interested in Noon's technological identity and the specter of culture that territorializes her. Alongside Sanger, Noon denotes a vital science fictional element in the narrative and in Mallory's consciousness, rendering him a cybernetic being. We could even read the river as a technology, a tool whereby Mallory, if only in his own head, innovates his surroundings, ecologically and socially.

Noon's exposure to technology begins with a government radio station. She grows bored with it and turns to cassette tapes that she finds on the *Salammbo*, which Mallory stole from Kagwa, who hunts him in an attack helicopter because his beloved Mercedes is on the boat (Kagwa is a cybernetic being, too, motivated by desires for technology). The tapes contain "popular guides to political philosophy, colonial history and third-world resources" and are Noon's "basic English language course, the first tuition of any kind that she had received in her life" (Ballard, *Day* 117). Once she discovers television and Sanger's documentary footage of Africa, including clips of herself, she abandons the tapes for "the transparent flattery of the lens. . . . [Mallory] could see her among the cabinets and control panels stacked beside the Mercedes, playing the film cassettes on the battery-powered monitor and miming to her own images on the screen. . . . Having discovered vision, the sound-world palled. Speech bored her, and the alphabet and syntax of the film were all she needed" (159). Noon (a.k.a. *no one*) (d)evolves into a Sangerian object, singing the body electric of his credo—"Sooner or later, everything turns into television" (62)—with her newfound desire and perception. One reviewer of the novel rightly said that she "progresses in a matter of weeks from Stone Age primitivism to a fascination with technology" (Rev. of *Day*), but it is more than mere fascination. It is a matter of ontology.

Sanger personifies and disseminates this ontology. Cast from the same techno-pathological mold as Vaughan, Richard Wilder, and Dick Sutherland, he is an archetypal Ballardian cybernetician who "lived in a fictionalized world, remade by the cliches of his own 'wild-life' nature films. These were not soap operas but soap documentaries. The makers of TV documentaries were the conmen and carpetbaggers of the late twentieth century, the snake-oil and fast-change salesmen purveying the notion that a raw nature packaged and homogenized by science was palatable and reassuring" (57). An arbiter of culture and the loss of reality, Sanger / culture forms an opposing binary with

Mallory/nature, "the backwoods physician stuck in [his] ways and unable to accept the opportunities of the media landscape" (33), although both parties actively engage in technological production, one high (the tool of media), one low (the tool of water). And both parties increasingly need and feed off one another. Over time, the nature/culture binary falls into deconstructionist play as Sanger's electronic desires bleed into Mallory's. Sanger's "imaginary travelogue" breathes life into their "adventure" (286). Without that travelogue, there is no adventure.

The technology of Sanger sets the story in motion. Mallory "creates" the Mallory when a tractor bulldozes a symbolic tree of life to make way for Sanger's film and he discovers water in the leftover cavity. He uses technological rhetoric to describe his initial perception of the water: "A thin stream . . . crept towards my heels and touched them, moving in a zigzag of lateral and forward movements that seemed to notch up a series of coded messages, computerizing itself around my feet" (40). Sanger makes altruistic claims to spread awareness about the situation in Port-la-Nouvelle, but really he wants to revive his ailing television career "with his threadbare mercy mission" (35). His interest shifts to Mallory himself, however, "the subject of a new documentary about a man who invents a river" (63).

Mallory abhors and resists him. Slowly, the technology of Sanger assimilates him, and he gets to a point where, like Noon, he can't dissociate himself from the electronic image. "I felt curiously detached from my own body with its pains and fevers, and closer to the abstract and stylized image on the small screen. The pearly rectangle . . . shrank me down to size, like everything else on which the camera turned its eye, and stripped away the irrelevancies of emotion, pain, and motive. Only my obsession endured, a great dream made small by failures of nerve, but a great dream nevertheless" (248).

Sanger's determination to film Mallory stokes his quest for the source, the discovery of which will be the film's climax. He is the voice of culture whispering into nature's ear, subjecting Mallory's would-be "organic" desires to the high-tech authority of the media environment. "The truth is merely the lie you most wish to believe. . . . After all, your creation of the river has sprung from a familiar repertory of childhood clichés. I even suspect that your wish to destroy it is really an attempt to destroy television's image of the world" (176). Fittingly, only Mallory and Sanger, nature and culture, arrive at the source. They are one entity, one imploded idea, the boundary between them evaporated along with any designs for good intentions. All that matters to them now is the denouement of their celluloid dream. Mallory confronts and witnesses the "death" of the river by himself, but he carries the cross of Sanger, who allows him to conjure (and kill) god. "Prepare yourself, Mallory," Sanger preempts him, "now we reach our climax . . . now God exists, Mallory, perhaps you have returned to Eden to destroy Him . . . a messiah for the age of cable television" (280).

Theoretically, culture does not assimilate or destroy nature, but it does *alter* nature, at least with regard to how Mallory perceives and experiences the natural world and himself (as an outgrowth of the natural world). Ballard demonstrates a similar differential playfulness in *Hello America* and *Rushing to Paradise*, both of which portray bipolar Edens with protagonists who must negotiate the schizophrenic flows of culture.

In "Hello, Baudrillard," James Reich deftly compares *Hello America* to Jean Baudrillard's *America*, calling them companion pieces whose "encounters with holographic, fictive America are inherently nostalgic" and whose "pop-cultural existentialism of Las Vegas is articulated through obsessive simulation and simulacra, hyperreality, and gambling under neon" (101, 102). Ballard and Baudrillard explore the impact of culture on the American landscape geographically, socially, and psychologically, "enter[ing] the fiction of America, enter[ing] America as a fiction. It is, indeed, on this fictive basis that it dominates the world" (Baudrillard, *America* 29). The result is science fiction that culminates in technological deterritorialization and estrangement.

America was published five years after *Hello America*. Ballard loved it, saying that the "only real rival is something like Swift's *Gulliver's Travels* in terms of brilliance" ("Interview," Lewis 261). He wondered about how Americans might receive it in that "what is absent from the book . . . is a *single American*" (261). Baudrillard's point of view is unapologetically European, theoretically subjective, and lacks the affection that Ballard had for American culture even as he parodied it. This may have something to do with the introduction he wrote for *Hello America* in 1994. Ballard discusses the Baudrillardian texture of American simulacra and image-culture in conjunction with the categorically Ballardian notion that even "the American people one meets in hotel lobbies and department stores seem like actors in a huge televised sit-com" (3). His thesis is that "the hidden logic of the American dream might one day lead to a President Manson playing nuclear roulette in Las Vegas" (4), an idea spurred by the nomination of Ronald Reagan, whose first year in the White House coincided with the publication of *Hello America*. Even so, he argues that his novel "is strongly on the side of the USA, and a celebration of its optimism and self-confidence, qualities that we Europeans so conspicuously lack" (4).

Ballard could have made this disclaimer in an effort not to ostracize US readers and hinder book sales overseas, but it seems true to his feelings about America, and it illuminates a fundamental disconnect between the novelist and the theoretician (Baudrillard mostly regards the US with disdain). The disclaimer couldn't hurt; *Hello America* wasn't picked up by an American publisher until 1988—the last year of Reagan's second presidential term. Reviewers panned the novel on several fronts, ranging from Ballard's naiveté about the US, which he didn't visit, to his uncouth extrapolation of Charles Manson, who remained a household *stain* well after the rise of his cult and his conviction of conspiracy to commit multiple murders in 1971.

For me, these factors enhance the novel. Kafka never visited the US either before writing *Amerika* (1927) and his lack of experience yielded imagery that reinforced the profound irreality of his landscapes, such as the Statue of Liberty brandishing a sword instead of a torch. Ballard set his America not in the time of his novel's composition but in the twenty-second century (2114 A.D.) after a postapocalyptic event; the landscape has undergone drastic changes, and a working knowledge of what it was like in the twentieth century isn't mandatory for extrapolation on this scale. Conceptually, Ballard's method perfectly aligns with his aggrandizement of the imagination and the power of American media: *Hello America* is the imaginative product of what he knew and learned about America from movies, television, magazines, and the news. And while Ballard also draws on the personas of Howard Hughes and Richard Nixon for his antagonist, Manson is ideal for the role, a sort of backwoods doppelgänger for Reagan, or the id that escaped the cage of Reagan's straight-shoulder suit, plastic smile, and Ken Doll hairdo. The media popularized Mason's pathology. Manson even lifted the name for his apocalyptic scenario "helter skelter" from a pop song by The Beatles.

That *Hello America* was poorly received is ironic. It's Ballard's most science fictional novel and follows the rules of the genre more than any other major work. As in the natural-disaster quartet, the environment is contaminated, mutated, hazardous. In this disaster novel, however, Ballard clearly identifies a future setting—not a potential alternative to reality but a direct extension of it—and he spends ample time explaining how that future came to be, devoting an entire chapter to info-dump that effectively romanticizes and ridicules the practice in pulp science fiction. *Hello America* is also the only Ballard novel that features androids. It encapsulates genre science fiction more than *The Wind from Nowhere*, but with distinctive Ballardian mannerisms, an attentiveness to inner space, and a satirical edginess.

Based on the 1976 story "The Ultimate City," *Hello America* combines the desert of *The Drought* and the jungle swamp of *The Drowned World* with the media psychosis of *The Atrocity Exhibition*. Umberto Rossi identifies a close alliance with *The Drowned World* given the novels' apocalyptic representations of the "Dead City," but their dates of publication are separated by almost two decades during which Ballard's writing evolved as important events took place in world and literary history ("Images" 81). I wouldn't say that *Hello America* is a wiser novel or even a better one. But it does offer "a lucid and ironic anatomy of the American Myth (but we could call it the American Dream)" (86).

The unborn desires of Ballard's protagonists flow from the ducts of American pathology. To be Ballardian is to be an *American* desiring-machine whose agential psychodrama erupts from the technology, media, values, and ethics of the US more than the UK (or, for that matter, China). *Hello America* is a telltale, as the narrator implies: "The United States had based itself on the proposition that everyone should be able to live out his furthest fantasies, wherever they might lead, explore every opportunity, however bizarre" (106). Under this aegis, the title of the first American edition of *The Atrocity Exhibition, Love and Napalm: Export USA*, signifies the Ballardian and defines Ballard himself, a Shanghai "export" who, from childhood, was drawn to American culture, loving it yet wary of its destructive fundament.

In the novel, a massive energy crisis precipitates the decline and fall of the US, whose excessive consumption of natural resources reached a breaking point in the late twentieth century. The fate of the American people is sealed when all the automobile manufacturers go bankrupt, depriving them of their cars and symbolically castrating them. Unable to sustain the changing seasons without gas or electricity, "the entire population of the United States migrated back to its original ethnic departure points in Europe and Africa, Asia and South America, a vast reverse migration duplicating the original westward passage two hundred years earlier" (47). By 2030, almost everybody had fled the continent. Decades later, a crew of European explorers sails to the US on the *SS Apollo*, an allusion to the NASA spaceflight program rendering postapocalyptic America an undiscovered planet that the crew aspires to rediscover and recolonize. They find an ecologically inverted landscape. The "wild west" has turned into a subtropical "forest world of fast-running jungle rivers, hundreds of lakes glutted by monsoon rain" (113). The urban east, in turn, has become a wasteland of dunes, cacti, and tumbleweed, a "desert replica of itself . . . transformed into a set for the ultimate western" (35).

After landing in New York harbor, repeating the immigration pattern of their European ancestors, the crew of the *Apollo* make their way across the continent toward California. In Las Vegas, they discover a paranoid, nuke-crazed monomaniac who has installed himself as the President of this New American Eden. He calls himself Charles Manson, but he is much more than this reference. A psychotic amalgam of media personalities, he reigns from the suite at the Desert Inn that used to belong to Howard Hughes.

Manson incarnates a technocultural extremism that is reified by the media-lacquered layout of the suite. Ballard's initial description of him is scientific, mechanical, cybernetic: "A metallic blue light, as if in some hospital intensive care unit, shone down on the marble-skinned body of a middle-aged man lying on a surgical couch in front of a battery of television screens. He was naked except for the towel around his waist, and held an aerosol inhaler in one hand, a remote-control TV unit in the other" (127). Not only is he metaphorically wired to technology via television, he literally relies on technology to breathe, "a modern Pharaoh holding the orb and sceptre of his office. The mosaic of images flicker . . . down on his unhealthy face" (129). Ballard associates him with Nixon, the president "he could imitate . . . more convincingly than any other" (128), but as Reich indicates, his persona chiefly points to Reagan and his Hollywood image: "Ballard's President Manson is a schizoid simulacra of the original psychopath, an anachronism . . . Manson simulates the latent psychopathy and imposture of all presidents. Publishing in the first term of the most synthetic of all presidents, *Hello America* fulfills Ballard's desire to fuck Ronald Reagan" (102). Manson's constant projection of pop Americana holograms onto the screen of clouds over Vegas further reifies his synthetic status, as do the swarms of attack drones he maneuvers around the sky, extending his technological subjectivity to the heavens of this postapocalyptic reality studio.

In the tradition of the pulp aesthetics that Ballard extirpates, many of the characters in the novel are stereotypes (femme fatale Anne Summers, mad scientist Dr. William Fleming, hard-nosed military veteran Captain Steiner). They aren't without depth or complexity, however, notably Steiner, a Ballardian eccentric who "prefers to think of America as just the ultimate backdrop to his fantasies of being alone" (87), and Fleming, an emeritus professor of computer science and builder of the android ex-presidents.

Manson's counterpart is Wayne, a twenty-one-year-old Scottish stowaway on the *Apollo*. He owns the signature and mythos of actor John Wayne, who, throughout his career, made over eighty western films and "personified for millions the nation's frontier heritage" (Davis 6). He has symbolic ties to nature and the natural world; not only is he a John Wayne, he is a "seaborne Tom Sawyer, with his thatch of blond hair, legs like stilts, eyes lit by all kinds of strange dreams" (10). Still, a nostalgia for American *culture* (dis)possesses him, and he comes to know the culture from residual media. Captivated by the classic and contemporary American dreams of striking gold and encountering celebrity, Wayne begins the expedition as a bastard hanger-on and ends up not only as the leader of the expedition but as vice president of the United States. Admiring his ambition, his Cogburnesque "true grit," Manson appoints him, and after the ex-presidents turn against and kill Manson, Wayne takes over the presidency.

Wayne's social and hierarchical upward movement accompanies his migration across America from sun-dried east to techno-Edenic west. This migration is both geographical and inner spatial, "a safari across the diameter . . . of [his] own skull" (73), and it is accompanied by the unearthing of his latent cultural identity. In spite of Manson's hypochondriacal fear of germs and disease, Wayne respects his "Yankee virtues" (146): "Manson had established the only base of organised power that had existed in north America for a hundred years. The reclamation of this jungle city, the millions of colored lights that shone through the tangled ferns and palms, the elaborate television and communications gear, the renovation of at least part of the old Hughes empire, together rekindled something of the power of the United States, and hinted at what could be done in the future" (131). Manson is the science fiction—the lost prospect of futurity—that reminds him why he had come to America in the first place: "to turn his back forever on an exhausted Europe" (14). He allows Wayne to enter that science fiction and plunge into the future by reterritorializing history.

This reterritorialization accelerates en route to Manson. Certain signposts chart Wayne's cultural progress and development. For example, he teams up with a group of "Indians" or "real Americans"—not natives, but "direct descendants of the few thousands who had stayed behind when the rest of the United States emigrated to Europe. [They] were among the last remnants of one of the dozen tribes that roved the continent" (63). Heinz, Pepsodent, GM, and Xerox adopted their names from "the products manufactured by the great corporations in Manhattan" (63), commodifying their signatures by default, but only under the canopy of history (technically, American commodity-culture is extinct). Their capitalist mythic origins make them "real" and encode Wayne's great American nostalgia. Above all, they represent how the "artificiality of American consumer culture has now become retroactively its natural origin" (Paddy 185)—the epitome of the Baudrillardian simulacrum.[6]

Heinz, Pepsodent, GM, and Xerox usher Wayne into the Promised Land of his American dreams. He encounters another crucial talisman in the chapter titled "Giants in the Sky." It takes place near Boot Hill Cemetery in iconic Tombstone, Arizona. Delirious, Wayne slumps against a gravestone and perceives a mirage of western movie stars looming overhead, including his namesake, "the film actor he had first seen in *Stagecoach*" (97), Henry Fonda, "dressed as Wyatt Earp in the old western [he] had seen so many times, *My Darling Clementine*," and Gary Cooper "with the tired, stoical expression he had worn in *High Noon*" (97, 98). For Wayne, the hallucination is a rite of passage from the realms of nature into culture, consciousness into unconsciousness, reality into image, ego into id, history into myth. Shortly thereafter, he meets Manson, icing the cake on his identity as a new Adam who has been freshly mediatized/baptized.

Hello America plays with numerous binaries that come to bear in the interplay between Wayne and Manson. There are a number of reversals, too.

Beyond reverse colonization, we see a reverse autogeddon—not "a continuous artificial horizon . . . of metallized creatures . . . formed by the raised parapets and embankments of motorways and their access roads and interchanges," (*Crash* 53, 199), but a weather-worn landscape rusting in the sand and swamp—and a reverse western, the "adventure no longer . . . in the discovery and conquest of virgin territory, but in the rediscovery of a culture in ruins, formulated as an inner landscape" (Costa 169). By moving backward over and across the High Plains of earth, time, and psyche, the novel moves forward. Whether that forward movement leads to fortuitous ends remains open for discussion. Ballard would have it no other way. He leaves his readers with another pickle to chew on.

In the end, Wayne, robots, and the remainder of his crew set off toward California in a squadron of light planes with hopes of establishing a(nother) New Eden. They call themselves the "Sunlight Fliers." But won't this Eden be a(nother) simulacrum, *de*territorializing the *re*coded flows of history and futurity? "The old dreams were dead, Manson and Mickey Mouse and Marilyn Monroe belonged to a past America. . . . It was time for new dreams, worthy of a real tomorrow" (224). Does this assertion "point to further delusion on Wayne's part, or is there a significant difference between Mickey Mouse and the flying automata?" (Paddy 189). Delusional or authentic, it seems that the future (and the collective memory of its hyperreal origin) will be thoroughly technological, a product of the dreams of science fiction that *Hello America* taps into and teases out as Ballard pays homage to American culture while expressing an acute ambivalence about its ongoing evolution.

Hello America was originally conceived as in illustrated book for young readers, one of several efforts by Ballard to write for children that didn't pan out, and he intended the title to be a joke. He expanded it into a novel about modern America.[7] *Rushing to Paradise* appeared in 1994, over a decade later. The autobiographical demons had been more or less exorcized from the body of his fiction, and he was on the cusp of entering the final phase of his career during which he would do the same thing in one novel after another, looking awry and darkly at lifestyles of the rich who live in communities where culture has devoured the last vestiges of nature. Siphoning material from the cultural resin of the present, Ballard attributed this decade-long fixation to a "bourgeoisification [and] suburbanization of the soul" ("Reading" 410), a process that endlessly fascinated him. Like *Hello America* and *The Day of Creation*, *Rushing for Paradise* fosters an interesting relationship between nature and culture, one that gestures toward "paradise" but prohibits its embodiment by the impossibility of the relationship. It is the last novel in which Ballard converges on the natural world.

Environmentalist and animal-rights activist Dr. Barbara Rafferty travels with a small crew to a Polynesian atoll called Saint-Esprit, a French military installation and former nuclear testing site. She intends to film a documentary about the endangerment of albatross. They land illegally, and a sixteen-year-old crew member, Neil Dempsey, is shot in the foot by a French soldier. Neil and "Dr. Barbara" become media celebrities during news coverage of the incident. They return to Saint-Esprit with more people, and Barbara establishes a small colony. At first, they work together to make the island a nature preserve where any animal can take refuge, but she becomes a Kurtzian psycho and wants the island to be a reserve for women only, a dark and twisted version of Charlotte Gilman Perkins's *Herland* (1915), where men (and the history of aggression perpetuated by men) are only as good as their capacity to impregnate women.

In order to cultivate this female ecotopia, the male integer must be removed from the social equation. Barbara slowly kills all the men on Saint-Esprit; she even suffocates a male baby. She spares Neil, the island's dominant sperm donor and worker who is also her lover; like Wayne for Manson, Neil contracts Stockholm syndrome, at once repelled, tyrannized, bewitched, and enchanted by her. Predictably, Barbara goes off the deep end and tries to kill everybody, women and men and even all the albatross. The French navy rescues Neil and the remaining islanders. Notwithstanding Barbara's insanity, Neil dreams of a future in which he and the wayward matriarch will be reunited and start a new "colony of threatened species" presided over by her "cruel and generous heart" (239). As in so many novels before it, *Rushing to Paradise* ends on a note of transcendent wishful thinking by the protagonist.

Respective emblems of cinematic ontology and media lunacy, Sanger and Manson are science fictional emissaries in *The Day of Creation* and *Hello America*. No major character in *Rushing to Paradise* is so profoundly defined by and dependent on technology. Everybody relies on technology, though, and the landscape of Saint-Esprit reflects it. Granted, Irving Boyd, the financier and "entrepreneur [who] saw the expedition to Saint-Esprit as little more than the reconnaissance for a television programme," who perceives "reality [as] a public service channel," and for whom "everything turns into television" (49), embodies the same capitalist, hyperreal ethics as Sanger, but he is a minor character limited to a few scenes.

Possessed by a death drive comparable to Jim's in *Empire of the Sun*, Neil views the island through the lens of a dark romanticism: "For all of Dr. Barbara's passion for the albatross, the nuclear testing-ground had a stronger claim on his imagination. No bomb had ever exploded on Saint-Esprit, but the atoll, like Eniwetok, Mururoa, and Bikini, was a demonstration model of Armageddon, a dream of war and death that lay beyond the reach of any moratorium" (15–16). Neil had been a part-time projectionist at the University of Hawaii's film school. Barbara hired him to shoot footage for her documentary. Media technologies and image-culture enabled his "fascination with nuclear weapons and electro-magnetic death" as he "screened cold-war newsreels for the modern-history classes in the film school theatre . . . star[ing] in awe at the vast detonations over the Eniwetok and Bikini lagoons, sacred sites of the twentieth-century imagination" (33). Neil is another imaginative Odysseus whose desires flow from visual culture and the machinery of violence. This becomes even more pronounced when he turns into an "all-purpose media star" (39), his image "bounced between the satellite dishes of the world, an electronic ambassador for Saint-Esprit" (96).

It would seem that Barbara's environmentalist desires flow from a diametrically opposed wellspring—not the machinery of violence, but an ideology of preservation. In fact, media technologies endorse and disseminate her activism, and without those technologies she would cease to maintain that subject-position, for better and for worse. Earlier in her career, she euthanized patients with terminal diseases and was brought up on charges. "A public debate ensued, during which she appeared prominently on television arguing her case with a passion and stridency that to some observers verged on the self-righteous. Alienated by her chilling manner, even her closest colleagues turned away from her. From then on she was unable to practice as a doctor" (40). Barbara's mediatized image—the electronic dissemination of her "chilling manner"—results in her disbarment.

After years in exile, she devotes herself to animal rights. Again television determines ontology; her efforts to save the albatross rely on media exposure.

Once television led to her downfall; now it will see her—and by "seeing" her, *make* her—rise to stardom. Ballard even describes Barbara's physiognomy and physique in cinematic terms, like an actor in a movie. And when a camera sees/makes her, she comes to life: "She rallied when Neil raised the camera and began to film her. A low cloud ceiling extended to the horizon, below which lay a grey, marbled air, the perfect film-light. Despite her ragged clothes, the sores on her lips and fraying hair, the camera lens instantly restored Dr. Barbara's confidence in herself" (18).

The natural world, too, abides by the laws of cinema, the air and light of the island figuring more as an artificial set than an actual setting, at least considering how it is perceived by Neil, which is to say, by the camera, the proboscis of Neil's body and mind. The island is a terrestrial formation, "a chain of sand-bars and coral islets, the rim of a submerged volcanic crater that enclosed a lagoon five miles in diameter" (15). It is also a technological geometry installed with concrete bunkers and camera-towers once used to record atomic tests, and Ballard frequently refers to it as a stage-set for the drama of Barbara's philanthropic exploits.

I'm not suggesting that Saint-Esprit is an (anti)character like the landscapes of *The Drowned World*, *The Drought*, and *The Crystal World*—Ballard doesn't sensualize the atoll, give it a backstory, describe it in suggestive detail or surreal language, or otherwise enliven it. Yet Saint-Esprit does operate as an externalization of the encultured inner space of Barbara and Neil. The subjectivities of the antagonist and protagonist affirm how reliant on technology we have become, not just for business-related purposes (altruistic, capitalist, or otherwise) but for the business of existence and everyday life, even if our goal is to "save" the nontechnological environment. Under these auspices, however, an argument could be made that the nontechnological environment is a fantasy at best. If a tree falls in the woods and nobody is there to *film* it, does it exist? *Rushing to Paradise* poses this timeworn philosophical question, but it links subjectivity and technology, proposing that seeing (and being) can be sanctioned only by the machinic "extensions of man."

Instead of a savior, Barbara paradoxically becomes a mass murderer. This makes sense in the context of the Ballardosphere: characters thrive on extremes whose manifestations sweep morality under the rug. There can be no middle ground, and what is "good" is what pushes an idea or an action to the limit, if not beyond. On the level of psychic flows, advocating or practicing violence or nonviolence doesn't matter so much to Barbara as the perpetual kindling and rekindling of desire.

Pringle speculates that Ballard may have based Barbara on a few sources, primarily Margaret Thatcher, but also Petra Kelly, a German Green Party politician with an Irish name, and Dr. Barbara Moore, a British engineer, long-distance walker, and "breatharian" who gained notoriety in the 1960s for her views about nutrition and physiology ("Re: Rushing"). The latter influence seems particularly apt given Moore's hunger for publicity and her eccentric beliefs, such as the idea that she cured herself of leukemia with an experimental diet and that people could live to be two hundred years old if they ate correctly and didn't drink, smoke, or have sex. Near starvation and bull-headed to the end, she died at age seventy-three ("Dr. Barbara Moore" 36). Dr. Barbara Rafferty holds fast to her resolve (and eccentricity) as well. And she turns out like so many of Ballard's protagonists before her, driven by her obsessions and more interested in creating a sanctuary for herself than in anyone or anything else.

In spite of her actions, she is no more pathological at the end of the novel than at the beginning; as a desiring-machine, she remains constant. The issue in question regards her shift from nonviolence to violence, which climaxes in her belief that men are "the greatest genetic defect of all" (205). Later, she applies this logic to all of humanity and the creatures of the earth—everybody and everything but her. A determination to escape the camera and the technological construction of her identity precipitates this shift. For Barbara, the media transmutes from a source of empowerment to an agent of rack and ruin. She comes to perceive the journalists, television crews, and photographers that besiege the island as monsters who wield "unlimited destructive power at every finger-tip" (91). Weary from the attention, she tells Neil: "I want the world to leave Saint-Esprit and forget us. Then we can find who we really are!" (112).

What she finds isn't conducive to any form of community or social order, be it utopian or dystopian. She wants "her new Eden" all to herself (95); nobody else lives up to her twenty-four-carat pathology. What she finds, in other words, is that she *needs* the world (really, the technology of culture) to make her human—a demonstrably science fictional quandary. In Barbara's fanaticism, Ballard produces another extreme metaphor, inverting traditional literary representations of technology, which is usually equated with aggression and violence. But she becomes aggressive and violent in her flight from technology into obscurity. Put differently, she molts culture and loses herself and her humanity in nature. The greater implication is that the mediatized, late capitalist world has fashioned us all into cybernetic beings, and any attempt to jack out of the matrix of our science fictionalized reality is an attempt to literally dehumanize ourselves. The result: obscenity. *Rushing to Paradise* shows us how twentieth-century culture has evolved us to be most human when we are situated like actors—by circumstance or force of will—on the stage of the technological theater.

ZONES OF TERROR AND ENNUI

Running Wild (1988) • *Cocaine Nights* (1996) • *Super-Cannes* (2000) • *Millennium People* (2003) • *Kingdom Come* (2006)

All authors with long, prolific careers are naturally prone to repetition of everything from word usage and prose structure to thematic refrains and story arcs. Ballard's repetitive tendencies began at an early stage and generated criticism. Peter Brigg comments on these and other tendencies in the conclusion of his study: "Ballard has failings as a writer and as a writer of science fiction. He is somewhat repetitive, or perhaps obsessed, and his highly pictorial imagination can lead to relatively static plotting or relatively aimless action. He does not treat character in the fashion of mainstream novelists nor does he settle for the stereotypes that people a good deal of science fiction" (109).

No author is without shortcomings, but I take issue with these particular claims, especially the idea that it was a bad thing for Ballard to swim against the current of the mainstream. Isn't the opposite true? It's what makes Ballard so compelling and extraordinary, what has drawn so many readers to his work, and what contributed to the sales of his books (remember, he died a millionaire). Likewise does his pictorial imagination distinguish him, and the "static plotting or relatively aimless action" can be attributed to the surreal texture of his narratives; the unfolding of his stories and the direction of his action sequences often feel more at home in dreams, however subtle their execution. It is the subtlety of Ballard's surreality that makes it so idiosyncratic and thought provoking. As for repetition, I find his recurrent use of certain pieces of language, tracts of syntax, and thematic foci intriguing and meaningful. On the larger scale of plot and character, I wanted far more variation in the last decade of his career when Ballard shifted the gears of repetition into full throttle, concentrating exclusively on the same angle of repose in his longer works, which explore the potential repercussions of terminal culture. These works are also quite pedantic and long-winded, replete with expository passages and exchanges in which resident zeitgeists are speculated upon and hammered home—a common occurrence in utopian literature, which isn't known for exciting action sequences or making readers care about and empathize with characters, among other things.

The novels I examine in this section are all set in gated communities, problematize the social and psychological effects of consumer-capitalist life, and hinge on an existential fear of bourgeois ennui, the pursuit of agential violence, and the discovery of truth and freedom in madness. Ballard returns to the principles of *High-Rise* and stays on that marker, recycling characters, plotlines and subject matter with unparalleled rigor. While these (re)visions are curious, if not downright superfluous and bizarre, they show him ending his career on the note of pathological obsession, a trait exhibited by so many of his Adams and now more than ever by their author and creator.

This obsession underscores another seminal theme: the performative nature of reality. Tzachi Zamir writes: "Repetition is intrinsic to theater. Besides theater's improvisational forms, a theatrical performance presents before its audience a sequence of events that the actors have rehearsed and acted many times. More than a contingent requirement of theater, repetition is intimately linked with aesthetic value" (365). Actors must rehearse again and again, repeating the articulations of their words and bodies to achieve the greatest sense of verisimilitude and/or artistic appeal. Whether he was conscious of it or not (probably not), I like the idea that Ballard partakes in this process even as his characters continue to offhandedly mistake their existence in the real as a performance in a film.

In 1986 Ballard said: "It seems to me that what most of us have to fear for the future is not that something terrible is going to happen but rather that *nothing* is going to happen, that we may live, or my children may well live, in a boring world, in what I would call an eventless world, a world where nothing happens. What I fear this will lead to is an atrophy of the imagination" ("Future" 228). This anxiety spurs the final novels in which the *bored*-geois elite commit crimes to breathe life back into the cadavers of their respective "zones of terror" and ennui, or rather, zones of ennui galvanized by terrorism. Some reviewers have called them crime or thriller novels. It is no surprise that they deviate from standard genre fare, as Benjamin Noys suggests, subverting and probing

> the transgressive gesture within the thriller or crime form, both of which rely on the exploitation of transgression. . . . Although [these] novels are organised around the investigation into a crime, in each case the element of mystery is often lacking. This is particularly true for the reader of more than one of these novels who soon notes the repeated pattern. In this way Ballard refuses to provide us with the usual enjoyment of the detective form: the process whereby an initial state of disorder is gradually restored to order by the work of the detective. Instead of the focus on a particular crime we witness the gradual emergence of what we could call criminality itself, in the form of organised and licensed transgression. (402)

In addition to this repeated pattern, the novels retain the technological and media estrangement that typified his earlier science fiction while displaying stock Ballardian themes of isolation, hedonism, the reality studio, primordial violence, and the psychopathology of everyday life. Most of all, they capitalize on Ballard's lifelong narrative quest for a new Eden, which is represented by the techno-capitalist resorts Estrella del Mar in *Cocaine Nights*, Eden-Olympia in *Super-Cannes*, Chelsea Marina in *Millennium People*, and Brooklands in *Kingdom Come*. The problem with any Eden, new or old, real or imagined, lies in the subjectivity of experience. What may be utopian for one individual or community will be dystopian for others. In the Ballardosphere, the deterministic factor is, once again, class.

In *Super-Cannes*, for instance, resident psychiatrist Wilder Penrose says: "The rich know how to cope with the psychopathic. The squirearchy have always enjoyed freedoms denied to the tenant farmers and peasantry. De Sade's behaviour was typical of his class. Aristocracies keep alive those endangered pleasures that repel the bourgeoisie. They may seem perverse, but they add to the possibilities of life" (96). Penrose's sentiment recalls the bourgeois utopia *Looking Backwards* in which Edward Bellamy designs what he thinks is the perfect social, cultural, and economic matrix. Bellamy erects his utopia upon the foundation of bourgeois, urban, socialist codes and mores, envisioning it as an ideal society for everybody, regardless of social standing and upbringing. In *News from Nowhere* (1890), William Morris responded to Bellamy with an alternative, pastoral utopia that demonstrates a slight awareness of subjectivity but still operates under the assumption that utopia can be achieved on a grand scale. During the twentieth century, efforts to map out viable utopias gave way to the dystopian exploits that largely define the science fiction genre today. There were occasional exceptions, such as B. F. Skinner's *Walden Two* (1948) and Kim Stanley Robinson's *Pacific Edge* (1980), but overall, utopia became synonymous with fantasy.

Ballard's characters neurotically pursue psychological utopias across the expanse of various dystopian landscapes.[8] In these novels, his methodology bears a likeness to Aldous Huxley's in *Brave New World* (1931)—a title, incidentally, extracted from a passage in *The Tempest*, the literary text that Ballard most frequently alludes to and revamps in his novels, along with *Heart of Darkness* and *Robinson Crusoe*. Huxley's novel prefigured numerous consumer technologies and architectures (pharmaceutical drugs, mega-malls, the porn industry, the delirium of celebrity culture, and so on). Margaret Atwood explains: "*Brave New World* is either a perfect-world utopia or its nasty opposite, a dystopia, depending on your point of view: its inhabitants are beautiful, secure and free from diseases and worries, though in a way we like to think we would find unacceptable." Ballard, too, depicts an ambiguity of emotion and enjoyment, but whereas Huxley accounts for an entire five-tier caste system, Ballard focuses on the top tier, cultivating dissension in the rank. For Huxley, the catalyst is a scientifically engineered atrophy of affect kept at bay by genetic predetermination, social conditioning, and drug use. For Ballad, it is an entropy of affect bred by super-rich leisure culture, a *fourth* world "waiting to take over everything" (*Cocaine* 216). Rebellion, violence, death—and, of course, "happiness"—result in both cases.

Cocaine Nights, *Super-Cannes*, *Millennium People*, and *Kingdom Come* are Ballard's most realistic novels, even more realistic than *Empire of the Sun* and *The Kindness of Women*. As Jeannette Baxter contends, however, they do "constitute another phase of formal and generic experimentation along Surrealist lines of influence" (*Surrealist* 192), with all of them centering on what Andre Breton called the ultimate surrealist act: "to go out into the street and fire a revolver at random into the crowd" (Ballard, "Interview," Revell 46). Meaningless violence is the guiding light of Ballard's later career. In Penrose's words, it "may be the true poetry of the new millennium. Perhaps only gratuitous madness can define who we are" (*Super-Cannes* 262). Invoking his Surrealist roots, Ballard signals the dawn of a bleak postcapitalist future grounded in a fully realized/mediatized psychopathology that is already upon us.

The first gated community book, *Running Wild*, is a short twenty-five-thousand-word epistolary novella. Ballard wrote it for Hutchinson Novellas, a series published in the late 1980s that also featured writing by Brian Aldiss, Anthony Burgess, Malcolm Bradbury, and Paul Theroux. It's a scaled-up version of his story "The Object of the Attack," which first appeared in *Interzone* in 1984 and reads like a blueprint for the final novels, although the antagonists are not discontent doctors, lawyers, and stockbrokers. They are the children of these upper-class professionals. Ballard portrays them as victims of an excess of structure and order that prompted them to revolt against and murder their parents.

Ballard formats *Running Wild* as the "Forensics Diaries of Dr. Richard Greville, Deputy Psychiatric Adviser, Metropolitan Police" (3). Greville's entries document his investigation of a massacre that occurred in Pangbourne Village, an exclusive suburban estate near London. Thirty-two adult residents are mysteriously killed, and it is initially believed that unknown assassins abducted their thirteen children. Greville develops a theory that the children are the assassins, collectively murdering their parents because of a paradoxical "despotism of kindness" and "tyranny of love and care," then running away (59). A fascist desire to control and surveil their children produced adverse effects. This desire stems from social and cultural stagnation, and the children's revolt is an effort not only to get rid of their oppressors but to escape the imaginative atrophy imposed on them. Greville writes:

> At Pangbourne Village . . . time could run backward or forward. The residents had eliminated both past and future, and for all their activity they existed in a civilized and eventless world. In a sense, the children rewound the clocks of life.

> . . . The children were desperate for the roughage of real emotions, for parents who now and then disapproved of them, became annoyed and impatient, or even failed to understand them. They needed parents who weren't interested in everything they did, who weren't afraid to be irritated or bored by them, and didn't try to rule every minute of their lives with the wisdom of Solomon. (62, 65)

In other words, children (and human beings in general) need leeway to *run wild*. Denied that basic aggressive compulsion, they will lash out. Ballard plays on William Golding's *Lord of the Flies* (1954), but on the turf of a very different playground. The devolution of Golding's children into savagery takes place on a tropical island, and a Darwinian portrait of human nature arises within the flora and fauna of the natural world. Ballard's children turn savage on the technological island of Pangbourne Village, a dense media complex rife with entertainment and surveillance equipment that Greville itemizes during his investigation, much of which requires him to put facts together by reviewing cassette tapes and recordings of events leading up to the massacre. "They were being watched every hour of the day and night. This was a warm, friendly, junior Alcatraz" (41). It is a media-saturated Alcatraz to boot, illuminated by television screens and monitored by arsenals of cameras, as if a failure to record what happens will render existence a myth. (This apprehension has materialized in the twenty-first century on a much larger scale with cellphones and social networks alone.)

Greville first confirms his suspicion that the children are the murderers by watching "yet another *Newsnight* recapitulation of the tragedy" about a girl who escaped or was released by the kidnappers (49); she is catatonic, but he detects the bearing of guilt in the camera light reflected off of her eyes and teeth. Later, and more substantively, he sees a home movie that presents life in the suburb as quiescent and adopts "the style of a real-estate developer's promotional video" (71). The copy Greville obtains has been doctored by the children. "This carried the identical jovial soundtrack, but Jasper and Amanda had added some twenty-five seconds of footage, culled from news documentaries, of car crashes, electric chairs and concentration-camp mass graves. Scattered at random among the scenes of their parents, this atrocity footage transformed the film into a work of eerie and threatening prophecy" (71). Technology, then, provides the impetus for the massacre, mediates Greville's enquiry, and allows him to solve the crime. Screening the home movie, he realizes that the children have turned into psychopaths, "willing themselves into madness as a way of finding freedom" (72). In the domain of the Ballardian, technology almost always determines the flows of madness and freedom.

The novels that take their cue from *Running Wild* expand on the novella's themes and unfold in similar Alcatrazes. Before turning to them, I want to say something about the problem of making judgments or quantifying an author based upon his or her later work. David James brings this to light in "Late Ballard," explaining:

> There may be no clear rationale for turning to a writer's final work as a distinctive phase in its own right, an independent chapter of creativity. Yet it's equally tempting to make the case for the opposite: to reconnect that last body of writing with its younger corpus, maybe with the expectation of finding a certain self-consciousness in a writer's later style, or at least some sign of belated reflection on all that both precedes and informs his or her closing texts. (160)

These elements are certainly visible; not only can we see a self-consciousness in *Cocaine Nights* and the subsequent postmillennial novels, Ballard even parodies his own style, making fun of himself while trying on a new, simpler suit of prose and tone.[9]

James proposes that Ballard wanted to agitate readers by "risking simplicity (in syntax, vocabulary, and perspectivism alike)" and (de)sensitizing them to the "apathetic disenchantment of the communities that [his characters] are drawn into" (161, 162). This notion is compounded if we consider the last three novels as rewritings or reshapings of *Cocaine Nights*, as if Ballard were monomaniacally trying to perfect the same narrative, a Moby-Dick that chronically eluded him. When critics accused him of being a copycat of himself, he cited famous historical writers like Kafka, Dickens, and Shakespeare, each of whose major works "seem to be the same" yet contain pivotal and evocative differences. "Every writer is locked into the sort of room of his or her mind. . . . You can't escape the basic elements of your own character, but if you've got a strong imagination you can transcend those" ("All" 398). That's a fair defense. But the differences between, say, *Cocaine Nights* and *Super-Cannes* are much slighter than between *The Trial* and *The Castle* (1926), *A Tale of Two Cities* (1859) and *Great Expectations* (1861), or *Twelfth Night* (1601) and *The Tempest.*

Individually the final novels are strong, intricate works of literature that beckon critical attention and corroborate the skill of a veteran author, but they lack the gravel and cunning of earlier novels, and Ballard will likely not be remembered for them. In the universe of science fiction, they are furthest away from the sun than anything else in his canon. Then again, they take place in postcapitalist realities and foreground themes of media pathology, technological subjectivity, and utopia and dystopia—all basics of the genre, and all connected to the epidemic of beach fatigue that runs through the stories in *Vermilion Sands*, only here we might call it media or culture fatigue.

Several articles and chapters have been written on the intertextuality and reciprocity of these four novels. Some scholars maintain that the first three constitute a trilogy. Others group the latter three together. Nicholas Royal says *Super-Cannes* "reads as a companion piece to *Cocaine Nights* but takes ideas from that novel and runs further." Actually, it's a protracted version with more nuances, characters, and exposition on the nature of agential crime and "the forced leisure that fossilized the nervous system" (*Cocaine* 34). The title refers to a high-tech business park for the European elite in the hills of Cannes called Eden-Olympia, an amplification of *Cocaine Nights*'s Estrella Del Mar.[10] Both follow the format of the crime novel—murder, investigation, suspense / deflection, reveal, payback—and the protagonists (Charles Prentice and Paul Sinclair) each come to be enamored of the ideas and worldviews of the antagonists (Bobby Crawford and Wilder Penrose). At the end, the protagonists slip into the roles of becoming-Adams, adopting the desires of the antagonists with the intention of acting on them.

There are similar gradations of character and plot in *Millennium People* and *Kingdom Come*, with protagonists David Markham and Richard Pearson falling under the spells of, respectively, mad psychiatrist Richard Gould and messianic adman David Cruise, but they entertain more advanced stages of the revolution gestating in *Cocaine Nights* and *Super-Cannes*, which occupy the same stage. The revolution is premised on meaningless transgressive behavior (ranging from vandalism, burglary, rape, drugs, porn, murder, and pedophilia to bombings, racial assaults, and terrorist attacks) that certain characters believe will resuscitate the corpse of affect terminated by media culture.

In "Situating the Violence of J. G. Ballard's Postmillennial Fiction," Philip Tew writes:

> In all three novels . . . troubling events become associated both in thought and action with the death of an individual who is socially adjacent to the protagonist (the putative former lover of a wife in *Super-Cannes*, a former wife who has remarried in *Millennium People*, and an estranged father in *Kingdom Come*). This trilogy thus reproduces the plot dynamics first seen in *Cocaine Nights*, a more conventional murder mystery and exploration of the meanings of murderous violence. . . . In contrast to *Super-Cannes*, *Millennium People* and *Kingdom Come*, the earlier text is less concerned with what one might term a radical sense of evil. (108)

I concur with Tew. If *Running Wild* is the seed, *Cocaine Nights* is the sprout, and the rest are the tree. All of them revolve around "consumerism dominat[ing] everything. . . . The message . . . is that all we've got left is our own psychopathology. . . . I keep repeating that in a totally sane society the only freedom is madness" ("All" 399, 400). Advanced technology dictates terms—the tree and its roots are electric and mechanical, products of culture, not nature. An early exchange in *Super-Cannes* illustrates this point. Police Chief Pascal Zander informs Sinclair about the social and architectural climate of Eden-Olympia, assuring him that crime doesn't exist. "In fact," he boasts, "I can say that the whole concept of criminality is unknown here." Sinclair admits that he hasn't even seen the mark of a litterbug. Zander replies: "The idea is unthinkable. There are no pine cones to trip you, no bird shit on your car. At Eden-Olympia even nature knows her place" (83). Culture has swallowed, digested, and processed nature into a hyperreality; there is no more interplay between the two. In Ballard's terminal New Edens, consumerism has evicted the jungle.

Cocaine Nights is a misleading title. The drug, let alone the word "cocaine," scarcely makes an appearance. It's more of a signifier for breaking the law and tapping jouissance from the cask of illicit behavior. The blasé days thread into "cocaine nights" in this novel and the subsequent trilogy that it scaffolds. What begins in *Running Wild* with an account of mediatized social relations in an exclusive neighborhood develops into a scathing critique of the capitalist landscape in *Kingdom Come*, where the gates of heaven are the revolving doors of a mega-mall, and God, in Baudrillard's words, "has become hyperreal" (*Simulacra* 159), an all-seeing Big Brother with camera lenses for eyes.[11]

Narrated exclusively in the first person, the novels become more and more about Ballard's experience in his home country.[12] *Cocaine Nights* and *Super-Cannes* have Mediterranean settings. Ballard sets *Millennium People* and *Kingdom Come* in England and explores what he knows best: the psychogeography of suburban London. He called *Kingdom Come* "a full-frontal attack on England today" erected upon his devout "feeling about this country—that we have nothing left but consumerism" ("Rattling" 433). But it's more than a devout feeling. The novel is agedly didactic and fraught with urgency and anxiety; Ballard pounds the pointer against the blackboard, and even though the conclusion does contain that familiar subthrob of madness and ambiguity, I was reminded more than ever of antiquated utopian novels in which the plot is subsidiary (if not disposable) to the author's exposure / exposition of a new and different world conveyed by a character in the know to another in tow. The satirical and self-effacing elements don't compensate for or counter Ballard's heavy-handed critique of a rising postcapitalism. Perhaps he wanted to give us a relatively unadulterated two cents in his final work, which culminates with the guy getting the girl, a great rarity, but probably a joke, the closest he would ever come to the matrimonial ending of a Jane Austen novel.

Deleuze and Guattari assert that "there is only desire and the social, and nothing else" (*Anti-Oedipus* 29). The social field is always invested by desire, the flows of which determine cultural production. Individually and collectively, what we make derives from what we want, and yet what we really want is to be enslaved, to be led and told what to do—hence capitalism, a system of our own creation that glints with the illusion of freedom, control, and power but ultimately subjugates us. In their volumes on capitalism and schizophrenia, Deleuze and Guattari develop innovative ways of reading and negotiating this dynamic. Michel Foucault called the first volume an "introduction to non-fascist life" (xiii), taking the schizoanalytic stance that the human condition is basically fascist. Ballard takes an analogous stance. A preoccupation with consumer fascism pervades these books and rises to a crescendo in *Kingdom Come*.

According to Brooklands high-school teacher David Sangster, "consumer fascism provides its own ideology, no one needs to sit down and dictate *Mein Kampf*. Evil and psychopathy have been reconfigured into lifestyle statements. It's a fearful prospect, but consumer fascism may be the only way to hold a society together. To control all that aggression, and channel all those fears and hates" (168). The ideology of consumer fascism, however, cannot remain static; constantly dislocated by the flows of desire, it demands change. A psychiatrist at a local mental hospital, Tony Maxted, corrects Sangster: "Consumerism is running out of road, and it's trying to mutate. It's tried fascism, but even that isn't primitive enough. The only thing left is out-and-out madness" (242). This is an antifascist solution. In a sense, "out-and-out madness" is Deleuze and Guattari's solution, too, a counterstrike to the Freudian apparatus they write against and aspire to subvert.

For all his characters' enthusiasm about "elective," "voluntary," or "willed" insanity and the violence required to enact it, Ballard didn't want to see it happen in the real world. Discussing *Cocaine Nights*, *Super-Cannes*, and *Millennium People*, he clarified that the "notions about the benefits of transgression in my last three novels are not ones I want to see fulfilled. Rather, they are extreme possibilities that may be forced into reality by the suffocating pressures of the conformist world we inhabit. Boredom and a deadening sense of total pointlessness seem to drive a lot of meaningless crimes" ("Reading" 412).

Ballard's interest in the consumer landscape entered his writing in the 1960s, most noticeably in *The Atrocity Exhibition*. Since then, it has become a defining feature of the Ballardian; literature, music, cinema, and art referred to as such should have something to do with the psychopathology of commodity culture. Likewise with electronic technology and media, offshoots of the consumer-capitalist apparatus that, no matter where we locate Ballard on or with respect to the science fiction register, are determining factors in his literary vision and central to his extrapolations. In these novels, I was struck particularly by the emphatic recurrence of diegetic uncertainty, a related theme and another Ballardian staple. Characters habitually confuse the real with the reel. Unlike Ballard's former usages of this trope, though, the reel, not the real, has become the dominant mode of psychological existence.

"Film is the way we see our world," proselytizes the oracular antagonist of *Cocaine Nights* (261). This is reinforced by a mnemonic component. Bobby Crawford adds: "There's a kind of amnesia at work here—an amnesia of self. People literally forget who they are. The camera lens needs to be their memory" (262). Film, then, doesn't just inform Ballard's psychoactive Edens and their "computerized" inhabitants (*Super-Cannes* 90); it is an ontological prerequisite. In effect, the diegeses of the novels are just that—cinematic environments—and the characters and narrators perceive and articulate them in terms of cinematic production.

In *Super-Cannes* Sinclair feels as if he and the Eden-Oympianites "were extras in a tourist film" (40), "actors appearing in under-rehearsed roles" (52), "dreamer[s] who had strayed onto a film set" (156) while the architecture of the business park seems "like a film set waiting for the opening credits" (178). In *Millennium People*, Markham compares himself to "a visitor to an abandoned film set" in the second sentence (3), then "an actor searching for the right stage set" (10), "a prisoner . . . trapped among the dreams of melodramas I had seen years earlier" (57), "a trapped spectre" on the "metabolized skin" of a movie screen (121), and "an actor standing in for [his] real self" (127). In *Kingdom Come*, Pearson, a former advertising executive, sees Brooklands as "a stage set, an adventure playground haunted by malicious and incendiary children" (125), and Cruise, a McLuhanesque "messiah without a message" (256), is the director of those children whose "entire career was built on illusion and a set of emotional three-card tricks" (142). At every turn, Ballard *cinematically undermines* the foundation of reality and the prospect of a fixed, stable identity.

The idea isn't new. It dates back to the Frankfurt School. In *Dialectic of Enlightenment*, for example, Max Horkheimer and Theodor W. Adorno famously hypothesized that "real life is becoming indistinguishable from the movies. The sound film, far surpassing the theater of illusion, leaves no room for imagination or reflection on the part of the audience, who is unable to respond within the structure of the film, yet deviate from its precise detail without losing the thread of the story; hence the film forces its victims to equate it directly with reality" (126). Ballard's characters are chronic manifestations of this affliction—only for them, the experience of the movies has leaked into the practice of real life. Horkheimer and Adorno, however, feared the same thing as Ballard: a widespread imaginative degeneration perpetuated by the culture industry and the commercialization of the arts and the psyche. Published at the end of World War II, *Dialectic of Enlightenment* emerged from a climate of moral panic, social upheaval, and unmitigated violence. In Ballard's novels, this climate emerges as the Final Solution to imaginative degeneration in communities where the culture industry has achieved a terminal status.

The title *Kingdom Come* not only resonates because of its biblical connotations (that is, its apocalyptic conflation of the divine with the consumer-capitalist) but also because of its station in Ballard's canon, both as his final novel and as the last installment in his final, culture-centric quartet of novels, a kind of foil and accompanying frame for his first, nature-centric quartet of novels. In *Kingdom Come* he fully enunciates the concepts he introduces and cultivates in *Cocaine Nights*, *Super-Cannes*, and *Millennium People*. The characters are exceedingly wooden, even for Ballard, more mouthpieces for his ideas than people, although their actions (or lack thereof) reflect the zones of ennui that they inhabit: by all means, they are products of their culture. Ballard made this broad statement about his postmillennial protagonists: "My characters try to remythologise themselves to recharge the batteries of their imaginations. They're trying to decode reality" ("Technology" 381). The death of affect is a symptom of consumer-capitalist technologies and media, which establish the code that *de*mythologizes and turns his characters into blip, blasé subjects who struggle to individuate and reimagine themselves. This can be said for almost every one of Ballard's protagonists.

But there is a stark difference between the protagonists of late and early Ballard. A comparison of Richard Pearson, David Markham, and Paul Sinclair with *The Crystal World*'s Edward Sanders, *The Drought*'s Charles Ransom, and *The Drowned World*'s Robert Kerans reveals distinctly Ballardian similarities (obsession, existential dissatisfaction, a desire for solitude, and sensitization). Sanders, Ransom, and Kerans, however, seek a remythology of the self in and via *nature*; the architecture of their inner spaces and the agency they crave is determined by the natural landscapes of their respective postapocalyptic futures. For Pearson, Markham, and Sinclair, nature is gone—everything is consumerism, television, *culture*. And in a sheer cultural matrix, Ballard's only viable agency is primal aggression.

Freud expresses a deep anxiety about aggression in *Civilization and Its Discontents*, speculating that the forces of nature may succumb to cultural law and lead to mass destruction. If nothing else, he foresees "a pathology of cultural communities" (110). This is Ballard's point of departure. He echoes Freud through the mouthpiece of Maxted, who predicts that the "future is going to be a struggle between vast systems of competing psychopathies, all of them willed and deliberate, part of a desperate attempt to escape from a rational world and the boredom of consumerism" (*Kingdom* 105).

The means to domination begins and ends with violence. There is no Ballardian without it. Most of his writing hinges on violent acts that manifest physically, psychologically, emotionally, and socially. The fiction itself is violent, too, breaking the rules of narrative, jolting readers back and forth between interior and exterior landscapes, writing toward the New by writing against the Old. Innovation is always destructive if only because it is disruptive. Given Ballard's childhood and the violence he witnessed in Shanghai and Lunghua, he ends his career with what is technically an extended meditation on the subject. While the characters who sing the praises of violence and psychopathology are often persuasive and weirdly sensible, as Ballard doubtless intended, their worldviews serve more to punctuate the aestheticization of violence by consumer-capitalist culture. Jeannette Baxter has said that the "increasing stylisation and banalisation of violence in films, computer-games and advertising merely cultivate a de-sensitised and insatiable appetite for more spectacular displays of brutality. Ballard maps out the addictive and corrosive effects of violent spectacles" (*Surrealist* 194). Inherent in this map is a nostalgia for nature. And a requiem for the loss of nature. Here may be the essence of Ballard's science fiction. Banished from the wilderness to the absurdist pleasure dome of culture, his mediatized freedom seekers commit *pathologies de l'acte* that are themselves efforts to escape the reality studio and reconnect with the most basic human instincts and impulses.

CONCLUSION

A recent novel by Christopher Fowler, *The Sand Men* (2015), adopts many of Ballard's signature moves. On the surface, it seems to be a viable candidate for the Ballardian label. The novel depicts a super-rich resort in near-future Dubai called Dream World that, like the building in *High-Rise*, is completely self-contained, offering every conceivable service and facility its wealthy residents need for daily life. Gradually, Fowler exposes Dream World's underbelly and disrupts the social register. He prefaces *The Sand Men* with a quote from *Super-Cannes*: "The ultimate gated community is a human being with a closed mind." The press release says that the book "is a Ballardian twist on *Desperate Housewives* for the *Gone Girl* generation, set in a world of uncertainties and paranoia, where cultures clash and human universals are stripped bare." Despite these marketing ploys, however, I was impressed with how *un*-Ballardian *The Sand Men* turned out to be. Fowler is a seasoned, prolific, and extremely talented author with over forty books to his name, but instead of enacting a "twist," he untwists Ballardian dynamics and lays them much flatter, falling into conventional narrative traps and simplifying what, in my estimation, no Anglophone writer has managed to do as Ballard had. This seems to be the way it goes with most authors (or admen, for that matter) who make concerted attempts to ally themselves with his oeuvre. The closer they stake a claim, the further they move away . . .

A possible exception to the rule is English novelist and journalist Will Self, who thought of Ballard as a mentor and was a close friend in his later life. At a memorial celebration in 2009, Rick McGrath provides an account of Self's tribute:

> Will amused us all by reading out a handwritten letter—actually, two of JG's ubiquitous postcards—he received 16 years ago. Will had written JG, tentatively suggesting he might be the man to write a screenplay for *Crash*. The reply was short on encouragement, but long on suggestions: JG recommended Will immediately go out and buy a book called *The Black Box*, which featured the final recordings of crews involved in aircraft crashes. "I'm thinking of writing a novel based entirely on black box recordings," JG enthusiastically wrote, then suggested it might be a technique Will might try. "He was always suggesting story ideas to me," Will intoned in a lazy, eccentric drawl oddly reminiscent of JG's dulcet tones. "I knew it was because he had already thought about it and had abandoned the concept." Much laughter. Will also revealed a bit of JG's horror of all things literary and fête. When JG won a PEN Award four months before his passing, it was Will who accepted on JG's behalf. When he delivered the award, JG took pains to warn Will about the "tweedy" side of the literary world: "It's very good of them to give me the award, but we must always remember" (here, Will's voice drops conspiratorially) *"they are the enemy."* ("Rick")

Pitting himself against the main and consistently straining to tap into uncharted, uncanny realms, Ballard carved out a special niche for himself that remains daunting in scope, style, execution, and the efficacy with which it represents technological subjectivity and society. He is simultaneously one of science fiction's most important authors, ardent critics, and distant nomads, conjuring prophecy with one hand, paradox with the other. Andrei Gasiorek nicely summarizes his relationship with the genre: "Ballard's election of science fiction as a valid literary mode . . . [was] predicated on his refusal of the very features that made it successful and popular . . . the tightly coded, formulaic products of the pulp era" (Gasiorek 6).

Ballard's reach extends beyond science fiction into other kinds of literature and media, ranging from cinema, television, and the visual arts to philosophy, cultural theory, and music, and as I indicated in my introduction, there is an active fan base of Ballardians, some of whom are his earliest reviewers and critics. During my research for this book, I came to know many of them. I have never encountered a community formed around a science fiction author like these accomplished intellectuals and artists. Just as Ballard's characters use obsession for a compass, so do Ballardians obsess over Ballard. Their tenacious devotion to his writing and legacy is an insignia of its power, impact, and endurance.

Since Spielberg's *Empire of the Sun* in 1987, several major motion pictures have been adapted from Ballard's works, most recently Ben Wheatley's *High-Rise* (2016), a superstylized rendering of the source material but, as with other adaptations, a rendering that belongs more to the filmmaker than the fiction writer. Ballard's surreal conflation of inner space and objective reality is simply too complex to portray onscreen in its totality. Unlike the glut of authors who are encouraged by editors and publishers to compose movie-ready novels and stories more akin to screenplays, he wrote to be read first, and in many ways, he was a writer's writer. Wheatley's film generated new and renewed interest in Ballard's novel, though, and considering the accumulative buzz about forthcoming adaptations, it may be primarily through the medium of film that the word of Ballard seeds itself in future generations, especially as cinematic technologies continue to evolve and develop the capacity to better visualize the surreal, technocratic, imploded diegeses he envisioned in so many works of fiction.

J. G. Ballard will always be an icon of science fiction against which other authors measure themselves. This will be the case whether or not we think he abandoned the "genre of ideas" because it ironically put restrictions on imagination. The fact is Ballard's career charts the path of science fiction for the second half of the twentieth century into the dawn of the twenty-first, illustrating how its imagined landscapes, alternate realities, electric dreams, and machinic desires have been subsumed and standardized by the futures we have come to inhabit.

A J. G. Ballard Bibliography

In this primary bibliography, I account for Ballard's fiction and nonfiction works. I list short fiction by each story's original publication, then by the original publication of each fiction collection. In cases where stories were first published under a different title, I make note of it. All story citations in this book come from *The Complete Short Stories of J. G. Ballard*. Citations from novels come from recent editions, but I have included the original publication information. For specific articles cited in *A User's Guide to the Millennium*, refer to the last section in the secondary bibliography. All primary sources are presented in chronological order of publication.

NOVELS

The Wind from Nowhere. New York: Penguin, 1976. First published by New York: Berkley Medallion, 1962.

The Drowned World. London: Fourth Estate, 2012. First published by New York: Berkley Medallion, 1962.

The Drought. London: Fourth Estate, 2011. First published as *The Burning World* (in an abridged form) by New York: Berkley Medallion, 1964.

The Crystal World. London: Fourth Estate, 2011. First published by London: Cape, 1966.

The Atrocity Exhibition. London: Fourth Estate, 2006. First published by London: Cape, 1970. Published as *Love and Napalm: Export USA* by New York: Grove, 1972.

Crash. New York: Picador, 2001. First published by London: Cape, 1973.

Concrete Island. London: Fourth Estate, 2011. First published by London: Cape, 1974.

High-Rise. London: Fourth Estate, 2011. First published by London: Cape, 1975.

The Unlimited Dream Company. London: Fourth Estate, 2011. First published by London: Cape, 1979.

Hello America. London: Fourth Estate, 2011. First published by London: Cape, 1981.

Empire of the Sun. New York: Simon and Schuster, 2005. First published by London: Gollancz, 1984.

The Day of Creation. London: Harper Perennial, 2006. First published by London: Gollancz, 1987.

Running Wild. (Novella.) New York: Noonday, 1998. First published by London: Hutchinson, 1988.

The Kindness of Women. New York: Picador, 2007. First published by London: HarperCollins, 1991.

Rushing to Paradise. London: Fourth Estate, 2011. First published by London: Flamingo, 1994.

Cocaine Nights. London: Flamingo, 1997. First published by London: Flamingo, 1996.

Super-Cannes. London: Fourth Estate, 2011. First published by London: Flamingo, 2000.

Millennium People. London: Fourth Estate, 2011. First published by London: Flamingo, 2003.

Kingdom Come. London: Fourth Estate, 2012. First published by London: Fourth Estate, 2006.

SHORT FICTION (ORIGINAL PUBLICATIONS)

"The Violent Noon." *Varsity*, May 26, 1951.

"Escapement." *New Worlds* 54 (December 1956).

"Prima Belladonna." *Science Fantasy* 20 (December 1956).

"Build-Up" (renamed "The Concentration City"). *New Worlds* 55 (January 1957).

"Mobile" (rewritten/renamed "Venus Smiles"). *Science Fantasy* 23 (June 1957).

"Manhole 69." *New Worlds* 65 (November 1957).

"Track 12." *New Worlds* 70 (April 1958).

"The Waiting Grounds." *New Worlds* 88 (November 1959).

"Now: Zero." *Science Fantasy* 38 (December 1959).

"The Sound-Sweep." *Science Fantasy* 39 (February 1960).

"Zone of Terror." *New Worlds* 92 (March 1960).

"Chronopolis." *New Worlds* 95 (June 1960).

"The Last World of Mr. Goddard." *Science Fantasy* 43 (October 1960).

"The Voices of Time." *New Worlds* 99 (October 1960).

"Studio 5, the Stars." *Science Fantasy* 45 (February 1961).

"Deep End." *New Worlds* 106 (May 1961).

"The Overloaded Man." *New Worlds* 108 (July 1961).

"Mr F. Is Mr F." *Science Fantasy* 48 (August 1961).

"Storm-Wind: Part 1" (serialized version of *The Wind from Nowhere*). *New Worlds* 110 (September 1961).

"Storm-Wind: Part 2." *New Worlds* 111 (October 1961).

"Billenium." *New Worlds* 112 (November 1961).

"The Gentle Assassin." *New Worlds* 113 (December 1961).

"The Drowned World" (novella version). *Science Fiction Adventures* 24 (January 1962).

"The Insane Ones." *Amazing Stories* 36, no. 1 (January 1962).

"The Garden of Time." *Magazine of Fantasy and Science Fiction* 22, no. 2 (February 1962).

"The Thousand Dreams of Stellavista." *Amazing Stories* 36, no. 3 (March 1962).

"Thirteen to Centaurus." *Amazing Stories* 36, no. 4 (April 1962).

"The Cage of Sand." *New Worlds* 119 (June 1962).

"Passport to Eternity." *Amazing Stories* 36, no. 6 (June 1962).

"The Watch-Towers." *Science Fantasy* 53 (June 1962).

"The Singing Statues." *Fantastic Stories of Imagination* 11, no. 7 (July 1962).
"The Man on the 99th Floor." *New Worlds* 120 (July 1962).
"The Subliminal Man." *New Worlds* 126 (January 1963).
"The Sherrington Theory" (renamed "The Reptile Enclosure"). *Amazing Stories* 7, no. 3 (March 1963).
"A Question of Re-Entry." *Fantastic Stories of Imagination* 12, no. 3 (March 1963).
"The Time-Tombs." *Worlds of If* 13, no. 1 (March 1963).
"Now Wakes the Sea." *Magazine of Fantasy and Science Fiction* 24, no. 5 (May 1963).
"End-Game." *New Worlds* 131 (June 1963).
"Minus One." *Science Fantasy* 59 (June 1963).
"The Encounter" (renamed "The Venus Hunters"). *Amazing Stories* 37, no. 6 (June 1963).
"The Sudden Afternoon." *Fantastic Stories of Imagination* 12, no. 9 (September 1963).
"The Screen Game." *Fantastic Stories of Imagination* 12, no. 10 (October 1963).
"The Delta at Sunset." *The Terminal Beach* (UK edition). 1964.
"The Drowned Giant" (renamed "The Souvenir"). *The Terminal Beach* (UK edition). 1964.
"The Gioconda of the Twilight Noon." *The Terminal Beach* (UK edition). 1964.
"The Volcano Dances." *The Terminal Beach* (UK edition). 1964.
"Time of Passage." *Science Fantasy* 63 (February 1964).
"Prisoner of the Coral Deep." *Argosy* 358, no. 3 (March 1964).
"The Lost Leonardo." *Magazine of Fantasy and Science Fiction* 26, no. 3 (March 1964).
"The Terminal Beach." *New Worlds* 140 (March 1964).
"The Illuminated Man." *Magazine of Fantasy and Science Fiction* 26, no. 5 (May 1964).
"Equinox: Part 1" (serialized version of *The Crystal World*). *New Worlds* 142 (May/June 1964).
"Equinox: Part 2" (serialized version of *The Crystal World*). *New Worlds* 143 (July/August 1964).
"The Day of Forever." *The Impossible Man*. 1966.
"The Impossible Man." *The Impossible Man*. 1966.
"Confetti Royale" (renamed "The Beach Murders"). *Rogue* 11, no. 1 (February/March 1966).
"You and Me and the Continuum." *Impulse* 1, no. 1 (March 1966).
"The Assassination Weapon." *New Worlds* 161 (April 1966).
"You: Coma: Marilyn Monroe." *Ambit* 27 (Spring 1966).
"The Assassination of JFK Considered as a Downhill Motor Race." *Ambit* 29 (Autumn 1966).
"The Atrocity Exhibition." *New Worlds* 166 (September 1966).
"Storm-Bird, Storm-Dreamer." *New Worlds* 168 (November 1966).
"Tomorrow is a Million Years." *New Worlds* 169 (December 1966).
"The Death Module" (renamed "Notes Towards a Mental Breakdown"). *New Worlds* 173 (July 1967).
"Venus Smiles." *Worlds of If* 17, no. 9 (September 1967).
"Cry Hope, Cry Fury!" *Magazine of Fantasy and Science Fiction* 33, no. 4 (October 1967).
"The Recognition." *Dangerous Visions*, October 1967.
"The Cloud-Sculptors of Coral D." *Magazine of Fantasy and Science Fiction* 33, no. 6 (December 1967).
"Why I Want to Fuck Ronald Reagan." (Chapbook.) Unicorn Books. January 1968.

"The Dead Astronaut." *Playboy* 15, no. 5 (May 1968).
"The University of Death." *Transatlantic Review* 29 (Summer 1968).
"The Great American Nude." *Ambit* 36 (Summer 1968).
"The Generations of America." *New Worlds* 183 (October 1968).
"The Comsat Angels." *Worlds of If* 18, no. 12 (December 1968).
"The Summer Cannibals." *New Worlds* 186 (January 1969).
"Crash!" *ICA Eventsheet.* February 1969.
"The Killing Ground." *New Worlds* 188 (March 1969).
"Tolerances of the Human Face." *Encounter* 33, no. 3 (September 1969).
"A Place and a Time to Die." *New Worlds* 194 (September/October 1969).
"Coitus 80." *New Worlds* 197 (January 1970).
"Journey across a Crater." *New Worlds* 198 (February 1970).
"Princess Margaret's Face Lift." *New Worlds* 199 (March 1970).
"Mae West's Reduction Mammoplasty." *Ambit* 44 (Summer 1970).
"Say Goodbye to the Wind." *Fantastic Stories* 19, no. 6 (August 1970).
"The Side-Effects of Orthonovin G." *Ambit* 50 (Spring 1972).
"The Greatest Television Show on Earth." *Ambit* 53 (Winter 1972/73).
"My Dream of Flying to Wake Island." *Ambit* 60 (Autumn 1974).
"The Air Disaster." *Bananas* 1 (January/February 1975).
"Low-Flying Aircraft." *Bananas* 2 (Summer 1975).
"The Ultimate City." *Low-Flying Aircraft.* 1976.
"The Life and Death of God." *Ambit* 66 (Spring 1976).
"The 60 Minute Zoom." *Bananas* 5 (Summer 1976).
"The Invisible Years." *Ambit* 68 (Autumn 1976).
"The Smile." *Bananas* 6 (Autumn/Winter 1976).
"Queen Elizabeth's Rhinoplasty." *TriQuarterly* 35 (Winter 1976).
"The Dead Time." *Bananas* 7 (Spring 1977).
"The Index." *Bananas* 8 (Summer 1977).
"The Intensive Care Unit." *Ambit* 72 (Summer 1977).
"Theatre of War." *Bananas* 9 (Winter 1977).
"Having a Wonderful Time." *Bananas* 10 (Spring 1978).
"One Afternoon at Utah Beach." *Anticipations*, June 1978.
"Zodiac 2000." *Ambit* 75 (Summer 1978).
"Motel Architecture." *Bananas* 12 (Autumn 1978).
"A Host of Furious Fancies." *Time Out*, December 19, 1980.
"News from the Sun." *Ambit* 87 (Autumn 1981).
"Myths of the Near Future." *Myths of the Near Future.* 1982.
"Memories of the Space Age." *Interzone* 2 (Summer 1982).
"Report on an Unidentified Space Station." *City Limits* 7, no. 10 (December 1982).
"The Secret Autobiography of J. G. B******." *Ambit* 96 (Spring 1984). (Originally published in French: "L'Autobiographie Secrete de J. G. B******." *Etoile Mécanique.* July 1981–March 1982.)
"The Object of the Attack." *Interzone* 9 (Autumn 1984).
"Answers to a Questionnaire." *Ambit* 100 (Spring 1985).
"The Man Who Walked on the Moon." *Interzone* 13 (Autumn 1985).
"Love in a Colder Climate." *Interview.* January 1988.

"The Secret History of World War 3." *Ambit* 114 (Autumn 1988).
"The Largest Theme Park in the World." *The Guardian*, July 7, 1989.
"The Enormous Space." *Interzone* 30 (July/August 1989).
"War Fever." *Magazine of Fantasy & Science Fiction* 77, no. 4 (October 1989).
"Jane Fonda's Augmentation Mammoplasty." *Semiotext(e) SF* 14 (December 1989).
"Dream Cargos." *Shincho* (September 1990).
"Neil Armstrong Remembers His Journey to the Moon." *Interzone* 53 (November 1991).
"A Guide to Virtual Death." *Interzone* 56 (February 1992).
"Report from an Obscure Planet." *Leonardo*, April 1992.
"The Message from Mars." *Interzone* 58 (April 1992).
"The Dying Fall." *Interzone* 106 (April 1996).

COLLECTED SHORT FICTION (ORIGINAL PUBLICATIONS)

The Voices of Time and Other Stories. New York: Berkley Medallion, 1962.
Billennium. New York: Berkley Medallion, 1962.
The Four-Dimensional Nightmare. London: Gollancz, 1963.
Passport to Eternity. New York: Berkley Medallion, 1963.
The Terminal Beach. London: Gollancz, 1964.
Terminal Beach. New York: Berkley Medallion, 1964. (The contents of this US edition differ from the UK edition above.)
The Impossible Man and Other Stories. New York: Berkley Medallion, 1966.
The Disaster Area. London: Cape, 1967.
The Day of Forever. London: Panther, 1967.
The Overloaded Man. London: Panther, 1967.
Vermillion Sands. New York: Berkley Medallion, 1971.
Chronopolis and Other Stories. New York: Putnam's, 1971.
Low-Flying Aircraft. London: Cape, 1976.
The Best of J. G. Ballard. London: Futura, 1977.
The Best Short Stories of J. G. Ballard. New York: Holt, Rinehart and Winston, 1978.
Myths of the Near Future. London: Cape, 1982.
Memories of the Space Age. Sauk City: Arkham House, 1988.
War Fever. London: Collins, 1990.
The Complete Short Stories. London: Flamingo, 2001.
The Complete Short Stories: Volume 1. London: Harper Perennial, 2006.
The Complete Short Stories: Volume 2. London: Harper Perennial, 2006.
The Complete Short Stories of J. G. Ballard. New York: Norton, 2009.

NONFICTION

A User's Guide to the Millennium: Essays and Reviews. London: Flamingo, 1997. First published by London: HarperCollins, 1996.
Miracles of Life: Shanghai to Shepperton, An Autobiography. New York: Liverlight, 2013. First published by London: Fourth Estate, 2008.

NOTES

INTRODUCTION

1. Jeannette Baxter uses this term in reference to Ballard, claiming that his "authorial ex-centricity is clearly delineated in his initial decision in the 1950s to reject the dominant mode of social realism and the extreme innovations of literary modernism in favour of science fiction" ("Introduction" 3).

2. Ballard has discussed Burroughs at length in interviews and essays. Invariably, his sentiments point to this assertion: "I think without a doubt he's the greatest American writer since WWII" ("Interview," Juno and Vale 6). At the same time, he eschewed comparisons between them. "I recognise the similarities [between our writing] instantly whenever I read Burroughs. People say I have been heavily influenced by him, but I don't think I have at all. My fiction is highly structured, I know where I am going, I always plot my novels and short stories very carefully, I always write an extended synopsis. Burroughs doesn't do this at all. . . . I think my approach is basically a speculative one. Therefore my emotions remain uncommitted to whatever imagination happens to generate. This is not true of Burroughs. He believes everything he writes. He lives in a paranoid micro-climate of his own" ("Conversations" 316).

3. "I've always wanted really to be a painter. . . . I've said somewhere else that all my fiction consists of paintings. I think I always was a frustrated painter. They are all paintings, really, my novels and stories" ("Interview," Goddard and Pringle 9). Ballard made the same basic assertion in many other interviews.

4. "A poet such as Ray Bradbury can accept the current magazine conventions and transform even so hackneyed a subject as Mars into an enthralling private world" ("Which" 195).

5. I use this expression in reference to Douglas Kellner and Stephen Best's *The Postmodern Turn*, an important analysis of the cultural transition between modernity and postmodernity (see chapter 4). Jeannette Baxter has vehemently disparaged the idea that Ballard's work occupies the playground of postmodernism. So has Ballard himself, saying that "the postmodern novel represents a dead-end, a desperate admission that the author has nothing to say and can only think of ever-more devious ways of disguising the fact" ("Ballard's Anatomy" 71). Nonetheless, *The Atrocity Exhibition* exhibits multiple elements of the postmodern in form, style, and content, including significant playfulness.

6. "Ballard's prose has been described as poetic. It is not. His methods, his intensification of his language and his imagery, are often those of the poet, but his prose . . . can sometimes be awkward" (Moorcock, "Modern" 60).

7. At Kosmopolis International Literature Fest in 2008, Ballardians V. Vale and Simon Sellars sat on a panel with Bruce Sterling called "Myths of the New Future." Impresario of the cyberpunk movement, Sterling had this to say about Ballard's impact: "In the circle of American science fiction writers of my generation—cyberpunks and humanists and so forth—[Ballard] was a towering figure. We used to have bitter struggles over who was more Ballardian than whom. We knew we were not fit to polish the man's boots, and we were scarcely able to understand how we could get to a position to do work which he might respect or stand, but at least we were able to see the peak of achievement that he had reached."

CHAPTER 1. J. G. BALLARD, A.K.A. SHANGHAI JIM

1. According to Rick McGrath, Baxter's unauthorized, erroneous, underdocumented biography is a "book-long fantasy" ("John"). Baxter is also a fiction writer and admired Ballard's work, but he evidently didn't like him as a person. McGrath's conclusion is that Baxter's book "encapsulates a certain amount of professional jealousy. This so-called biography has more holes in it than the Albert Hall." In "Dissecting John Baxter's J. G. Ballard Bile-ography," McGrath, David Pringle, Mike Holliday, and others hold Baxter in contempt, pointing out errors regarding Ballard's method of composition, self-promotion (as a consummate "adman"), and hell-bent determination to portray Ballard as a psychopath prone to violence and fits of wild abandon.

2. Ballard explains the fictionalization of Jamie in a 1984 interview for "Writers in Conversation": "I wasn't faced with having to feed myself on quite that sort of day by day, hour by hour level that my young hero is. I base Jim's experiences in the book partly on my own but more on a boy who's a close friend of mine in the camp who lived a few rooms away from my family in G block . . . and who was . . . separated from his parents who were trapped in North China. He was virtually orphaned by the war and he spent the war in this room with a family (husband, wife and a young child) in circumstances rather like Jim's in the book. So it's an amalgam of experiences but it's basically a fiction."

3. In 1984, Ballard frankly admitted: "Of course, I don't like England *at all*. If my children weren't living here I think I would move" ("Interview," Juno and Vale 31).

4. In 2006 Ballard attributed a good part of his relationship with his parents to the war: "I think it probably reflects my rather ambivalent feelings towards my own father . . . from whom I was pretty estranged. . . . Something that went back to the war. . . . One effect of being interned in a camp for nearly three years with my parents was the estrangement. I never really felt that close to my parents afterwards, because my parents, like all other adults with children, could not feed me, clothe me, keep me warm, give me any hope for the future—they were often frightened, more frightened than I was. . . . [O]ne effect of civil war of any kind is that children look to their parents. . . . And if the parents are powerless, and they usually are, civilian parents, they can do nothing. And that's damaging. Very damaging" ("Dangerous" 426).

5. "Having said this," Rossi adds, "it would be both naive and reductive to think that *Miracles* offers a definitive version of J. G. Ballard's life" ("Mind" 68). The autobiography doesn't provide the answers some readers may have expected and wanted, in that it ignores many key aspects of Ballard's personal, professional, and public life. "Neither

does it contain a checklist which can be used to explain away key Ballardian obsessions or repeating motifs such as drowned cities, crashed cars and dead astronauts" (ibid.). As such, *Miracles* can function like his fiction: elusive and ambiguous.

6. See Goddard and Pringle's "An Interview with J. G. Ballard" (10–11).

7. "The shabby barrack huts, the cement dormitory blocks, the worn parade ground and the guardhouse with its leaning watchtower lay together in the June sun, a rendezvous for every fly and mosquito in the Yangtze basin" (Ballard, *Empire* 130).

CHAPTER 2. THIS WAY TO INNER SPACE

1. In addition to *Empire of the Sun*'s seedling "The Dead Time," most notable are "The Illuminated Man," the story that Ballard expanded into *The Crystal World*, and "Crash!," a chapter in *The Atrocity Exhibition* that was extrapolated into the novel of the same name.

2. "Many people tell me I should write more short stories—and I reply that I don't know where I'd publish them. When I began writing them fifty years ago, it was completely different: nearly every paper and magazine in those days published short stories, some of them even every day. And then there were of course the science fiction magazines, which had an almost insatiable appetite for short stories. The SF magazines in those days were an entirely wonderful training space for budding authors—one could pursue one's obsessions, one's fantasies; one could discover what kind of writer one wanted to be" ("I Really").

3. In 1968 Ballard explained the effect that his early interaction with science fiction fandom had on him: "I don't have any contact with fans. My one and only contact with fandom was when I'd just started writing, twelve years ago, when the World Science Fiction Convention was being held in London, in 1957, and I went along to that as a new writer hoping to meet people who were interested in the serious aims of science fiction and all its possibilities. In fact there was just a collection of very unintelligent people, who were almost illiterate, who had no interest whatever in the serious and interesting possibilities of science fiction. In fact I was so taken aback by that convention that I more or less stopped writing for a couple of years. Since then I've had absolutely nothing to do with fans, and I think they're a great handicap to science fiction and always have been" ("Interview," Storm 20–21).

4. In a 1979 interview, Ballard states: "It so happens that my first stories were being published at almost exactly the time that Sputnik One . . . was launched in 1957. At the time I remember a great mood of optimism in science fiction circles. It seemed that the Sputniks had ushered in the Space Age, and that everything that the science fiction writers had been predicting for 100 years was coming true. Now I remember paradoxically responding to this general euphoria by being intensely pessimistic . . . I felt very strongly that the age of space, as far as science fiction was concerned, was *ending* rather than beginning. And indeed the Space Age did *end* and far from lasting hundreds or even thousands of years, its total lifespan was hardly more than a decade" ("The Space," Evans 123). In Ballard's view, the Space Age officially ended when the final Skylab mission landed on Earth—it was the first landing not to be televised, which signified a dramatic shift in popular attention. The best source for short fiction dealing with the subject is *Memories of the Space Age* (1988). It features Cape Canaveral-based

stories published between 1962 and 1985 that, with the exception of the eponymous entry, appear in earlier collections.

5. Ballard recycled the surname "Maitland" from the protagonist of *The Wind from Nowhere*. He used it again for the lead in *Concrete Island*. This recurrence is particularly meaningful if we think about the surname as a portmanteau word that combines "mate" and "land," the union of one man (and one man's psyche) with a landscape that is simultaneously hazardous and seductive. I unpack this idea in chapter 4.

6. Ballard elaborates: "In a certain way 1975 was the end of a period. I'd written four books all tending in one particular direction, if one counts *The Atrocity Exhibition*, all dealing with the communications landscape and modern technology. Afterwards I'd simply had enough of it and I went off towards other themes. That will . . . be apparent in . . . *Myths of the Near Future*" ("Interview," Fuchs and Körber 144).

7. See Mike Holliday's "Ballard and the Vicissitudes of Time" for a cogent reading of these stories. With "Myths of the Near Future" and "News from the Sun," Holliday also discusses "Memories of the Space Age," saying that these three works are "all concerned with a psychological disturbance of our perception of the flow of time, a dislocation that has been caused, somehow, by human space-flight. These stories are so similar to each other that one might suspect self-plagiarism, were they not written by Ballard."

8. Jeannette Baxter makes an excellent point about "Ballard's reviews of other people's lives," which "exist in an uneasy relation with the narration of his own life stories: (un) homely memories return to pose disquieting questions about origins and identity" ("Uncanny" 57).

CHAPTER 3. DISASTER AREAS

1. For the best readings of the Freudian drives and other psychoanalytic issues, refer to Samuel Francis's *The Psychological Fictions of J. G. Ballard*.

2. *Red Mars* (1992), *Green Mars* (1993), and *Blue Mars* (1996). Each color denotes a different stage of terraformation, although the planet is still very much "alive" when it is dead and red.

3. An early, serialized version of the novel first appeared in two parts as "Storm-Wind" in *New Worlds* under the editorship of John Carnell.

4. "I thought I'd use all the clichés there are, the standard narrative conventions" ("Interview," Goddard and Pringle 21).

5. In a 1982 interview, Ballard claimed that he did not keep any archives whatsoever. That may have been true at the time, but thereafter he did save some materials. Acquired by the British library at Ballard's request prior to his death and made available to the public in 2011, these items came from fifteen storage boxes and included manuscripts, photographs, notebooks, letters, and other miscellany. However, "Ballard's literary suitcases at the British Library . . . will disappoint the customs officials of biographical research. . . . [T]he sparkle and clutter of everyday ephemera that will often swell collections of personal papers in enlightening ways is entirely absent from Ballard's archive. The limited range of personal material that is present—school certificates and reports, some photographs, and a seemingly personal bundle of primary documentation from Lunghua Camp—has not survived because the author treasured such material through the years" (Beckett, "Progress").

6. In "J. G. Ballard: The Quest for an Ontological Eden," Gregory Stephenson convincingly refutes critics who called Ballard pessimistic and says that the "disaster motif in Ballard's fiction is thus grounded, not in nihilism, but in the desire for transcendence" (39).

7. Ballard invented the concept of archaeopsychic time as an alternative to more generic uses of the time travel theme, hoping it would catch on. "Instead of treating time like a sort of glorified scenic railway, I'd like to see it used for what it is, one of the perspectives of the personality, and the elaboration of concepts such as the time zone, deep time and archaeopsychic time" ("Which" 198).

8. According to Ballard, all of the characters in *The Drowned World* partake in a kind of spinal descent. "In a certain sense, [the characters] climb down their own spinal column. They traverse down the thoracic vertebrae, from the point at which they are air-breathing mammals, to the lumbar region, to the point at which they are amphibious reptiles. Finally they reach the absolute past, which on one hand represents the birth of life itself in the hot womb of the primeval jungle, and which in another sense represents their own origins and birthplace in the mother's womb. I show humanity face to face with the difficulty of making sense of this decline in their status to non-entities. I use this portrait of the spinal column as a vessel containing a reflection of the memory of the past, and the details of the entire evolutionary development of the human race, as a literary device, as I was dissatisfied with the traditional forms used by SF writers to realise time travel" ("Interview," Uncredited 11).

9. John Baxter plays up Ballard's capacity for self-promotion in his biography, systematically referring to him as a chronic adman willing to do anything to sell more books. As usual, Baxter's provocations are overblown.

10. Reviewers widely compared *The Drowned World*, *The Drought*, and *The Crystal World* to *Heart of Darkness*. Ballard may not have read Conrad's novel until later. In 1975 he said that any similarities were probably coincidence: "I don't know whether I'd read *Heart of Darkness* at the time I wrote *The Crystal World*. I honestly don't think I was influenced by Conrad. I don't mind being influenced—after all, we're all influenced to some extent—but if you're talking about conscious imitation: certainly not" ("Interview," Goddard and Pringle 16).

11. My argument here stems from "The Undivided Self," an article in which Nick Perry and Roy Wilkie suggest that Sanders and Ventress can be envisioned as two facets of the same character, with the crystal world signifying the (d)evolving self.

CHAPTER 4. PSYCHOPATHOLOGIES OF EVERYDAY LIFE

1. From the cover description of *The Postmodern Turn*.

2. The textual collages of "Project for a New Novel" were later published in *New Worlds* in 1978.

3. An example of such artwork was a collage by Richard Hamilton. It featured *Forbidden Planet*'s Robbie the Robot cradling a passed-out, half-naked woman in his giant mechanical arms. Beneath them crouched a smaller Marilyn Monroe in the iconic pose from *The Seven Year Itch* (1955) with the skirt of her white dress blown up by a gust of air from a subway vent.

4. Elsewhere Ballard admitted that *Crash* could be read as science fiction "because it contains elements of political and 'sociological' thought which one finds in certain works of the genre," but he worried that readers might be "fenced in by the limitations . . . that are habitually attributed to science fiction" ("Crash," Louit 73).

5. As B. W. Powe writes in *Marshall McLuhan and Northrop Frye: Apocalypse and Alchemy*, Ballard and his cyberpunk protégé William Gibson both "acknowledged their imaginative debts to McLuhan's technological vision of extended psyche and nerve ends, discarnate body, imploding senses: flesh and steel, cells and microchips now the battleground" (67). Simon Sellars infers that Ballard anticipated McLuhan (and Jean Baudrillard), demonstrating "how encroaching advertising and mass consumer culture played on submerged desire, implanting new, artificial subjectivities to create a schizophrenic underclass" ("Introduction" xii).

6. In an annotation to the first chapter, Ballard says: "The many lists in *The Atrocity Exhibition* were produced by free association, which accounts for the repetition but, I hope, makes more sense of them" (14).

7. David Porush emphasizes the importance of metaphor and authorship in *The Soft Machine: Cybernetic Fiction*: "Cybernetic fiction responds to the invitation to use the machine icon as a metaphor for authorship, a metaphor combining the strict structuralist view of the text as a 'code' (whose 'objectively present' meanings can be derived from an algorithm for reading) with the cybernetic view of the author as machine" (16). *Atrocity* exemplifies this dynamic and is the point of departure for a veritable fetishization of the author and the self that Ballard further develops in *Crash* and his autobiographical novels.

8. In *Technologized Desire: Selfhood and the Body in Postcapitalist Science Fiction*, I argue that Deleuze and Guattari's machinic ethos belongs to cyberpunk literature, building on Scott Bukatman's claim in *Terminal Identity: The Virtual Subject in Postmodern Science Fiction* that they "are cyberpunks, too, constructing fictions of terminal identity in the nearly familiar language of a techno-surrealism" (326).

9. "Nader has only just survived into the 1990s, and it's difficult now to imagine his name leaping to anyone's lips, but at the time he sent a seismic tremor through the mind of the US consumer, challenging the authority of the greatest of all American icons, the automobile. Every car crash seemed a prayer to Ralph Nader. . . . Looking back, one can see that Nader was the first of the eco-puritans, who proliferate now, convinced that everything is bad for us" (38n, 127).

10. "Dr. Nathan represents the safe and sane voice of the sciences. His commentaries are accurate, and he knows what's going on. On the other hand, reason rationalizes reality for him, as it does for the rest of us, in the Freudian sense of providing a more palatable or convenient explanation, and there are so many subjects today about which we should not be reasonable" (89n).

11. "A complete discontinuity existed between Reagan's manner and body language, on the one hand, and his scarily simplistic far-right message on the other. Above all, it struck me that Reagan was the first politician to exploit the fact that his TV audience would not be listening too closely, if at all, to what he was saying, and indeed might well assume from his manner and presentation that he was saying the exact opposite of the words actually emerging from his mouth" (169n).

12. For a full account of the proceedings, see Holliday's "'A Dirty and Diseased Mind': The Unicorn Bookshop Trial."

13. Over a decade after the publication of *Crash*, John Money coined this term in "Paraphilias: Phenomenology and Classification," a 1984 article that appeared in *American Journal of Psychotherapy*. He classifies symphorophilia as a "sacrificial paraphilia . . . in which one or both of the partners must atone for the wicked and degenerate acts of

defiling the saint with ecstatic lust by undergoing an act of penance or sacrifice" (168). Strangely, Money does not mention Ballard.

14. The review appeared in *Reader's Report* and was written by the wife of a psychiatrist. Ballard loved it because "it meant total artistic success! For a *psychiatrist* to say 'you're beyond psychiatric help'—in a way, that's the greatest compliment you can be paid!" ("Interview," Revell 49).

15. Asked what he was cautioning against in 1997, Ballard replied: "Well, cautionary tales take many forms. One of the most famous of all, Swift's *Modest Proposal*, employs the deadpan approach. It seems to embrace the very subject that is the target of Swift's anger. I'd like to think that *Crash* lies in the tradition of that type of cautionary tale. I mean, when I was writing *Crash*, I certainly didn't think I was writing a cautionary tale. What I thought I was doing was following certain trends that I saw inscribed in the sensation-hungry, rather affectless landscape that was emerging in the '60s. I was following these trends that I saw inscribed across the graph paper to the point where they seemed likely to intersect, you know, way off the page. I saw this new logic, a nightmare logic, emerging, and this was what I was exploring. I was, in a sense, carrying out an autopsy before the cadaver was cold" ("Body" 78).

16. Published in French as "Ballard's *Crash*" in 1976, Baudrillard's essay was translated into English and first appeared in *Foundation: The International Review of Science Fiction* in 1984.

17. See "Ballard / *Crash* / Baudrillard," in which Ruddick maintains that Baudrillard's essay is "a serious misreading, possibly even a shameless distortion, of *Crash*'s themes" (356).

18. Ballard expresses his feelings about postmodern criticism most acidly in a special 1991 issue of *Science Fiction Studies* on the topic of postmodernism and science fiction.

19. Ballard supplied the full list of his favorite books in the 1992 anthology *The Pleasure of Reading*, a collection of essays by prominent writers: "*The Day of the Locust*, Nathanael West; *Collected Short Stories*, Ernest Hemingway; *The Rime of the Ancient Mariner*, Samuel Taylor Coleridge; *The Annotated Alice*, ed. Martin Gardner; *The World through Blunted Sight*, Patrick Trevor-Roper; *Naked Lunch*, William Burroughs; *The Black Box*, ed. Malcolm MacPherson; Los Angeles *Yellow Pages*; *America*, Jean Baudrillard; *The Secret Life of Salvador Dali*, Salvador Dali" ("Pleasures" 182).

20. The car crash expo has been discussed extensively by Ballard and critics. A concise but representative account by Ballard can be found in a rare interview he did in 1975 for the one-issue publication *Repsychling: A Magazine for the Unborn*.

21. For a superb essay on this subject, read Valentini Polcini's "Ancient Mariner's of Inner Space and Robinson Crusoes in Reverse: Literary Myths in J. G. Ballard's Science Fiction."

22. See Chris Beckett's "J. G. Ballard's 'Elaborately Signalled Landscape': The Drafting of *Concrete Island*."

23. In *The Psychological Fictions of J. G. Ballard*, Francis discusses the influence of Laing in *Concrete Island*, *Super-Cannes*, and *Millennium People*, but curiously not in *High-Rise*. He doesn't even mention *High-Rise*—a missed opportunity.

CHAPTER 5. EMPIRES OF THE SELF

1. *VALIS* (1978), *The Divine Invasion* (1980), *The Transmigration of Timothy Archer* (1982), *Radio Free Albemuth* (1985), and the unfinished *The Owl of Daylight*, which Dick had been writing at the time of his death.

2. Bolstering Blake's multivalence, *Unlimited* incorporates themes and elements from Ballard's previous works, such as "the harsh starkness of reality (concrete motorways, tower blocks, washing machines and TV sets reminiscent of the cultural disaster trilogy, and the exotic images of fantasy (tropical flora and fauna reminiscent of *The Drowned World* and *The Crystal World*, [which are] explored in depth by David Pringle in *The Four-Fold Symbolism of J. G. Ballard*)" (McGrath, "Re: Unlimited").

3. Cessna Aircraft Company was founded in 1929. During World War II the RAF acquired 180 T-50s ("Cessna"). Ballard may have flown them years later in 1954–55 when he was stationed in Canada, but probably not. In *Miracles*, he states: "I enjoyed flying the heavy Harvard T-6, with its huge radial engine, retractable undercarriage and variable pitch propeller" (148). Cessna's most notable models are small aircraft powered by piston engines. Ballard likely elected to feature one in *Unlimited* because, by the 1970s, they were the best-known light planes in the world.

4. This added similarity with Maitland, whose life had been in dire straits prior to crashing his Jaguar, reifies the intimate bond between *Unlimited* and *Concrete Island*. They are different imaginings of the same core narrative and closer to one another than any of Ballard's books.

5. Among these natives are "three small children. Two boys and a girl, they sat side by side on a swing like monkeys huddled together on a perch, smiling hopefully at whatever game the young woman [Miriam St. Cloud] was trying to arrange for them" (17). Ballard said this about them: "Maybe those three children were really standing in for my own children. Maybe the woman doctor is a stand in for my late wife—or, rather, an amalgam of my late wife and one or two other women who have been very close to me over the years" ("Unlimited" 8).

6. "Despairing at last" alludes to Jesus's final words on the cross: "Father, why have you forsaken me?" And Jesus, too, "decided to die."

7. "Jim gazed at the young pilot, doing his best to grasp the miracle that had taken place. By touching the Japanese he had brought him to life; by prizing his teeth apart he had made a small space in his death and allowed his soul to return" (*Empire* 271). Thereafter Jim imagines himself raising everybody from the dead, even those who have not yet died, including himself.

8. For a detailed account of how Ballard deviates from factual occurrences in this novel, see David Pringle's "Fact and Fiction in J. G. Ballard's *The Kindness of Women*."

9. Evans's research was instrumental to Ballard's writing. In 1982 he said: "Chris Evans—now dead, sadly . . . worked at the computer laboratories of the National Physical Laboratory. . . . We had an arrangement that lasted for years. He was in charge of a large computer laboratory and he sent me the contents of his wastepaper baskets. His material would come in big envelopes; about once a week his secretary would send me scientific handouts, giveaway magazines, bulletins, printouts that weren't needed anymore . . . any sort of laboratory detritus. . . . [O]nce a week this huge envelope would arrive, *packed* with the contents of his wastepaper basket. And it was a *gold mine*. . . . It's impossible to exaggerate how exciting these strange crossovers from the communications world were: psychopathology, experimental and applied psychology, commercialism . . . all those, overlaid together, provided a wonderful sort of *compost* which my imagination could feed on" ("Interview," Juno and Vale 9, 10).

10. Both Miriam and Mary died in 1964 in Spain, but as I pointed out in chapter 2, Mary died from pneumonia. Regarding this alteration, Pringle says: "Presumably, in the novel he has changed the circumstances slightly in order to make the event seem more dramatic and sudden" ("Fact"). I suspect Ballard made changes of this kind almost exclusively for dramatic effect.

11. Tandy clarifies that Sinclair is talking about 1960s and 1970s fiction, "but the idea could be applied to much of Ballard's other work" (276n).

12. In the quotes within this citation, Rossi cites Roger Luckhurst's *"The Angle between Two Walls": The Fiction of J. G. Ballard.*

CHAPTER 6. THE ROAD TO CULTURE

1. *Pattern Recognition* (2003), *Spook Country* (2007), and *Zero History* (2010). Like Ballard, Gibson has a penchant for novel sequences, writing two before this one, the Sprawl trilogy in the 1980s and the Bridge trilogy in the 1990s, all works of dystopian cyberpunk.

2. David Paddy identifies these literary citations: "Mallory's namesake—Thomas Malory, the author of *Le Morte d'Arthur*—Conrad's *Heart of Darkness*, Shakespeare's *The Tempest*, and numerous Biblical references (from the novel's title, the Garden of Eden, Noah's Ark, Adam's act of naming [see the title of chapter 15] and a day of rest on the seventh day of travel [chapter 14])" (219).

3. The title of the last chapter echoes the first sentence of the novel: "Dreams of rivers, like scenes from a forgotten film, drift through the night, in passage between memory and desire" (7).

4. Ballard "never visited the part of central Africa where he had set [*The Day of Creation*] and felt that to do so was unnecessary. 'The landscape convinced me as I wrote it, and hopefully it will convince the reader.' He believes in both the resources of the imagination and its limits. He would never attempt to write about Antarctica, say—'a landscape which I've never been comfortable with'" ("J. G. Ballard Discusses").

5. Whereas Kagwa and Harare represent male aggression, Mrs. Warrender and her minions represent female aggression. Both can be read as shades of Mallory's persona. Regarding the latter, Marie-Pascale Buschini writes: "The names of Mallory's ferry, the *Salammbo*, and Mrs. Warrender's brothel-ship, the *Diana*, both refer to moon goddesses (in Flaubert's novel, Salammbo is a priestess of Tanit), which stresses the importance and the ubiquity of the female side of the psyche in Mallory's quest." As with so many of his novels, Ballard suggests that everybody and everything may only exist in the mind of an Adam.

6. For a fascinating contemporary version of this kind of commodity-naming, see Max Barry's *Jennifer Government* (2003), which appears to take a cue from *Hello America*. Barry envisions a postcapitalist near-future where US citizens are given corporate surnames that bind them subjectively and ontologically to capitalist enterprise (for example, John Nike, Hayley McDonalds, Rendell ExxonMobil, and Buy Mitsui).

7. In 1979 Ballard said: "I'm writing a novella now, rather similar to 'The Ultimate City,' for a publisher of illustrated books, Pierrot . . . [*Hello America*] was a title I suggested as a joke. Philip Dunn of Pierrot said, 'marvellous title, it's got to be called that!' So I said, 'Well, wait a minute . . . ' But, you know . . . Simon and Schuster are prepared to buy

40,000 copies or something on the strength of that title. . . . But we'll see. It's not a bad title, actually, when I think about it. I'm about half way through it. I suppose it'll be about 30 to 40,000 words, a bit longer than 'The Ultimate City.' That sort of thing, in the same sort of setting—the United States, in the future" ("Interview," Pringle, *Thrust* 19). It turned out to be in the vicinity of sixty-six thousand words.

8. "From Kerans in *The Drowned World* to Mallory in *The Day of Creation*, most of his central characters, and many of the peripheral figures in his loosely structured pilgrim bands, reach (or at least glimpse) that highest point accessible to consciousness. If 'utopia' is a place where all is well, a place of joy and perfection, then the psycho-physical landscapes of Ballard's fictions are manifestly such places" (Wagar 54).

9. In 2006, Ballard told an interviewer: "I can't resist having a dig at myself" ("Rattling" 432). For example, in *Kingdom Come* he refers to his protagonist as being "beyond psychiatric help," "a deliberate little in-joke for those who are interested. The publisher's reader for *Crash* made that comment years and years ago, so I couldn't resist inserting it" (ibid.).

10. Jeannette Baxter says Eden-Olympia was "modelled on the actual business park of Sophia-Antipolis, a few miles north of Antibes" (*Surrealist* 199). In a foreword to my edition of the novel, Ballard elaborates: "Super-Cannes is a luxury enclave on the heights above the Croisette, but the term might well refer to that whole terrain of science parks and autoroutes on the high ground above the Var plain. Together they make up Europe's silicon valley, a world away from the casinos and belle epoque hotels that define the Riviera of old."

11. Baudrillard theorizes the capitalist mediatization of the biblical God via the American family: "[A] typical American family, California home, three garages, five children, assured social and professional status, decorative housewife, upper-middle-class standing. In a way it is this statistical perfection that dooms it to death. Ideal heroine of the American way of life, it is, as in ancient sacrifices, chosen in order to be glorified and to die beneath the flames of the medium, a modern *fatum*. Because heavenly fire no longer falls on corrupted cities, it is the camera lens that, like a laser, comes to pierce lived reality in order to put it to death." (*Simulacra* 28). Ballard's fictions address these same concerns. Baudrillard even invokes one of Ballard's favorite sidebars in this passage: the imploded, cinematic texture of reality, life, and death.

12. "With the publication of *Millennium People*, Ballard shifted his focus in his 'crime' novels from the British expatriate enclaves of southern Europe to middle-class revolt fomented in the high-security gated communities of central London" (O'Hara, Introduction 407).

BIBLIOGRAPHY OF SECONDARY SOURCES

Popular and literary criticism on Ballard is extensive. Over twenty book-length monographs and collections have been published in multiple languages, and there are thousands of reviews and stand-alone essays that analyze Ballard's stories and novels or that read other narratives through the lens of the Ballardoscope.

This bibliography includes books published in the English language, interviews, anthologies, Web sites and other sources (most of them related to science fiction) that I have used to support my arguments. It is by no means exhaustive but rather intended to give readers a solid foundation of scholarship to date. For an excellent selection of book chapters and journal articles published up to 2008, I point readers to the reference guide at the end of Jeannette Baxter's *Contemporary Critical Perspectives: J. G. Ballard*. Also useful is Umberto Rossi's secondary bibliography in Rick McGrath's *The J. G. Ballard Anthology 2014*.

The final section of my bibliography lists specific sources cited in this study.

MONOGRAPHS AND KEYWORDS

Baxter, Jeannette. *J. G. Ballard's Surrealist Imagination: Spectacular Authorship*. Surrey: Ashgate, 2009.

Baxter, John. *The Inner Man: The Life of J. G. Ballard*. London: Orion, 2011.

Brigg, Peter. *Starmont Reader's Guide 26: J. G. Ballard*. Mercer Island, Wash.: Starmont House, 1985.

Cord, Florian. *J. G. Ballard's Politics: Late Capitalism, Power, and the Pataphysics of Resistance*. Berlin: De Gruyter Mouton, 2017.

Delville, Michel. *J. G. Ballard*. Plymouth, UK: Northcote House, 1998.

Francis, Samuel. *The Psychological Fictions of J. G. Ballard*. London: Continuum, 2011.

Gasiorek, Andrzej. *J. G. Ballard*. Contemporary British Novelists. Manchester: Manchester University Press, 2005.

Greenland, Colin. *The Entropy Exhibition: Michael Moorcock and the British "New Wave" in Science Fiction*. 1983. Boston: Routledge, 2013.
Luckhurst, Roger. *"The Angle between Two Walls": The Fiction of J. G. Ballard*. Liverpool: Liverpool University Press, 1997.
Oramus, Dominika. *Grave New World: The Decline of the West in the Fiction of J. G. Ballard*. 2007. Toronto: Terminal, 2015.
Paddy, David Ian. *The Empires of J. G. Ballard: An Imagined Geography*. Canterbury: Glyphi, 2014.
Pringle, David. *Earth Is the Alien Planet: J. G. Ballard's Four-Dimensional Nightmare*. San Bernardino, Calif.: Borgo, 1979.
Sinclair, Iain. *Crash: David Cronenberg's Post-Mortem on J. G. Ballard's "Trajectory of Fate."* London: BFI, 1999.
Stephenson, Gregory. *Out of the Night and into the Dream: A Thematic Study of the Fiction of J. G. Ballard*. London: Greenwood, 1991.
Tandy, Pippa. *Writing World War III: J. G. Ballard's Field Guide to the Cold War*. In McGrath, *Deep Ends: 2015*, 178–294.

ANTHOLOGIES

Baxter, Jeannette, ed. *Contemporary Critical Perspectives: J. G. Ballard*. London: Continuum, 2008.
Baxter, Jeannette, and Rowland Wymer, eds. *J. G. Ballard: Visions and Revisions*. New York: Palgrave Macmillan, 2012.
Black, Candice, ed. *Terminal Atrocity Zone: J. G. Ballard 1966–73*. San Francisco: Sun Vision, 2013.
Goddard, James, and David Pringle, eds. *J. G. Ballard: The First Twenty Years*. London: Bran's Head, 1976.
Juno, Andrea, and V. Vale, eds. *RE/Search 8/9: J. G. Ballard*. San Francisco: RE/Search, 1984.
McGrath, Rick, ed. *The J. G. Ballard Book*. Toronto: Terminal, 2013.
———. *Deep Ends: The J. G. Ballard Anthology 2014*. Toronto: Terminal, 2014.
———. *Deep Ends: The J. G. Ballard Anthology 2015*. Toronto: Terminal, 2015.
———. *Deep Ends: The J. G. Ballard Anthology 2016*. Toronto: Terminal, 2016.
Ryan, Mike, and V. Vale., eds. *J. G. Ballard: Quotes*. San Francisco: RE/Search, 2004.
Sellars, Simon, and Dan O'Hara, eds. *Extreme Metaphors: Interviews with J. G. Ballard, 1967–2008*. London: Fourth Estate, 2012.
Vale, V., ed. *J. G. Ballard: Conversations*. San Francisco: RE/Search, 2005.

INTERVIEWS WITH J. G. BALLARD

"Against Entropy." 1984. Interview by Peter Rønnov-Jessen. In Sellars and O'Hara, *Extreme Metaphors*, 199–210.
All We've Got Left Is Our Own Psychopathy: J. G. Ballard on *Millennium People*." 2003. Interview by Chris Hall. In Sellars and O'Hara, *Extreme Metaphors*, 396–406.
"The Art of Fiction." 1984. Interview by Thomas Frick. In Sellars and O'Hara, *Extreme Metaphors*, 181–98.

"Ballard's Anatomy: An Interview with J. G. Ballard." Interview by Paul Di Filippo. *Science Fiction Eye* 8 (1991): 66–75.

"Body Work." Interview by Andrew Hultkrans. *Artforum* 35, no. 7 (March 1997): 76–81, 118.

"A Conversation with J. G. Ballard." 1988. Interview by James Verniere. In Sellars and O'Hara, *Extreme Metaphors*, 231–40.

"Conversations: J. G. Ballard." 1995. Interview by Will Self. In Sellars and O'Hara, *Extreme Metaphors*, 299–319.

"Crash and Learn." 1974. Interview by Robert Louit. In Sellars and O'Hara, *Extreme Metaphors*, 72–80.

"'Dangerous Bends Ahead. Slow Down': J. G. Ballard on *Kingdom Come*." 2006. Interview by Toby Litt. In Sellars and O'Hara, *Extreme Metaphors*, 415–30.

"Everything Is Science Fiction!" 1970. Interview by James Goddard. In McGrath, *J. G. Ballard Book*, 16–31.

"Future Now." 1986. Interview by Solveig Norlund. In Sellars and O'Hara, *Extreme Metaphors*, 224–30.

"Historian of the Future." 2007. Interview by Hari Kunzru. In Sellars and O'Hara, *Extreme Metaphors*, 463–72.

"In Conversation with J. G. Ballard." Interview by Christopher Bigsby. In Bigsby, *Writers in Conversation with Christopher Bigsby*, 1: 71–86. Norwich: EAS, 2000.

"Interview by Graeme Revell." 1984. In Juno and Vale, *RE/Search 8/9*, 42–52.

"Interview by Toby Litt." In Sellars and O'Hara, *Extreme Metaphors*, 415–30.

"An Interview with J. G. Ballard." 1968. Interview by Jannick Storm. In Sellars and O'Hara, *Extreme Metaphors*, 14–21.

"Interview with J. G. Ballard." 1968. Uncredited interview. Trans. Dan O'Hara. In Sellars and O'Hara, *Extreme Metaphors*, 10–13.

"An Interview with J. G. Ballard." 1975. Interview by James Goddard and David Pringle. In Goddard and Pringle, *Ballard: First Twenty Years*, 8–35.

"Interview with J. G. Ballard." 1975. Interview by Philippe R. Hupp. In Sellars and O'Hara, *Extreme Metaphors*, 78–80.

"Interview with J. G. Ballard." 1979. Interview by David Pringle. *Thrust* 14 (Winter 1980): 12–19.

"An Interview with J. G. Ballard." 1982. Interview by Werner Fuchs and Joachim Körber. In Sellars and O'Hara, *Extreme Metaphors*, 132–45.

"An Interview with J. G. Ballard." 1991. Interview by Jeremy Lewis. In Sellars and O'Hara, *Extreme Metaphors*, 248–62.

"Interview with J. G. Ballard: Psychoanalyst of the Electronic Age." 1985. Interview by David Pringle. In McGrath, *J. G. Ballard Book*, 8–15.

"Interview with JGB by Andrea Juno and Vale." 1982. Interview by Andrea Juno and V. Vale. In Juno and Vale, *RE/Search 8/9*, 6–35.

"'I Really Would Not Want to Fuck George W. Bush!' A Conversation with J. G. Ballard." Interview by Werner Fuchs and Sascha Mamczak. Interview by Dan O'Hara. *Ballardian.com*, May 17, 2008.

"J. G. Ballard." 1973. Interview by Peter Linnett. In Sellars and O'Hara, *Extreme Metaphors*, 48–55.

"J. G. Ballard." Interview by Charles Platt. In Platt, *Dream Makers: Science Fiction and Fantasy Writers at Work*, 87–96. New York: Ungary, 1987.

"J. G. Ballard." 1978. Interview by Jon Savage. In Sellars and O'Hara, *Extreme Metaphors*, 106–20.
"J. G. Ballard Discusses *The Day of Creation*." Interview by Michelle Field. *Publishers Weekly*, March 11, 1988.
"J. G. Ballard: A Few Brief Queries." 2005. Interview by Samuel Francis. In McGrath, *J.G. Ballard Book*, 142–61.
"The J. G. Ballard *Repsychling* Interview." Anonymous interview. In McGrath, *J. G. Ballard Book*, 32–39.
"J. G. Ballard's Cinema in the Slipstream of Discontent." 1999. Interview by Iain Sinclair. In Sellars and O'Hara, *Extreme Metaphors*, 364–73.
"JGB Interviewed by Mark Pauline." In Vale, *Ballard: Conversations*, 127–59.
"'Marinated in War and Violence': Phillip Dodd Interviews J. G. Ballard." Interview by Phillip Dodd. *Ballardian.com*, February 7, 2008.
"Memento: J. G. Ballard." 1993. Interview by Joan Bakewell. In Sellars and O'Hara, *Extreme Metaphors*, 274–82.
"The New Science Fiction." Interview by George Macbeth. In *The New SF: An Original Anthology of Modern Speculative Fiction*, edited by Langdon Jones, 52–60. London: Arrow, 1969.
"Nothing Is Real, Everything Is Fake." 2003. Interview by Hans Ulrich Obrist. In Sellars and O'Hara, *Extreme Metaphors*, 383–95.
"Rattling Other People's Cages." 2006. Interview by Simon Sellars. In Sellars and O'Hara, *Extreme Metaphors*, 431–42.
"Reading the Signs." 2004. Interview by Jeannette Baxter. In Sellars and O'Hara, *Extreme Metaphors*, 407–14.
"Sci-fi Seer." 1970. Interview by Lynn Barber. In Sellars and O'Hara, *Extreme Metaphors*, 22–35.
"The Space Age Is Over." 1979. Interview by Christopher Evans. In Sellars and O'Hara, *Extreme Metaphors*, 121–31.
"Technology Is Always a Facilitator: J. G. Ballard on *Super-Cannes*." 2000. Interview by John Gray. In Sellars and O'Hara, *Extreme Metaphors*, 374–82.
"Unlimited Dreams?" Interview by Alan Dorey and Joseph Nicholas. *Vector* 96 (December/January 1979–80): 4–9.
"The Visitor." 1992. Interview by Phil Halper and Lard Lyer. In Sellars and O'Hara, *Extreme Metaphors*, 263–73.
"Writers in Conversation: J. G. Ballard with Matthew Hoffman." 1984. Interview by Matthew Hoffman. *YouTube*. Accessed March 6, 2013.

WEB SITES

Bonsall, Mike, ed. *J. G. Ballard: The Concordance*. 2008. www.bonsall-books.co.uk/concordance.
Goddard, James, ed. *J. G. Ballard: 20th Century Chronicler*. www.solaris-books.co.uk/Ballard.
Holliday, Mike, ed. *J. G. Ballard: A Collector's Guide*. www.holli.co.uk/JGB/ballard.htm.
McGrath, Rick, ed. *JGBallard.ca*. www.jgballard.ca.
Sellars, Simon, ed. *Ballardian.com*. www.ballardian.com.

BIBLIOGRAPHY OF SECONDARY SOURCES

Adachi, Ken. "Novelist Kept Putting Off Book about War Experiences." *Toronto Star*, December 14, 1987.

Adorno, Theodor W. "The Essay as Form." 1958. *Notes to Literature: Volume 1*. New York: Columbia University Press, 1991.

Adorno, Theodor W., and Max Horkheimer. *Dialectic of Enlightenment*. 1944. New York: Continuum, 2000.

Aldiss, Brian. "The Wounded Land: J. G. Ballard." 1965. In Goddard and Pringle, *Ballard: First Twenty Years*, 38–48.

Amis, Martin. "Introduction." In Ballard, *Complete Stories*, xi–xiv.

Andrews, Stephen E., and Nick Rennison. *100 Must-Read Science Fiction Novels*. New York: Black, 2008.

Arnold, Kyle. *The Divine Madness of Philip K. Dick*. Oxford: Oxford University Press, 2016.

Ashley, Mike, and Peter Nicholls. "Golden Age of SF." *The Encyclopedia of Science Fiction*. April 9, 2015. Accessed March 9, 2016, at http://sf-encyclopedia.com/entry/golden_age_of_sf.

Atwood, Margaret. "Everybody Is Happy Now." *The Guardian*, November 17, 2007.

Ballard, J. G. "Apocalypse How?" *Spin*, November 1995, 77–84.

———. "Cataclysms and Dooms." 1977. In Ballard, *User's Guide to the Millennium*, 208–9.

———. "Crash and Learn: J. G. Ballard's Introduction to the French Edition of *Crash!*" *JGBallard.ca*, 1974.

———. "Fictions of Every Kind." Rev. of *The Shattered Ring*, by Lois and Stephen Rose. 1971. In Ballard, *User's Guide to the Millennium*, 205–7.

———. "The Future of the Future." 1977. In Ballard, *User's Guide to the Millennium*, 224–27.

———. "Images of the Future." 1966. *JGB News* 19 (1993). *JGBallard.ca*, n.d.

———. "New Means Worse." 1981. In Ballard, *User's Guide to the Millennium*, 189–91.

———. "The Pleasures of Reading." 1992. In Ballard, *User's Guide to the Millennium*, 178–82.

———. Rev. of *La Jetée* (dir. Chris Marker). 1966. In Ballard, *User's Guide to the Millennium*, 28–29.

———. "Science Fiction Cannot Be Immune from Change." In *SF Symposium*, edited by Jose Sanz, 157–59. Rio de Janeiro: Instituto Nacional do Cinema, 1969.

———. "Second Thoughts: Sculptors Who Carve the Clouds." *The Independent*, October 24, 1992.

———. "A User's Guide to the Millennium." 1987. In Ballard, *User's Guide to the Millennium*, 17–22.

———. "Which Way to Inner Space?" 1962. In Ballard, *User's Guide to the Millennium*, 195–98.

"Ballardian." *Collins English Dictionary*. Accessed September 2, 2014, at www.collinsdictionary.com/dictionary/English.

Barthes, Roland. "The Death of the Author." 1967. In Barthes, *Image-Music-Text*, 142–48. New York: Hill and Wang, 1978.

Baudrillard, Jean. *America*. 1986. London: Verso, 1989.

———. *Simulacra and Simulation*. 1981. Ann Arbor: University of Michigan Press, 2000.

Baxter, Jeannette. "Introduction: J. G. Ballard and the Contemporary." In Baxter, *Contemporary Critical Perspectives*, 1–10.

———. "Uncanny Forms: Reading Ballard's 'Non-Fiction.'" In Baxter and Wymer, *J. G. Ballard*, 50–68.

Baxter, Jeannette, and Rowland Wymer. Introduction to *J. G. Ballard: Visions and Revisions*, 1–15.

Beckett, Chris. "J. G. Ballard's 'Elaborately Signalled Landscape': The Drafting of *Concrete Island*." *Electronic British Library Journal*. 2015. Accessed December 8, 2015, at www.bl.uk/eblj/2015articles/article5.html.

———. "The Progress of the Text: The Papers of J. G. Ballard at the British Library." *Electronic British Library Journal*. 2011. Accessed July 7, 2015 at www.bl.uk/eblj/2011articles/article12.html.

Best, Steven, and Douglas Kellner. *The Postmodern Turn*. New York: Guilford, 1997.

Bradbury, Malcolm. "Fly Away." Rev. of *The Unlimited Dream Company*, by J. G. Ballard. *New York Times*, December 9, 1979.

Bukatman, Scott. *Terminal Identity: The Virtual Subject in Postmodern Science Fiction*. Durham, N.C.: Duke University Press, 1993.

Burke, Christopher. "Four Stories: 'The Drowned Giant' by J. G. Ballard." *Weird Fiction Review*, November 5, 2014.

Burroughs, William S. "Introduction." *Queer*. New York: Penguin, 1985.

———. *Nova Express*. 1964. New York: Grove, 1994.

Buschini, Marie-Pascale. "J. G. Ballard's *The Day of Creation*: Copying God and (Re)Creating One's Self." *Etudes Britanniques Contemporaines* 5 (1994). Accessed March 25, 2016, at http://ebc.chez-alice.fr/ebc.html.

"Cessna History: 1940–1949." *Cessna.com*, 2009.

Clute, John, and David Pringle. "Ballard, J. G." *The Encyclopedia of Science Fiction*. December 14, 2014. Accessed January 22, 2015, at http://www.sf-encyclopedia.com/archives/ballard_j_g/109358.

Costa, Jordi. "Ballardoscope: Some Attempts at Approaching the Writer as Visionary." In McGrath, *J. G. Ballard Book*, 162–71.

Crosthwaite, Paul. "'A Secret Code of Pain and Memory': War Trauma and Narrative Organisation in the Fiction of J. G. Ballard." *JGBallard.ca*, 2005.

Davis, Ronald L. *Duke: The Life and Image of John Wayne*. Norman: The University of Oklahoma Press, 1998.

Dick, Philip K. *Ubik*. 1969. New York: Vintage, 1991.

Deleuze, Gilles, and Félix Guattari. *Anti-Oedipus: Capitalism and Schizophrenia*. 1977. Minneapolis: University of Minnesota Press, 1998.

———. *A Thousand Plateaus: Capitalism and Schizophrenia*. 1980. Minneapolis: University of Minnesota Press, 2000.

Donne, John. "Meditation XVII." *Selected Prose*. London: Penguin, 1987.

Dowell, Ben. Rev. of *Cocaine Nights*, by J. G. Ballard. *Manchester Evening News*. In Ballard, *Cocaine Nights*, 1. London: Flamingo, 1997.

"Dr. Barbara Moore, Who Walked across U.S., Is Dead at 73." *New York Times*, May 15, 1977.

Evans, Dylan. *An Introductory Dictionary of Lacanian Psychoanalysis*. London: Routledge, 1996.

Freud, Sigmund. *Civilization and Its Discontents*. 1930. New York: Norton, 1989.

———. *The Psychopathology of Everyday Life*. 1901. New York: Norton, 1989.

Gibson, William. "Talk for Book Expo, New York." In *Distrust that Particular Flavor*, 41–48. New York: Putnam, 2012.

———. "William Gibson Says the Future Is Right Here, Right Now." Interview by Mark Ward. *BBC News*, October 12, 2010.

Gordon, Joan. "Literary Science Fiction." In *The Oxford Handbook of Science Fiction*, edited by Rob Latham, 104–14. Oxford: Oxford University Press, 2014.

Groes, Sebastian. "From Shanghai to Shepperton: Crises of Representation in J. G. Ballard's Londons." In Baxter, *Contemporary Critical Perspectives*, 78–93.

———. "The Texture of Modernity in *Crash*, *Concrete Island* and *High-Rise*." In Baxter and Wymer, *J. G. Ballard*, 123–41.

Heller, Jason. "After the California Downpour, *The Drought* Offers Some Dry Reading." *NPR.org*, December 5, 2014.

Holliday, Mike. "A Dirty and Diseased Mind: The Unicorn Bookshop Trial." *Ballardian .com*, June 20, 2009.

———. "Ballard and the Vicissitudes of Time." *Ballardian.com*, July 3, 2008.

———. "Desperate Measures: A History of *The Atrocity Exhibition*." In McGrath, *J. G. Ballard Book*, 104–14.

———. "Short Story Collections." Holliday, *J. G. Ballard*, November 11, 2014.

James, David. "Late Ballard." In Baxter and Wymer, *J. G. Ballard*, 160–76.

Kaveney, Roz. "J. G. Ballard Between Derangement and Suburbia." Rev. of *The Inner Man*, by John Baxter. *Times Literary Supplement* 21 (November 2011). Accessed October 10, 2014, at www.the-tls.co.uk/articles/public/j-g-ballard-between-derangement-and -suburbia.

Kimberley, Nick. "The River from Nowhere." *City Limits*, September 10, 1987, 88.

Le Guin, Ursula K. *The Left Hand of Darkness*. 1969. New York: Ace, 2000.

———. "On the Verge of a Narrative Breakdown." *New York Times*, April 21, 1991.

Levin, A. E. "English Language SF as Socio-Cultural Phenomenon." Translated by Yuri Prizel. *Science Fiction Studies* 4, no. 3 (November 1977): 246–56.

Linnett, Peter. Rev. of *Concrete Island*, by J. G. Ballard. In Goddard and Pringle, *Ballard: First Twenty Years*, 71–73.

March-Russell, Paul. *Modernism and Science Fiction*. London: Palgrave Macmillan, 2015.

———. "The Writing Machine: J. G. Ballard in Modern and Postmodern Short Story Theory." In *Modernism, Postmodernism, and the Short Story in English*, edited by Jorge Sadico, 125–47. Amsterdam: Rodopi, 2012.

McGrath, Rick. "In the Beginning . . . 'The Violent Noon.'" *JGBallard.ca*, n.d.

———. "John Baxter: The Outer Child." *JGBallard.ca*, 2011.

———. "Re: HR." Message to D. Harlan Wilson. May 14, 2014. E-mail.

———. "Re: Unlimited." Message to D. Harlan Wilson. February 5, 2016. E-mail.

———. "Reconstructing *High-Rise*." *JGBallard.ca*, May 2004.

———. "Rick McGrath's Letter from London: The J. G. Ballard Memorial." *Ballardian .com*, November 30, 2009.

McGrath, Rick, David Pringle, Mike Holliday et al. "Dissecting John Baxter's J. G. Ballard Bile-ography." *JGBallard.ca*, 2011.

McLuhan, Marshall. *Understanding Media*. In *Essential McLuhan*, edited by Eric McLuhan and Frank Zingrone, 149–79. New York: Basic, 1995.

Melville, Herman. *Moby-Dick*. 1851. New York: Norton, 2002.

Money, John. "Paraphilias: Phenomenology and Classification." *American Journal of Psychotherapy* 38, no. 2 (April 1984): 164–79.
Moorcock, Michael. "Books for the Kids?" *New Worlds* 146 (January 1965): 115–19.
———. "Modern Metaphors." 1974. In Goddard and Pringle, *Ballard: First Twenty Years*, 60–62.
Nicholls, Peter, and David Pringle. "Disaster." *The Encyclopedia of Science Fiction*. October 12, 2014. Accessed June 21, 2015, at www.sf-encyclopedia.com/entry/disaster.
Noys, Benjamin. "*La libido réactionnaire?* The Recent Fiction of J. G. Ballard." *Journal of European Studies* 37, no. 4 (December 2007): 391–406.
O'Hara, Dan. Introduction to "Reading the Signs." 2004. Interview by Jeannette Baxter. In Sellars and O'Hara, *Extreme Metaphors*, 407–14.
———. "Reading Posture and Gesture in Ballard's Novels." In Baxter and Wymer, *J. G. Ballard*, 105–20.
Pardey, James. "Landscapes from a Dream: How the Art of David Pelham Captured the Essence of J. G. Ballard's Early Fiction." *Ballardian.com*, June 14, 2010.
Perry, Nick, and Roy Wilkie. "The Undivided Self: J. G. Ballard's *The Crystal World*." *Riverside Quarterly* 5, no. 4 (April 1973): 268–77.
Porush, David. *The Soft Machine: Cybernetic Fiction*. New York: Methuen, 1985.
Powe, B. W. *Marshall McLuhan and Northrop Frye: Apocalypse and Alchemy*. Toronto: University of Toronto Press, 2014.
Priestley, J. B. "They Come from Inner Space." *Thoughts in the Wilderness*. New York: Harper, 1957.
Pringle, David. "An Honest Madness." Rev. of *Crash*, by J. G. Ballard. In Goddard and Pringle, *Ballard: First Twenty Years*, 63–66.
———. "Ballard, J. G." *The Encyclopedia of Science Fiction*. September 16, 2015. Accessed October 30, 2015, at www.sf-encyclopedia.com/archives/ballard_j_g/127746.
———. "Books Received." *Interzone* 161 (November 2000): 64–67.
———. "Fact and Fiction in J. G. Ballard's *The Kindness of Women*." *JGB News* 20 (August 1993). Available at *JGBallard.ca*.
———. "Obituary: J. G. Ballard." *The Guardian*, April 19, 2009.
———. "Re: Rushing." Message to D. Harlan Wilson. June 10, 2015. E-mail.
———. "The Incredible Shrinking World." Rev. of *High-Rise*, by J. G. Ballard. In Goddard and Pringle, *Ballard: First Twenty Years*, 74–76.
Rev. of *The Day of Creation*, by J. G. Ballard. *Publishers Weekly*, April 1, 1988.
Robinson, Kim Stanley. "Interview with Kim Stanley Robinson." Interview by Andrew Liptak. January 26, 2015. Accessed January 26, 2015, at https://andrewliptak.com/2015/01/26/interview-with-kim-stanley-robinson.
Rossi, Umberto. "Images from the Disaster Area: An Apocalyptic Reading of Urban Landscapes in Ballard's *The Drowned World* and *Hello America*." *Science Fiction Studies* 21, no. 1 (March 1994): 81–97.
———. "Is the War Inside Your Mind? War and the Mass Media in J. G. Ballard's 'Theatre of War' and *War Fever*." *Interpretations: European Research Project for Poetics and Hermeneutics (Violence and Art)* 1 (2007): 157–76.
———. "Mind Is the Battlefield: Reading Ballard's 'Life Trilogy' as War Literature." In Baxter, *Contemporary Critical Perspectives*, 66–77.

Royal, Nicholas. "That Sublime Riviera Touch." *Independent*, September 1, 2000. Accessed January 18, 2016, at www.independent.co.uk/arts-entertainment/books/reviews/that-sublime-riviera-touch-625764.html.

Ruddick, Nicholas. "Ballard/*Crash*/Baudrillard." *Science Fiction Studies* 19, no. 3 (November 1992): 354–60.

Schuyler, William M. "Portrait of the Artist as a Jung Man: Love, Death and Art in J. G. Ballard's *Vermillion Sands*." *New York Review of Science Fiction* 57 (May 1993): 1, 8–11; and 58 (June 1993): 14–19.

Self, Will. *Junk Mail*. London: Penguin, 1996.

Sellars, Simon. "Introduction: A Launchpad for Other Explorations." In Sellars and O'Hara, *Extreme Metaphors*, xi–xx.

———. Introduction to "Speculative Illustrations: Eduardo Paolozzi in Conversation with J. G. Ballard." Interview by Frank Whitford. In Sellars and O'Hara, *Extreme Metaphors*, 36–47.

———. "Collecting 'The Violent Noon' and Other Assorted Ballardiana." *Ballardian.com*, February 5, 2007.

———. Rev. of *Crash*, by J. G. Ballard. *Ballardian.com*, September 17, 2006.

Shanghai Jim: Form Dictated by Time. Dir. James Runcie. Perf. J. G. Ballard, Michael Troughton, and Hans Gevruers. BBC Bookmark, 1991.

Simmel, Georg. "The Metropolis and Mental Life." 1903. *The Sociology of Georg Simmel*. New York: Free Press, 1950. 409–24.

Slavitt, David R. "The Monster He Became." *New York Times*, November 10, 1991. Accessed January 20,2014, at www.nytimes.com/books/98/07/12/specials/ballard-women.html?mcubz=2.

Stephenson, Gregory. "J. G. Ballard and the Quest for an Ontological Garden of Eden." *Foundation* 35 (Winter 1985–86): 38–47.

Sterling, Bruce. "Myths of the Near Future." Kosmopolis International Literature Fest. Centre de Cultura Contemporània de Barcelona. October 25, 2008. Panel Discussion.

———. "Preface." 1986. In *Mirrorshades: The Cyberpunk Anthology*, edited by Bruce Sterling, ix–xvi. New York: Ace, 1988.

Suvin, Darko. *Metamorphoses of Science Fiction*. New Haven, Conn.: Yale University Press, 1979.

Tew, Phillip. "Situating the Violence of J. G. Ballard's Postmillennial Fiction: The Possibilities of Sacrifice, the Certainties of Trauma." In Baxter, *Contemporary Critical Perspectives*, 107–19.

Wagar, W. Warren. "J. G. Ballard and the Transvaluation of Utopia." *Science Fiction Studies* 18, no. 1 (Mar. 1991): 53–70.

Wardle, Irving. "Review: *The Crystal World*." *Observer*, April 17, 1966.

Watson, Ian. "The Greening of Ballard: A Review of Concrete Island." In Goddard and Pringle, *Ballard: First Twenty Years*, 67–70.

Wilkins, Alastair. "Remembering J. G. Ballard's Science Fiction Legacy." *io9*, April 21, 2009.

Wilson, D. Harlan. *Technologized Desire: Selfhood and the Body in Postcapitalist Science Fiction*. Bowie: Guide Dog, 2009.

Zamir, Tzachi. "Theatrical Repetition and Inspired Performance." *Journal of Aesthetics and Art Criticism* 67, no. 4 (Fall 2009): 365–73.

Index

D. HARLAN WILSON is a professor of English at Wright State University–Lake Campus. He is the author of *Cultographies: They Live*, *Technologized Desire: Selfhood and the Body in Postcapitalist Science Fiction*, and over twenty novels and fiction collections.

Modern Masters of Science Fiction

John Brunner *Jad Smith*

William Gibson *Gary Westfahl*

Gregory Benford *George Slusser*

Greg Egan *Karen Burnham*

Ray Bradbury *David Seed*

Lois McMaster Bujold *Edward James*

Frederik Pohl *Michael R. Page*

Alfred Bester *Jad Smith*

Octavia E. Butler *Gerry Canavan*

Iain M. Banks *Paul Kincaid*

J. G. Ballard *D. Harlan Wilson*

THE UNIVERSITY OF ILLINOIS PRESS
is a founding member of the
Association of American University Presses.

University of Illinois Press
1325 South Oak Street
Champaign, IL 61820-6903
www.press.uillinois.edu